THE
WORLD
OF
SOUL

THE
WORLD
OF
SOUL

Black America's Contribution
to the Pop Music Scene

by Arnold Shaw

COWLES BOOK COMPANY, INC.
NEW YORK

To the black singers and musicians whose unique
and vital artistry has helped make American
pop music a world force.

CONTENTS

A Note to the Reader

American popular music is a mix, a product of the interplay between white Americans and black Americans, black musical originators and white polishers and popularizers.

As the black man has suffered discrimination, so has his musical contribution. Nowhere is this prejudice so apparent as in the area of the urban, ensemble, electrified blues known as rhythm-and-blues. One scans the work of dedicated historians like Sigmund Spaeth, Gilbert Chase, David Ewen, Wilfrid Mellers, to name a few, and is abashed at the utter absence of any mention of the work of hundreds of black singers, writers, musicians, and recording men.

Information about this "underground"—really segregated—music, created from the mid-forties to the mid-fifties is not readily available. Most of the recording was done by small, independent companies whose catalogs have gone out of print or been absorbed. Many of the individual creators and producers are gone, are not too communicative, and were not too careful about keeping records.

But scattered in the elusive catalogs of one hundred or more R & B labels are the works of the pioneer bluesmen who helped shape the Rock Revolution. The current R & B revival, accompanying the Soul movement, has helped us uncover the creations of the seminal artists like B. B. King, Chuck Berry,

Howlin' Wolf, Little Richard, Albert King, and Muddy Waters. It has not done much for less renowned figures like Amos Milburn, Lowell Fulson, Bullmoose Jackson, Memphis Slim, and Big Maybelle, not to mention Washboard Sam, Memphis Minnie, Joe Liggins, and Guitar Slim. If this section of my book is heavy in detail, put it down to the desire of a prospector anxious to leave as much of a record as possible for future adventurers. Adequately to cover the R & B period would require a volume larger than the present book.

In the course of my studies, I have become convinced that the role of black radio and black disk jockeys in the history of the blues has been grossly neglected. Because recordings are accessible long after they have been released, their impact on bluesmen has been stressed and overstressed. But cotton patch workers are not record collectors.

B. B. King launched his career on Memphis station WDIA, where Rufus Thomas of Stax Records is still spinning platters. Howlin' Wolf was a WKWM disk jockey for years before he embarked on a recording career. Elmore James was a WOKI (Jackson, Miss.) disk jockey. From 1938 intermittently for almost three decades, the second Sonny Boy Williamson broadcast daily on "King Biscuit Time" over WFFA of Helena, Arkansas, and WROX of Clarksdale, Mississippi.

Beginning in the forties WHAT of Philadelphia, WJLD of Birmingham, KXLW of St. Louis, and other local stations concentrated on black music. Apart from launching careers and influencing the musical taste of listeners, black radio played a large, underestimated role in spreading influences and shaping artists' styles. I have sought to right the balance, but it is a story that remains to be told in depth.

I was part of music business during the R & B and rock 'n' roll eras. My first magazine piece on pop music was about "Open the Door, Richard." The last disk I secured and promoted before I left the music business in 1966 was Damita Jo's recording of Jacques Brel's tortured ballad "Ne Me Quitte Pas," with American lyrics by Rod McKuen. As General Professional Manager of several major song-publishing companies, it was my job to find and develop hits. I had more than an average run of luck with black artists.

Attending Harry Belafonte's first RCA Victor date, I was able to acquire "Matilda, Matilda" for the firm I managed. The Chords' disk of "Sh-Boom" led me to purchase a 50 percent interest in its publishing rights. I bought "Piddily, Patter, Patter" for E. B. Marks after Herman Lubinsky played Nappy Brown's Savoy recording. From a small indie record manufacturer, I acquired the Tarriers' "Banana Boat Song" and the Four Fellows' "Soldier Boy," both songs that became best sellers with black artists.

Sarah Vaughan and the first black A & R producer on a major label, Clyde Otis, made a hit for me and writers Sherman Edwards and Hal David of "Broken-Hearted Melody." Guided by Otis, Dinah Washington revived "What a Difference a Day Makes," while Brook Benton scored a best seller with "Hotel Happiness."

I enjoyed the excitement of watching Oscar Brown, Jr., pop out of nowhere onto Columbia and of sponsoring most of his early songs. Partly through my efforts, Oliver Nelson, now a Hollywood composer-conductor, became the first black musician to arrange and conduct a TV dramatic series, "Mr. Broadway." With an integrated duo, I cut the original disk of "Lollipop," a song that was a Chordettes smash.

Personal immersion makes for immediacy, but it also tends to limit one's view of a field. Turning from the music business to writing about music necessitated an opening of the lens aperture. Here was where that abomination of the underground press, best-selling charts, became a source of objective information. Just as scoreboards are an index to baseball history, so music charts are the matrix of pop music history.

I first began thinking about this book in 1961 when I contributed a survey piece, "Popular Music from Minstrel Songs to Rock 'n' Roll," to *One Hundred Years of Music in America,* centennial publication of G. Schirmer, Inc. I am indebted to the publishers and editors of *Billboard,* and particularly to Lee Zhito and Paul Ackerman, for the opportunity, since 1966, of developing some of this volume's analytical ideas in articles I wrote for the annual editions of the magazine's "World of Soul." I owe a similar debt to another knowledgeable lunch companion, Russell Sanjek of *BMI: The Many Worlds of Music,* and to Doug Allen and Alan LeMond, publisher and editor of *Cavalier.*

References will be found in the text to recordings, magazine articles, and books that stimulated my thinking or yielded useful information. The work of a number of men requires special mention: Robert M. W. Dixon and John Godrich for *Blues and Gospel Records, 1902–1942;* Mike Leadbitter and Neil Slaven for *Blues Records, 1943–1966;* Leonard Feather for *The Encyclopedia of Jazz;* Nat Shapiro for the volumes of *Popular Music; An Annotated Index of American Popular Songs;* Pete Welding, whose research and Testament recordings have yielded basic documentation of the blues; LeRoi Jones for his provocative book *Blues People;* Charles Keil for his study *Urban Blues;* Paul Oliver for his books on Bessie Smith and the Blues; and Sam Charters, author of *The Country Blues* and *The Bluesmen,* and long a field researcher and producer of blues recordings. Many other people have given me the benefit of their thoughts. But I would feel remiss in failing to acknowledge the assistance of Ghita Milgrom, Ahmet Ertegun and Bob Rolontz of Atlantic Records, Herman Lubinsky of Savoy, Henry Glover of King Records, Bobby Shad of Time Records, Dave Axelrod of Capitol Records, and Catherine Fauver and Charles N. Heckelmann, my dedicated editor, at Cowles Book Company.

In this brief study I have attempted to trace the development of soul music, a vocal art, from its root beginning in country blues. As a pioneer survey, it has the limitations of any first trip. I have lingered too long in some places and moved too quickly over others. No material will be found on jazz, except for some of the singers, partly because it it an instrumental art and partly because it has been so extensively covered. I hope that I have succeeded in conveying some idea of the rich contribution of black artists to the growth and flowering of American Pop from 1920 to the present.

As a scholar who once was part of the scene, I hope also that I have been able to avoid the error of rock and blues purists who approach performers and creators as if they lived in a vacuum or on an esthetic cloud. To such dogmatists, it is a matter of grave concern that Howlin' Wolf idolized Jimmie Rodgers, Father of White Country Music, and that Albert King had an (impure) love for Woody Herman's band. They learn with despair that Albert King has said, "Sometimes I think I'd like to go back to driving a bulldozer. This music can get awful boring."

The compartmental approach is so destructive that, as an instance, an extremely well-informed music commentator devotes one paragraph in a book on the big bands to Bob Wills, whose Texas Playboys were giants of western swing and whose band was every bit as exciting as Glenn Miller or Tommy Dorsey, each of whom rates a long essay. The strength of American pop music is that it has never paid attention to categories, and has always been more concerned with communication than self-expression. Since the turn of the century it has welcomed the free interplay of black and white, the absence of which on the social, economic, and political levels today threatens the very foundations of our society.

Labor Day, 1969   ARNOLD SHAW

SOUL IS . . .

The fifth game of the World Series of 1968 began, as such public events do, with the singing of the national anthem. The young Puerto Rican chosen to sing "The Star-Spangled Banner," accompanied himself on an acoustic guitar. As he progressed through the song, some boos echoed across Detroit's Tiger Stadium. And hardly had José Feliciano completed his rendition, punctuated with a gentle "yeah, yeah" at the end, than angry phone calls began jarring NBC's switchboard, followed by a flood of telegrams and letters of outrage.

"I'm young enough," said the brother of a Tiger infielder, "to understand it, but I think it stank. It was nonpatriotic."

A Detroit housewife told a reporter, "It was a disgrace and an insult. I'm going to write my senator."

Verdict of the conductor of the U. S. Army Band: "Totally unacceptable."

Now, what had Feliciano done to create such a furor? Instead of using the traditional chords and adhering to the authorized melody line of "To Anacreon in Heaven"—the eighteenth century English drinking song to which Francis Scott Key, who was not a composer, had written the words of the national anthem—the Puerto Rican vocalist had occasionally substituted his own chords, manipulated the pitches, and altered the note values. As he had become more involved in the song, he had made considerable use of melisma, stretching one syllable over many notes. (Bluesmen call it "worryin' " a word.) In short, he had done what jazz singers, folk artists, and even pop singers sometimes do—changed the published version in accordance with his feelings.

"A man expresses love for his country any way he feels," said Feliciano, who was born blind, settled in Spanish Harlem in 1950, and grew up on Manhattan's slum West Side. "I did it with the intention of just communicating with young people. The anthem is a groovy thing and it should be upgraded. . . . It sure made people listen. . . ." That his treatment was heartfelt and intense no one questioned. But since it was "soul-spangled," as one newsman wrote, instead of star-spangled, it infuriated traditionalists.

Of course, there are those who would question the applicability of the word "soul" to Feliciano, since he is of Spanish and not African descent, is not an American Negro but a Puerto Rican, and is brown, not black. But there can be little doubt that his style was soulful, to substitute an esthetic for a racial concept.

As both a racial and an esthetic term, Soul has gained currency only recently. Station WOL of Washington, D.C., programming for black listeners, made its initial use of the phrase "Soul Radio" in July of 1965. Three years earlier, at the height of the twist craze, saxist King Curtis had had an R & B hit in an original instrumental titled "Soul Twist." While the term is to be found earlier in jazz and pop music criticism as an epithet of praise, the non-music world first discovered it during recent black ghetto uprisings when shopkeepers displayed Soul Brother signs in an effort to escape destruction and looting. In short, the concept took shape as an identifying symbol in the sixties.

Perhaps because of Soul's youth, definitions and descriptions vary greatly. "We don't really know what Soul it," says Ray Charles, one of its foremost musical exponents. "It's like electricity. It's a force that can light a room."

Kristin Hunter, author of *Soul Brothers and Sister Lou*, is not satisfied with such an abstraction. "It may be a mystique to some," she has said, "but to me it is a concrete reality. I find it in the singing of Ray Charles and Aretha Franklin, in the sermons of James Cleveland, in the rhetoric of two black spokesmen as dissimilar as Stokely Carmichael and Martin Luther King. . . . Not all black people have soul and not all white people are lacking in it . . . because soul is a way of being at home with yourself, at home with your body, at home in your world, and digging yourself and the world both happily and tragically."

"Soul is being natural," Al Calloway agrees, "telling it like it is." Though this statement by the publisher of the Afro-American magazine *The Probe* does not contain any color qualifications, all of his references do. The Soul Heroes on Chicago's Wall of Respect, at Langley Avenue and Forty-third Street, are all Afro-Americans, and specifically Afro-Americans "who have steered large masses of black people away from the 'assimilation complex' bag that Du Bois talked about, and guided them to the positive course of *digging* themselves. . . . The real genius of the Wall is that it generates African-American self-pride." Calloway concludes, "One thing is certain: soul would be nowhere without the great saviour, soul food," a thought that has stirred blue-eyed jazzmen and bluesmen to seek musical salvation in pig tails, knuckles, ears, snout, neck bones, tripe, ham hocks, hog maws, sowbelly, and chitterlings (the small intestines of a pig, pronounced "chit-lins"), not to mention turnip and collard greens, black-eyed peas, and sweet potato pie.

But black actress Gail Fisher asserts, "Soul is not just black. It's being groovy. Soul is everything that is good—love, warmth and rhythm, happiness and feeling."

Black comic Godfrey Cambridge does not share this sunshine view. "Soul is getting kicked in the ass," he says, "until you don't know what it's for. It's being broke and down and out, and people telling you you're no good. It's the language of the subculture; but you can't learn it because no one can give you black lessons."

It was not until 1967 and 1968 that the mass media, and even music trade papers, gave full recognition to the concept.

3

In June, 1967, *Billboard* issued the first in an annual series titled "The World of Soul," to document "the impact of Blues and R & B upon our musical culture."* In April, 1968, *Esquire* turned to author Claude Brown and publisher Al Calloway for "An Introduction to Soul," while *Time*'s cover story in June focused on Aretha Franklin, "Lady Soul: Singing It Like It Is."

By early '69, *Time* was advising that Soul had become such an in thing that soul food restaurants for white diners were springing up everywhere—West Boondock in Manhattan, Player's Choice in Hollywood, and Melvin's in Boston, to name a few. By that time there were at least three soul food cookbooks on the market, enabling suburban housewives to prepare dishes from items that once had been discards for plantation slaves from "the big house on the hill."

By '68 the scholars had also become involved with the concept. In its April issue, *Race*, the journal of the Institute of Race Relations, described "The Rhetoric of Soul: Identification in Negro Society." This is an extremely revealing study, both because the writer tried to be objective and failed, and because the field approach proved inadequate to bridge the culture gap.

Swedish ethnographer Ulf Hannerz found that the concept had emerged from the black ghettos of large northern cities to signify what is *essentially Negro*. But he contended that it was an ambivalent concept. Being a "soul brother" meant belonging to a *select* group rather than a segregated one, marked by a high rate of unemployment, incidence of crime, and percentage of broken families—and, to add items that Dr. Hannerz somehow neglected to mention: poor educational facilities, circumscribed social mobility, exorbitant rents and food costs, inferior housing, high interest rates, and discrimination.

* To that issue, the author of this book contributed "The Blues: A Definition," "100 Years of the Blues," "Billie Holiday and the Blues," "Gershwin, Arlen and The Blues," and "A Bookshelf of the Blues." For the 1968 edition, Arnold Shaw wrote "Piano Blues," "Blue-Eyed Soul," "The Blues Bands," and "Choreography & Soul." In the most recent edition (1969), Shaw is represented by "The Rhythm & Blues Revival: No White Gloved, Black Hits" and "Flipside Blacks Sing Country Music."

4

When it came to "soul music," the Swedish scholar found *Soul* no difficulty in identifying people (James Brown) and media *Music* (the Soul Shack, a record shop in Washington, D.C., WOL Soul Radio, and WWRL Soul Brother Radio). But he was able to discern only three themes: "lack of control over the social environment," "unstable personal relationships," and "a bitter-sweet experience" (?). The style, in his view, alter- *Style* nated "between aggressive, somewhat boasting behaviour and plaintive behaviour from an implicit under-dog position." Apparently Dr. Hannerz was not aware of Nina Simone's social fury, Otis Redding's high-voltage demand for "Respect," James Brown's jubilant eroticism, and the many other notes of pride, militancy, and anger sounded by the soul singers.

Granting that Soul had become publicly associated with black militancy as a result of the ghetto explosions, Dr. Hannerz saw "little basis for connecting the majority of 'soul brothers' with black militant nationalism." Obviously, he was correct simply in terms of numbers. But to think quantitatively instead of historically is to miss vital differences in temper and direction.

"Soul is sass, man," says Claude Brown, author of *Manchild in the Promised Land.* "Soul is arrogance. Soul is walkin' down the street in a way that says, 'This is me, muh-fuh!' Soul is that nigger whore comin' along . . . ja . . . ja . . . ja, and walkin' like she sayin', 'Here it is, baby. Come an' git it.' Soul is being true to yourself, to what is *you.* Now, hold on: soul is . . . that . . . uninhibited . . . no, *ex-tremely* uninhibited self . . . expression that goes into practi-cally every Negro endeavor . . . That's soul. And there's swagger in it, man."

The dots are Claude Brown's. But his conception embodies an all-essential time coordinate missing from Dr. Hannerz's view. Blind Lemon Jefferson has many points of contact with Ray Charles, as Bessie Smith has with Aretha Franklin and Leadbelly with James Brown. But the thundering contrasts are a product not merely of personality but of the temper of the times. The Blues, country and classic, is an expression of forti-tude in the face of frustration. After World War II, rhythm-

5

in-blues embodied the search for urban pleasures as well as the electrified resentment of a people for whom the grandiose slogans of the war had proved hollow promises. Soul is black, not blue, sass, anger, and rage. It is not just feeling but conviction. Not just intensity but involvement. A force as well as a style, an accolade as well as identification. It is an expressive explosiveness, ignited by a people's discovery of self-pride, power, and potential for growth.

As we shall see, Soul became a musical force in the mid-fifties with Ray Charles and James Brown. But it did not acquire its electric stridency and highly amplified tension, it did not become *possession* rather than expression, until the collapse of the biracial civil rights movement. Soul is black nationalism in Pop. Stylistically it can be imitated, as it has been by white singers and instrumentalists. But the native expression derives from people whose ancestors reached these shores in chains, who cooked soul food as a matter of survival, who attended religious services in storefront gospel churches, and who have a long history of deprivation, exploitation, and segregation behind them.

To understand Soul and put it in perspective, we must go back at least to the Blues and pursue its transformation into urban rhythm-and-blues. But the position of this study is that, while Blues is the root of Soul, it derives most immediately from gospel and black church music; to be precise, from shouting, handclapping, foot-stomping, jubilant, and frenzied storefront-church music.

Part I
BLUES

I wrote these blues, gonna sing 'em as I please,
I wrote these blues, gonna sing 'em as I please
I'm the only one like the way I'm singin' em, I'll
swear to goodness ain't no one else to please.

—Traditional

2

COUNTRY BLUES AND BOTTLENECK BLUESMEN

Soul music had its distant beginnings whenever "we" became "I" for black people, whenever "people" became "person," and, as a historical matter, when "slave" became "citizen." The Negro made music from his earliest days on this continent. But it was communal music: to pray to, to lighten labor, occasionally to dance to. In the work songs, with their strong rhythms and kinesthetic accents, we find root material of the blues. But the singer had to see himself as an individual and personalize the group's experience before the work song or the freer-flowing field holler could emerge as a blues.

Obviously, this could not become a sociohistorical reality until some time after the Emancipation Proclamation. The slave had to be separated from the land to which he had been feudally attached and given awesome mobility. The food and shelter provided on the plantation had to be taken away and the "freed" man given the freedom to starve and scramble for necessities. The new man had to discover the world of penitentiaries and chain gangs and romantic sex and a bottle of gin before he began to sing:

> When a woman takes de blues
> She tucks her head and cries.
> But when a man catches the blues,
> He catches er freight and rides.

9

If de blues was whiskey
I'd stay drunk all de time.
De blues ain't nothin'
But a poor man's heart disease.

As jazz was an urban, instrumental development, emerging from the marching meters of brass bands and the lively, improvised rhythms of entertainment tenderloins, the blues was rural in origin—the vocal ruminations of lonely men, hungry people, mistreated prisoners, and troubled hearts. Jazz was revelry, happy dance music. Blues was saying things "they wished they could say in real life."

Jazz was New Orleans, Memphis, brass instruments, woodwinds, whorehouses, tailgate wagons, and riverboats. The blues was the plains of Missouri and Texas, the delta region of Mississippi, a wheezing harmonica, a whining slide guitar, and a falsetto, nasal cry. Jazz was Louis Armstrong and the gold-toothed grin in the wide satchel mouth, Jelly Roll Morton and the diamonds in gold-jacketed teeth.

The country blues was Blind Lemon Jefferson, singing on southern street corners and working Texas tenderloins . . . Mance Lipscomb, a Brazos County sharecropper, who was never a "perfessional" musician like his father but remained "an open player by himself" for neighborhood parties . . . Speckled Red, born Rufus Perryman in Monroe, Louisiana, in 1892, a worker in sawmill camps and turpentine jukes, who wrote "The Dirty Dozens," the well-known talkin' dirty and insult song . . . Sleepy John Estes, the one-eyed Brownsville, Texas, bluesman whose style of "crying the blues," in Big Bill Broonzy's words, was first captured on wax in the twenties and who emerged again in the sixties, a wizened old man with a cane, to record for Delmark and enchant listeners at the Newport Folk Festival of 1964 . . . Skip James, a Yazoo County sharecropper, Arkansas sawmill worker, and Birmingham strip miner, who could not reconcile profane blues with his religious feelings and who, after entering the church in 1932, did not record again for thirty-two years.

Louisiana, Tennessee, and Texas have each been credited at

times with originating the blues. By now, scholars are agreed that the delta area of Mississippi is the most likely birthplace, if any one place can be so designated, or at least has produced the largest number of important bluesmen. While the blues has its roots in the various forms of black music that preceded it—work songs, hollers, ring shouts, and particularly the spirituals—it is basically a post-Civil War development.

Rural in origin, the earliest blues developed in places with limited instrumental resources and without a European instrumental tradition. The voice was used as an instrument. The music was a form of self-expression, self-contemplation, self-amusement, and only later a music for performance and entertainment. It also became a music for dancing, but in its earliest stage it was the itinerant music of men traveling from farm to farm, lumber camp to lumber camp, town to town, and, unquestionably, sweetheart to sweetheart.

Some efforts have been made to discern different blues styles in terms of rural, city, urban, and soul. These differences exist. But they are so tenuous as to make for confusion. I favor distinctions in terms of place and time, geography and era, though even these must be regarded as suggestive rather than precise. Speaking broadly, scholars find distinguishing characteristics that can be associated with three geographical areas: delta, including Mississippi, Arkansas, and Alabama; southwestern, including Oklahoma, Missouri, and Texas; and southeastern, meaning Tennessee, Georgia, and Florida.

Delta, or Mississippi, style is regarded as the most primitive and crude. As Pete Welding has described it in a recent *Down Beat* article, it is characterized by undeveloped lyrics, limited melody, spoken rather than sung words, and a delivery that is harsh and coarse. Among the bluesmen who fit into this category are Son House, Bukka White, John Lee Hooker, Mississippi John Hurt, and Robert Johnson. To Welding's characterization, I would add the illumination offered by Charles Keil in *Urban Blues*: "drones, moans, the bottleneck guitar technique, constant repetition of melodic figures, harmonica tremolos, a heavy sound and rough intensity." Big Bill

Broonzy, a Mississippi-Arkansas product, has said of his guitar style, "We push the strings."

Texas, or southwestern, style introduces elements of sophistication and refinement. Both playing and singing become cleaner, clearer, and more musical. Bluesmen who helped develop this style include Aaron T-Bone Walker, Charles Brown, Smokey Hogg, Amos Millburn, Lowell Fulson, and Percy Mayfield. In Charles Keil's description, Texas country blues tradition emphasizes "a somewhat lighter touch; guitar playing tends to be less chordal, with an emphasis on single-string melodic dexterity; more relaxed vocal qualities and an open rather than a dense accompaniment texture prevail."

The southeastern development is the most advanced and schooled of all, involving harmonic inventiveness, a disciplined sense of rhythm, and a search for musical expressiveness. Welding's epithets are "consonant," "rich," and "finely wrought." The singers working in this tradition include Little Milton, Junior Parker, Johnny Ace, Bobby Bland, B. B. King, and Albert King.

Born blind, illiterate, a man who ate with his hands and was paid off with a bottle of cheap whiskey and a prostitute when he recorded, Lemon Jefferson was nevertheless the man whose singing has been characterized as "the most exciting country blues singing of the 1920s." His life was short and not too pleasant despite his innate talent, and he did not leave a particularly good impression on those who knew him. But he did leave a legacy of tough recordings and gifted followers— among them, Josh White, Lightnin' Hopkins, Aaron T-Bone Walker, and Leadbelly.

Begging was, in those days, an inevitable occupation for a blind man without schooling. By the time he was fourteen, Jefferson had mastered the guitar and was singing on the streets of Wortham, Texas, close by Couchman, where he had been born in 1897. At twenty, when America was entering the war against the Kaiser, he left his parents' farm and traveled to Dallas. There is obvious autobiography in "Tin Cup Blues," which he later recorded:

I stood on the corner, and almost bust my head,
I stood on the corner, almost bust my head,
I couldn't earn me enough money to buy me a loaf of bread.

For a time, he earned money performing as a novelty wrestler in Dallas theaters; he was 250 pounds of blubber. Then he joined forces with Leadbelly: "With Huddie's mandolin," according to folklorists John and Alan Lomax, "and Lemon's Hawaiian guitar, [they] made a good living in the saloons and red-light district of East Dallas."

After eight years of rootless wandering through southern tenderloins—his lead boys reportedly included Josh White, Lightnin' Hopkins, Leadbelly, and Aaron T-Bone Walker—he became so widely known that Paramount recorded him and released two sides in April, 1926. "Booster Blues" and "Dry Southern Blues" attracted enough purchasers that the company had a new Jefferson disk on the market the following month. Although he cut two sides for Okeh, which tried to lure him away, he wound up making seventy-nine blues records for Paramount in the four years of his active recording career. By February, 1930, he was prematurely dead, a casualty of his blindness and, perhaps, drunkenness. Details are sketchy. But he was found in the snow one morning after he had recorded at Paramount's Chicago studios. Reports had it that he had gone to a house party after the session. His guitar lay in the snow beside the frozen body.

Twenty-four of the blues he recorded are readily obtainable in two albums released by Riverside Records. They are primitive in every respect except two. The lyrics are crude, often confused, and generally formless. The performance is likewise crude, frequently lacking meter and structure. But the accompaniments played by Jefferson are gems, revealing an innate musical sense and a feeling for expressive figuration. And though he is difficult, if not impossible, to understand, there is an intensity in the high-pitched whine of his voice that makes his bitterness, pain, and disappointment palpable.

Blind Lemon derived little from his short tenure on this earth. His blues abound in the negations that would assail a blind, fat, unattractive man of limited means and outlook. Sex was an obsession and women were untrustworthy:

> Peach Orchard Mama, you swore nobody'd pick your fruit but me,
> Peach Orchard Mama, you swore no one'd pick your fruit but me,
> I found three kid men shaking down your peaches free.

"Black Snake Moan," the highly successful recording that prompted an approach by Okeh Records, was an erotic adaptation of a narrative blues by Victoria Spivey. In Blind Lemon's version, the actual snake became a vivid sex image:

> Um-um, black snake crawling in my room,
> Um-um, black snake crawling in my room,
> Yes, some pretty mama better get this black snake soon.

Blindness meant constant dependence on others. Even his recording director was apparently not above taking advantage of him. Only in his music was Jefferson the complete master. In music he poured out the woes of all the helpless and exploited. And what of their hopes?

> Well, there's one kind favor I ask of you,
> One kind favor I ask of you,
> Lord, there's one kind favor I ask of you,
> Please see that my grave is kept clean.

(Bob Dylan is one of a number of contemporary artists who have recorded this blues.) Blind Lemon lies in an unmarked grave between his mother and sister in an overgrown field outside Wortham, Texas. But no marker is required to assure his place in the history of country blues.

The Blind Lemon collaborator who became known as Leadbelly—a nickname he allegedly acquired in a penitentiary because he had "guts of steel and could outwork, outsing and outlast everybody"—had a better command of language than his associate but hardly as good a command of his temper or fists.

Born of ex-slaves in Mooringsport, Louisiana, around 1888 and raised in Texas, Huddie Ledbetter was in and out of prison three times. From 1918 until he was pardoned in 1925, he was in a Louisiana penitentiary for having murdered a romantic competitor. From February, 1930, to August, 1934, he was in a Texas jail serving a sentence for attempted homicide. He was pardoned again. And during 1939-40, after coming north, he served a year in a New York prison on an assault conviction. Knife scars on his right cheek and throat were mute evidence of his tempestuous brawls.

A big man, over six feet tall, Leadbelly also had big ideas. He billed himself "King of the Twelve-String Guitar." In the Texas jail he earned the reputation of being the number-one man in the number-one gang on the number-one chain gang in the state. According to Alan Lomax, son of the archivist who befriended Leadbelly, "he could carry the lead row in the field for twelve to fourteen hours under the broiling July and August sun and then cut the fool for the guards all evening." Fellow convicts were snide about his readiness to perform for the whites. But Leadbelly's performances led to his becoming a trusty, an entertainer, and ultimately a healthy survivor of chain gang brutality.

Without compunction about being a con man, he apparently gloried in his feats of persuasion as well as brawn. It is now believed that the story of his pardon from the Texas pen in 1934 is apochryphal. But it was widely circulated—no doubt at his instigation—that when he learned of an impending visit of Governor Pat Neff to the prison, he hurriedly composed "A Plea for Mercy." Legend has it that the governor, who had sworn never to pardon a prisoner, was so moved by Leadbelly's singing that he ordered the release of the King of the Twelve-String Guitar. According to Alan Lomax, who repeated this tale in his introduction to a Leadbelly memorial album, Huddie "also met and conquered my father one summer afternoon in Louisiana so that John A. Lomax spent a year introducing him to the world."

The elder Lomax, with whom Leadbelly broke in bitterness after a year, arranged for him to make recordings for the archives of the Library of Congress. By that time Leadbelly had attained recognition nationally as an artist in the ethnic blues tradition and was making appearances in nightclubs, on the radio, and at colleges, where he reportedly both terrified and enchanted the students. Having moved to New York shortly after becoming Lomax's protégé, he worked closely with such folk artists as Cisco Houston, Sonny Terry, and Woody Guthrie.

In fact, the Oklahoma-born Dust Bowl folkster is said to have journeyed east in a mood of great depression to draw strength from the commanding presence and inspired artistry of the ex-con. (Curiously, young Bob Dylan made a similar hegira twenty years later to Woody Guthrie's bedside in a Brooklyn hospital.)

Leadbelly died in 1949, the year of a highly successful tour of France, a victim of the muscular atrophy disease that killed baseball's famed Iron Horse, Lou Gehrig. In that year the Almanac Singers, a *Talking Union* group that included Pete Seeger and Woody Guthrie, modulated into the Weavers, the brilliant quartet that made hit records of Guthrie's "This Land Is Your Land" and Leadbelly's tender love ballad, "Good Night, Irene."

It is interesting that both songs were germinated by the experiences of dispossessed and itinerant laborers, the one by Oklahoma Dust Bowl farmers and the other by Texas rivermen. Unfortunately for Leadbelly, "Irene" became a pop hit in the year after his death. Six years later, another song he had recorded, "Rock Island Line," became a best-selling disk for the British singer Lonnie Donegan, who received authorship credit for his version of the traditional folk ballad.

Among the most moving and exciting of all of Leadbelly's recordings is his version of "Midnight Special," based on the superstition that if the light of a train shines into a prisoner's cell at midnight he will soon be a free man. Leadbelly's affinity for prison and railroad songs was hardly surprising. But he also had a large repertoire of jigs, reels, slow drags, cakewalks, sukey-jumps, and almost anything else an audience might favor. He possessed the self-taught artist's ability to absorb and reproduce almost anything he heard, as the numerous recordings he made for Asch, Capitol, Columbia, Disc, Folkways, Musicraft, Victor, and Stinson (unquestionably his best) amply testify.

In the literature of the blues, there is perhaps no more disturbing disquisition on their nature than Leadbelly's. "All Negroes like blues," he says in the spoken introduction on his Stinson disk of "Good Morning Blues." "Why? Because they was born with the blues. And now, everybody have the blues." (Don't underestimate Leadbelly's scorn for Mr. Charley despite the big con.) "But when you lay down at night, turn from one side of the bed all night to the other and you can't sleep, what's the matter? Blues got you.

"Or when you git up in the mornin', sit on side of the bed—may have a mother or father, sister or brother, boyfriend or girlfriend, husband or wife around—you don' want no talk out of um. They ain't done you nothin', you ain't done them nothin'—what's the matter? Blues got you.

"Well, you get up and shev your feet down under the table and look down in your place—you may have chicken and rice, take my egvice, you walk away and shake your head, you say, 'Lord, have mercy. I can't eat, I can't sleep.' What's the matter? Why, the blues got you. They want to talk to you. You got to tell um something . . ."

Then Leadbelly begins singing the ironic "Good Morning Blues," but adds lines of his own:

> I was not sick, but I was dissatisfied . . .
> I went to eat my breakfast, the blues was in my bread . . .

These poetic lines lead to a complete non sequitur. "I got a new way of spelling Memphis, Tennessee," he sings, in an obvious attempt to dissolve despondency in flippancy.

But Leadbelly can also put on a front to hide disappointment. In "Big Fat Woman," cut, according to Alan Lomax, with a stout woman dancing for him in the Asch studio—talk about the search of teen-age rock groups for immediacy—he sings, "I woke up this mornin' and found my baby gone/I woke up this mornin' and found my baby gone/I was so mistreated but I wouldn't let on."

17

He can also mock his superiors. In "Take This Hammer," a ballad he learned while traveling with the Lomaxes, he sings, "Take this hammer (wow!) and carry it to the captain (wow!)/You tell him I'm gone (wow!)." And at the end "If he asks you (wow!) was I laughin' (wow!)/You tell him I was cryin' (wow!)."

In "Gray Goose," it's the Baptist preacher who becomes the object of extended derision. Instead of going to church, the preacher goes hunting and kills a tremendous bird. But even though the fowl is six weeks a-boilin' the fork wouldn't stick him, the knife wouldn't cut him, the hogs wouldn't eat him, the sawmill couldn't cut him, and the last time "I seed him, Lord, Lord, Lord, he was flyin' 'cross the ocean with a long string of goslins, and they all gwine, Quack, Quack."

The gray goose was sure a tough bird. But so was Huddie Ledbetter, who overcame the harsh limitations of being born to ex-slaves, having no education and a murderous temper, and succeeded in making himself a seminal figure among a generation of itinerant bluesmen.

The 1939 Carnegie Hall concert that introduced Leadbelly to New York and the national folk scene also featured an Arkansas country singer named William Lee Conley Broonzy. Known as Big Bill Broonzy, he was introduced as an ex-sharecropper. He had worked his own farm in 1915, shortly after his marriage, and later owned a farm in Pine Bluff, Arkansas. But at the time of the "Spirituals to Swing" shindig, he was a highly successful writer of blues and a best-selling recording artist on the Vocalion label. Unlike excitable Leadbelly and Blind Lemon Jefferson, whose style he copied in the early 1930s, Big Bill effectively made the transition from a rural country singer to an urban professional, though his audience remained largely black.

A man with a warm, ingratiating personality, he found the atmosphere of the South unbearable when he was mustered out of the army after World War I. Later he wrote a famous bitter quatrain:

> Now, if you're white
> You're all right.
> If you're brown,
> Stick aroun'.
> But if you're black
> Git back! Git back! Git back!

He admitted later that when he went north to Chicago in 1920, he had been determined to have everything white men had: sharp clothes, shiny cars, and white women. Although he took a job as a redcap with the Pullman Company, he began studying guitar with a Paramount blues singer, Papa Charlie Jackson. (As a boy, he had entertained at Arkansas picnics on a homemade fiddle constructed from a cigar box.) By keeping after Mayo Williams, head of Paramount Records, which recorded Blind Lemon, he managed to get a record released in 1927. He was then thirty-four years old, having been born in Scott, Mississippi, on June 26, 1893, one of twenty-one children.

It took seven more years of hard plugging before Big Bill began to make a dent in the record market. During those years, the recording industry suffered the throes of the depression that was shaking up the world's economy. Dwindling sales forced Columbia and its subsidiary Okeh into receivership, while Paramount Records shuttered its doors completely. And Broonzy was himself struggling, trying to find a style of his own.

The economic togetherness of the New Deal brought a racial rapport that made Josh White the Presidential Minstrel and a favorite of Franklin and Eleanor Roosevelt. Sparked by White, who added showmanship—the lit cigarette stuck behind the ear—bell-like diction, and male sex-manship to the blues, an audience for blues singers developed in white nightclubs. Broonzy made a well-deserved ascent, displaying a knowing way in charming white intellectuals and nightclub habitués both here and abroad.

A recording contract in 1934 with Bluebird, a new Victor subsidiary, yielded Broonzy's first big disk, "Take Your Hands

Off Her" (a rewrite of the ribald tent show ditty "Take Your Finger Off It") and "The Sun Gonna Shine in My Back Door Some Day" (an elaboration of Richard M. Jones's classic "Trouble in Mind"). These sides make it clear that he had developed from a raucous blues shouter in the Blind Lemon tradition to a mellow blues balladeer in the mode of Leroy Carr, then a reigning favorite.

Carr, who died prematurely in 1935, is credited with completely transforming the blues singing style. The writer of such fine and well-recorded songs as "How Long, How Long Blues" and "In the Evening When the Sun Goes Down," Carr and his gifted accompanist, Scrapper Blackwell, launched a tradition of sweet blues adorned with beautiful chording that was to culminate in the sophisticated blues singing of Josh White, Dinah Washington, Sam Cooke, Nat "King" Cole, Sarah Vaughan, and other black artists. Unquestionably, Carr's style went far to make the blues palatable to white listeners, who approached the form as entertainment rather than an experience. Carr frequently accompanied himself at the piano instead of using guitar, a procedure followed by Big Bill.

During the early forties, Broonzy served as accompanist to Lil Green, a well-loved Chicago blues singer whose first big hit on Bluebird was her own song, "Romance in the Dark." Touring Detroit and Chicago theaters with her, Big Bill wrote some of her favorite songs, including "Country Boy Blues," "My Mellow Man," and "Keep Your Hands on Your Heart."

By the end of World War II, Big Bill's popularity had dipped so badly that he took a job as janitor at Iowa State College. (It should be borne in mind that Negro songwriters and recording artists operated under a severe handicap at this time, and for years to come. Frequently they were given only outright payments—no continuing royalties—for their work.)

His comeback led eventually to a set of recording sessions out of which came one of the interesting audio documentaries on the blues. *The Bill Broonzy Story* consists of five Verve LPs excerpted from ten hours of singing, playing, and talking. Broonzy performs thirty-four selections, including work songs, spirituals, hollers, folk ballads, popular standards, a lullaby, and blues. The blues, which predominate, are mostly of his own creation but also include selections by Bessie Smith ("Backwater Blues"), Leroy Carr ("In the Evening"), Richard M. Jones ("Trouble in Mind"), and evergreens like "I'm Gonna Move to the Outskirts of Town."

In an interview with Chicago disk jockey Studs Terkel and Cleveland disk jockey Bill Randle, Broonzy reminisced about such contemporaries as Blind Lemon, Huddie Ledbetter ("We called him Lead because that's what he had in his breeches"), Howlin' Wolf, Muddy Waters, Big Boy Crudup ("you hear Elvis Presley and you hearin' Big Boy"), Speckled Red, Tampa Red ("he played guitar with a little bottleneck on his finger and everybody tried to play like him"), Kokomo Arnold, Sonny Boy Williamson, Blind Boy Fuller, and others.

He was affable, ingratiating, and outspoken, particularly when it came to the ladies ("Georgia White was the girl made 'Trouble in Trouble', but nobody could get to her 'cause her husband was always around"). He made probing observations about jazz and the blues, spirituals and the blues, playing the blues ("sure, the strings of my guitar are out of tune, how else can you play the blues?"). In short, here is an anthology, a technical study, and an autobiography, all in one.

The morning after the last of three sessions, Broonzy was operated on for lung cancer. He required a second operation. Then, on the morning of August 14, 1958, as an ambulance was rushing him to the hospital once again, Big Bill died. In his autobiography, *Big Bill Blues*, he wrote, "When you write about me, please don't say that I'm a musician or a guitar player—just write Big Bill was a well-known blues singer and player and has recorded 260 blues songs from 1925 up til 1952; he was a happy man when he was drunk and playing with women; he was liked by all the blues singers, some would even get a little jealous sometimes but Bill would buy a bottle of whiskey and they would all start laughing and playing again . . ."

At his funeral Mahalia Jackson, with whom he had toured a

number of times, sang "Just a Closer Walk with Thee," Win Stracke, a Chicago folklorist, sang "We're All Brothers," and Brother John Sellers rendered "Nobody Knows the Trouble I've Seen." Broonzy's own voice was heard via a taped recording of "Swing Low Sweet Chariot."

In 1928, in the period when talent scouts for the major record companies were roaming the South in a feverish search for authentic bluesmen, an Okeh man encountered Mississippi John Hurt in Memphis. The bluesman, who was born in Teoc, Mississippi, in 1894 and never went beyond second grade in school, came to New York and recorded "Spike Driver Blues," "Louis Collins," and "Frankie," among other blues.

Then he returned to his native state and disappeared in the delta cotton fields for thirty-five years. When a musicologist sought him out in 1963, he was working in the tiny town of Avalon, Mississippi, as a farmhand, and his wife as the farmer's cook. Together, they were earning twenty-eight dollars a month. "I thought he was the police," Hurt later said of the musicologist. "When he asked me to come north, I figured if I told him no, he'd take me anyway. So I told him yes."

Hurt came to Washington, D.C., where late in March and early in April of 1963 he cut thirteen sides for Dick and Louisa Spottswood's Piedmont label. These included several of the songs he had recorded for Okeh, "Avalon Blues" and the spicy "Salty Dog," "Candy Man" and "Richland Woman." A shy man, he was apologetic about the off-color lines and wanted to know whether he could sing them as he always did for his Mississippi friends:

> The rooster said, "Cock-a-doodle-doo,"
> Richland woman said, "Any cock will do."

That summer he sang at folk festivals in Newport and Philadelphia—and again returned to Mississippi to pick cotton at four dollars a day.

But by September, 1963, as interest in ethnic folk singers grew and his Piedmont album began to circulate, he embarked on a concert tour and played coffeehouses throughout New

England. Sixty-nine years old, he was now a full-time blues-man. He appeared at Newport again in '64, singing "Trouble, I've Had It All My Days" and other blues that were recorded live by Vanguard Records. In November, 1966, in Grenada, Mississippi, only three years after starting his new career, he died of a heart attack. He was an old-time delta bluesman, meaning really a farmer or laborer for whom playing the blues represented a mode of pondering and ruminating on his problems.

Although Hurt, Big Bill, and Leadbelly lived into modern times, they were part of the 1890s generation of bluesmen that included such pioneers as Charley Patton, Lonnie Johnson, and Mance Lipscomb. Even the next generation (Roosevelt Sykes, Son House, Big Boy Crudup, Bukka White, and others) and the succeeding generation (Lightnin' Hopkins, Robert Johnson, Homesick James Williamson, John Lee Hooker, and Elmore James) included men who were basically sharecroppers and farmhands, and only occasional performers and recording artists. It may well be that the emotionalism, intensity, and earthiness of their delivery, however crude, were the result of their attachment to the soil. Their hands and voices were not those of musicians but of working people.

To call country blues "bottleneck blues" is not entirely accurate. Many of the pioneer bluesmen were not slide gui-tarists. But it is a highly suggestive characterization. These guitars have a high-pitched, whining quality that is associated in contemporary ears with Hawaiian music. Steel bars are used to produce the smooth, rising glissandos of hula music. The delta bluesmen employed knives, metal tubes, cylindrical rings, and the necks of bottles. Small medicine bottles, placed on the third or fourth fingers of the left hand, or sometimes on the pinky, were utilized. When these were not available, the neck of a Coke bottle, skillfully broken off, served as well. These devices were slid along the strings from note to note, whence the style sometimes known as "slide guitar."

The accompaniment employed by Mississippi John Hurt and others was a unison following of the voice. Queried about the origin of the blues, Son House, born in Mississippi in 1902, said, "All I can say is that when I was a boy we always was singin' in the fields. Not real singing, you know, just hollerin'. But we made up our songs about things that was happening to us at the time, and I think that's where the blues started."

Like Charley Patton before him and Skip James of his own generation (the 1900s), Son House was torn by the inner conflict between the profane life of the blues and the sanctified life of the preacher. As a youth, working to gather moss out of trees for mattresses, picking cotton, or performing the chores of a cowhand, and later as a rural preacher, he was upset when he heard men singing the blues.

Only after he moved to St. Louis to work at the Commonwealth Steel plant at the fabulous pay of one dollar an hour did he become interested in playing-and-singing. It happened one day when he saw a crowd gathered around a man who was playing guitar with a small medicine bottle on his finger. The sound of the instrument struck his fancy.

Through Patton, who was fifteen years older, he made a test for a Paramount Records scout and then recorded at the company's studios in Grafton, Wisconsin, in July, 1930. "Preachin' the Blues" reflected his troubled state of mind, which he constantly characterized in live performances—"I can't hold God in one hand and the Devil in the other." "Dry Spell Blues," another of his identifying songs, graphically described the plight of southern farm people during a drought.

In the early 1940s Eddie James House, Jr., to give him his Christian name, moved to Rochester, New York, attracted by the wages paid in a war plant. After a time he became a rivet-heater in a dispatch shop of the New York Central, an association that led to his working as a railroad porter for a dozen years.

When his playing buddy, Willie Brown, died in 1948, he took it as a sign and put his instrument away. He did not record again until 1962, when Alan Lomax persuaded him to cut a batch of songs for the Library of Congress. All he received for his efforts was a bottle of Coke. But, he adds with a good-natured twinkle. "It was good and cold." Since the Newport

Folk Festival, when he and other ethnic bluesmen were re-discovered by a new generation of folksters, he has played and lectured at college concerts and folk fests, a living representative of the delta blues tradition.

Another bluesman who was introduced to New York by the Spirituals to Swing concert in 1938 was Saunders Terrell of Greensboro, Georgia, better known as Sonny Terry and seldom thought of without his long-time partner, Brownie McGhee of Knoxville, Tennessee. The two teamed up during the Broadway run of Tennessee Williams's play *Cat on a Hot Tin Roof* when they worked in a brief scene. One of the most lasting and productive of partnerships, it has yielded a large catalog of blues albums on many record labels.

Born in October, 1911, harpist Terry lost the sight of both eyes in his teens, one in a children's game and the other when he was struck by a chunk of iron. It was apparently DeFord Bailey, the first, and for a long while the only Negro to appear on the Grand Ole Opry, who motivated Terry to turn to harmonica playing for a livelihood. One of Bailey's rousers on the Nashville radio show was his realistic imitation of a railroad train. Admirers of Sonny Terry contend that his harp-cum-voice imitation was even more exciting. Before teaming with Brownie McGhee, Terry worked the streets of North Carolina's tobacco towns with Blind Gary Davis, later known as the Reverend Gary Davis, and Blind Boy Fuller, whose eyesight was destroyed by a jealous girlfriend and a dose of lye in his washing water.

When the influential Fuller died suddenly in 1940, some of Brownie McGhee's Vocalion disks were released, much to his displeasure, under the cognomen of Blind Boy Fuller No. 2. Walter Brownie McGhee, who was born in 1914, had a lame right leg, the result of an attack of polio in his preschool days. In his teens, he had a string band that featured two washboards and that was popular in his hometown of Knoxville. After teaming with Sonny Terry in the early forties, he opened a school for guitarists and singers in Harlem known as the House of the Blues. Like Fuller, McGhee early espoused a swinging, bluegrass style known as "jukin' " in the Piedmont area—the southeastern states of Georgia, Florida, and the Carolinas. Unlike Fuller, his singing style had polish and intimacy.

McGhee was in this respect close to Josh White, who became the most successful and most popular (for a time) of southern bluesmen, Piedmont or delta. Born in Greenville, South Carolina, in February, 1908, of a deeply religious family, White early left his schooling to become lead boy for a long series of blind bluesmen, among them Blind Arnold, Blind Blake, and even Blind Lemon Jefferson. It was Blind Joe Taggart who first brought him into a recording studio (Paramount) in 1928. But his recording career really began in the 1930s when he cut gospel songs as the Singing Christian and blues as Pinewood Tom.

White achieved fame in the 1940s when his popularity with President and Mrs. Franklin Delano Roosevelt, and his performances at the White House, led to his being hailed as the Presidential Minstrel. He had top-selling disks in a *Chain Gang* album and in songs like "John Henry," "Hard-Time Blues," "(I'm Gonna Move to) The Outskirts of Town," and particularly "One Meat Ball," a million-copy pop adaptation of an old blues.

But he achieved his greatest renown through appearances in East Side, in-group Manhattan clubs, where his good looks and slick showmanship made him a pre-Belafonte black sex idol. Onstage he wore an open-necked striped sports shirt and made a beguiling figure as he performed with a lit cigarette stuck behind one ear. To folk singing, if not the blues, he brought matinee sexuality, bell-like diction, and pop appeal— hardly qualities that endeared him to blues purists. He died in 1969 in Manhasset, Long Island, after several years of inactivity forced upon him by an automobile accident.

Sam Hopkins, born in the Texas country of Blind Lemon Jefferson, about halfway between Houston and Dallas, became

Lightnin' Hopkins in 1946–47. By then he was thirty-four years old and an accomplished country bluesman who had performed at hometown (Centerville) dances between chores as a cotton picker and sharecropper.

Journeying to Houston as World War II ended, rather than return to sharecropping—listen to "Tim Moore's Farm" for an autobiographical account of the cruelties and indignities he endured on a north-of-Dallas farm—he was helped by a cousin who had recorded for Okeh and Vocalion in the twenties. Texas Alexander used him as an accompanist in club work and introduced him to a piano player known as "Thunder" Smith. At the urging of a Houston businesswoman scouting talent for the Aladdin label, Smith and Hopkins journeyed to Hollywood for a recording session in November, 1946.

"When I did 'Rocky Mountain,' " Hopkins later revealed, "where I'm fast with my fingers, they said, 'We'll call you Lightnin'.' " It seemed natural to have the credits read "Thunder" Smith and "Lightnin' Hopkins."

The disk ("Can't You Do Like You Used to Do" backed with "West Coast Blues") hardly generated the excitement suggested by the two cognomens. Neither did the other sides he made in 1947 for the Aladdin label, then seeking a competitor to Capitol's Leadbelly. But in that same year he also began recording for a small Houston company, Gold Star, and these sides established his reputation. (Today, they are collectors' items.) Without advertising, "Baby, Please Don't Go" sold more than eighty thousand disks, a sensational quantity for a regional record. On these disks, Lightnin' worked without Thunder, accompanying his singing in true country style on an unamplified guitar.

In the next ten years Hopkins cut nearly two hundred sides, recording for many of the small, independent rhythm-and-blues labels like Jax, Time, Herald, RPM, Kent, Sittin' In With, and Ace. Then, with the advent of rock 'n' roll, he tried to adapt his style to the demands of the teen-age market. It was a mistake, which recent Newport folk festivals have corrected by reawakening interest in him as an ethnic bluesman.

"The white boys just don't have the voices for blues," he said not too long ago. "They're afraid to let go of themselves. Afraid it makes them look too much like a fool."

Regardless of the validity of the statement, Hopkins's power as a performer is precisely in the unbuttoned emotionalism of his style. Samuel B. Charters, who recorded him in 1959 in a run-down house on Hadley Street in Houston, reports, "After he had sung the magnificent 'Penitentiary Blues,' he went on to sing seven more blues and Blind Lemon's song, 'One Kind Favor I Ask of You.' He sang until he became so tense emotionally that it was impossible to talk to him."

Except for the brief interval when he tried to sing rock, Lightnin' has continued the tradition of the rural shouter launched by Lemon Jefferson. He first heard the fat, blind singer when he was eight and went to a Baptist picnic in Buffalo, Texas. He studied Jefferson's raw, freewheeling, frequently unmetrical style. He was also influenced by his cousin Texas Alexander, another bluesman in the tough country tradition. For all these country bluesmen, songwriting was a form of autobiographical expression and singing was an intense expression of life lived in poverty, want, emotional frustration, and social degradation. The Negro audiences that made up their fervent following came to hear them tell it like it was for them, too. It was not entertainment but emotional sublimation in the style of Greek tragedy.

"Lightnin' is a magnificent figure," Samuel B. Charters writes in his pioneering and valuable study *The Country Blues*. "He is one of the last of his kind, a lonely, bitter man who brings to the blues the intensity and pain of hours in the hot sun, scraping at the hardened earth, singing to make the hours pass. The blues will go on. But the country blues, and the great singers who created, from the raw melodies of the work songs and field cries, the richness and variety of country blues, will pass with men like this thin, intense singer from Centerville, Texas."

Born in Clarksdale, Mississippi, in 1915, John Lee Hooker grew up in Memphis, worked in Cincinnati, and matured in

Detroit. He did not begin recording until after World War II. But despite his urban upbringing and emergence in the R & B era, his style is archaic and he remains a rural bluesman whose accompaniment includes heavy foot-stomping.

Hooker learned guitar and repertoire from his stepfather, who came from Shreveport, Louisiana, and whose home was visited by Blind Lemon, Blind Blake, and Charley Patton during Hooker's boyhood. Like most delta bluesmen, he used open tuning—a G chord: D, G, D, G, B, D—and only later picked up standard tuning: E, A, D, G, B, E. Eschewing farm work, he ran off to live with an aunt in Memphis, where he worked as an usher in the W. C. Handy Theatre and jammed with bluesmen like Robert Nighthawk, Eddie Love, and Joe Willard. Later he went to live with an aunt in Cincinnati, where he also worked as an usher.

In Detroit, where he was married in 1943, he served as an orderly at a hospital, a janitor at the Dodge auto plant, and a janitor at the Comco Steel Company. At night he worked the clubs on Hastings Street with a small combo—bass, drums, piano, and second guitar. A representative of Modern Records heard him and arranged a session at Detroit's United Sound Studios. He cut in November, 1948, a date that yielded "Sally Mae" and "Boogie Chillen." These were the first released sides—"Highway Blues" and "Wednesday Evening Blues" have never been issued—in an amazing career that included over five hundred recordings.

Beginning in 1948, there was apparently such a demand for Hooker that he recorded for many labels under different names. On Modern he remained John Lee Hooker for five uninterrupted years. But he was Texas Slim during most of those years on King. On Regent in 1949 he was Birmingham Sam. On Staff he was Johnny Williams in 1949 and 1950, a name that he also used in 1952 and 1953 on Philadelphia's Gotham label. In 1951 he appeared as John Lee Booker on Acorn, Chance, Deluxe, Rockin', and Gone. On the last mentioned, he also was known as The Boogie Man.

After 1953 he began recording for labels other than Modern as John Lee Hooker, with Vee Jay of Chicago serving as a kind of home base from 1958 through 1963. Although his disks are to be found on Chess, Atco, Specialty, Riverside, Prestige, Vanguard, Impulse, Verve-Folkways, and most recently on Bluesway, the Crown LPs are generally regarded as the best embodiments of his urgent art. Listen to *The Blues* and *Folk Blues* for the delta sound that has made unforgettable titles of "Drifting from Door to Door," "Nightmare Blues," and "I'm in the Mood." If ever there was an old-style peripatetic bluesman in modern times, John Lee Hooker was it.

Of the Mississippi delta bluesmen, the seminal figure was Robert Johnson. Like John Lee Hooker, he was born near Clarksdale, Mississippi, but he was not nearly as prolific a recording artist as his contemporary. Johnson was an intensely emotional man for whom nothing seemed to matter except music and sex. Despite his impact on the Muddy Waters generation, he was only twenty-three or twenty-four when he died, a murder victim.

Son House, who probably influenced him most and whom he avidly studied when he was just a boy—lacking an instrument, he would follow finger movements with his eyes and during a group's "take five" would seize an instrument and try to duplicate what he had heard—Son House was amazed that he lived so long. "He'd go up to a gal he saw at one of those dances," Son recalls, "and try to take her off, no matter who was around, her husband or boyfriend or anybody. . . ."

Nobody really knows how Johnson died. But rumor has it that it was a woman, not a man, who either stabbed or poisoned him in a fit of jealousy. The year was 1937 and the month December, just six months after he had recorded for Don Law of American Recording Corporation in Dallas. The sides have recently been reissued on Columbia Records, which bought the ARC catalog years ago, thanks to the productive insights of Frank Driggs.

Johnson was an itinerant musician, either because that was the only way he could earn a livelihood—he never worked at anything else—or because he had an unconquerable restlessness. Johnny Shines and the later Walter Horton, two Chicago musicians out of Memphis, met him in Arkansas around 1933 and drifted with him for two years.

Both have vivid memories of a man who could not resist anyone's suggestion that they move on and who would literally take off in the middle of the night. Willie Johnson, another Memphis bluesman, recalls hearing him in juke joints of various Mississippi river towns and in roadhouses where levee-building work gangs repaired for entertainment.

References in a number of his songs hint at fears amounting to a phobia that may have contributed to his migratory tendencies. The sense of being pursued by Satan himself comes through in "Me and the Devil Blues" and in one of his best-known songs, "Hellhound on My Trail":

> I got to keep moving, I got to keep moving, blues
>   falling down like hail, blues falling down like hail,
> I got to keep moving, I got to keep moving, blues
>   falling down like hail, blues falling down like hail,
> And the day keeps on 'minding me there's a hellhound on my
>   trail, hellhound on my trail, hellhound on my trail.

Despite his persistent horniness and incessant movement, both of which brought him into contact with a large array of desirable females and tough males, he was a strangely shy man. Don Law, who also recorded him in San Antonio, Texas, for Vocalion Records, tells of how he asked Johnson to play for a group of Mexican musicians and of how the young Mississippian resisted, but finally yielded to the coaxing by playing with his face to a wall. It was not discourtesy, according to Law, but shyness. Henry Townsend, who played with him in St. Louis for about six months, remembers him as a self-contained man even when he was "pretty well torn up."

Clearly, Johnson's impact was less the product of personality than of superior musicianship. Bluesmen who heard him hurl superlatives when they talk of his instrumental mastery, audible on a Columbia reissue, *King of the Delta Blues Singers*. Johnson sang with such intensity that during record sessions first takes were generally more acceptable than later versions. Repetition produced a mounting excitement that caused him

31

virtually to lose control of his voice. "He was a great guy for inspiration," Townsend told Pete Welding. "He'd get a feeling and out of nowhere he could put a song together." But once the feeling was gone, he frequently could not repeat the song.

Johnson also had a way with words:

I got stones in my passway, and my road seems dark at night,
I have pains in my heart, they have taken my appetite.

And he could turn a phrase when it came to the blue side of the blues:

I'm going to get deep down in this connection, keep on tangling with
    your wires,
And when I mash down on your starter, then your spark plug will
    give me fire.

From Son House, he acquired stylistic traits and material—songs like "Walking Blues," "Preachin' the Blues," "Milkcow's Calf Blues," and "If I had Possession over Judgment Day."

He in turn exerted tremendous influence on at least two key figures of the post-World War II generation of Chicago musicians, Elmore James and Muddy Waters. The former made a theme song of Johnson's "I Believe I'll Dust My Broom" and called his group the Broomdusters. The latter's first recorded song was "Walking Blues," a side that was modeled on the 1936 Vocalion disk of the delta bluesman who brought bottleneck style to a peak of expressiveness.

Dead in 1963 (in his mid-forties) of complications brought on by asthma and Chicago's icy winds, James left a large legacy of recordings on offbeat R & B labels like Flair, Chief, Fire, Enjoy, and Sphere Sound. For a time, he worked as a disk jockey on Station WOKJ in Jackson where he also ran a radio shop. But his bottleneck guitar virtuosity led to his becoming an active performer and to his settling in Chicago. Although James continued to record into the early sixties, the delta blues on which he was raised had little meaning for the younger generation of Chicago blacks, whose bitterness found tougher expression in the music of his disciples of the Buddy Guy-Otis Rush-J. B. Hutto generation.

3

CLASSIC BLUES

Theater audiences know from Edward Albee's famous one-act play the troubling tale of Bessie Smith's death. But the number who know of her passing because a southern white hospital would not admit her very likely exceeds the number who have listened to her recordings and perceived the eloquence and artistry of her singing. The Empress of the Blues, as she was appropriately called, represents the peak of the classic blues era in the twenties.

It was another, unrelated Smith who created the market for the theatrical blues style that came to fruition in the roaring decade. In 1920 songwriter-pianist Perry Bradford persuaded the recording director of the newly established Okeh label to cut a young Harlem singer named Mamie Smith.

"Crazy Blues," a new Bradford song and Mamie's second platter, sold in such quantities that the label launched its Race Series—records produced for the Negro buyer. The success of Mamie Smith's disk made other labels aware that there was a market for the blues in northern cities as well as the rural south.

This development should have surprised nobody, since World War I had brought a large population shift, the mills and factories of northern cities affording employment not pre-viously accessible to Negroes. Until then, the blues had de-

33

veloped slowly as a folk art, transmitted orally by rural, itinerant performers—farmhands and laborers—not professional entertainers reworking the field hollers and work songs of plantation life. Although W. C. Handy's "Memphis Blues" has sometimes been erroneously credited, it was not the first blues in print, and was not really a blues.

As Samuel Charters notes in *The Country Blues,* "Dallas Blues" was the first published instance of the form, and, ironically, it was the creation of a white Oklahoma City musician named Hart Wand. The most famous blues, W. C. Handy's "St. Louis Blues," did not appear in print until two years later (1914), an expansion of the earlier "Jogo Blues" whose melody Handy admits he acquired from a Memphis Beale Street piano player. By then, almost everyone in New York's Tin Pan Alley—Negro writers like Perry Bradford, James P. Johnson, Noble Sissle, and Clarence Williams, as well as white songsmiths like Irving Berlin, Walter Donaldson, and Gus Kahn—was trying to produce blues song hits.

When the sales of Mamie Smith's Okeh disk of "Crazy Blues" continued to grow, other labels began a talent hunt for blues singers. In 1922 Paramount Records—owned by a Wisconsin furniture company that had entered recording in 1917 to sell phonographs—launched its invaluable 12,000 series of Race Records. In the succeeding five years, under J. Mayo Williams, its shrewd and enterprising director, it recorded a host of country blues singers whose work might have been lost to posterity, among them Charley Patton, Son House, Ed Bell, and Blind Lemon. Later, Gennett Records of Richmond, Indiana, moving its portable Electrobeam Studio throughout the South, began recording ethnic bluesmen.

As the black market for blues mushroomed before the onset of the depression, short-lived labels like Black Swan, Black Patti, Gold Star, Oriole, and many others began adding their product. It was a development not unlike the current revival of pioneer rhythm-and-bluesmen sparked by derivative rock singers. Country blues was put on disk and preserved through the success of the urban, classic performers nurtured on its material and styles.

After a time, Frank Walker, head of Columbia, remembered that he had heard a remarkable young girl singer in a Selma, Alabama, honky-tonk.

"She was just a kid of seventeen, maybe eighteen," he later said. "But I never heard anything like the torture and torment she put into the music of her people. . . . It was a matter of feeling. It was inside. . . . It all came out in her singing."

Walker sent Clarence Williams, a pianist who rehearsed and coached artists for the label, to find Bessie Smith.

"The girl Williams brought back," Walker recalls, "looked like anything but a singer. She looked about seventeen—tall and fat and scared to death—just awful! But all of this you forgot when you heard her sing, because when Bessie sang the blues, she meant it. Blues were her life. . . ."

To help get her acclimated, Walker settled Bessie in Harlem for several months before attempting to record her. Cut on February 17, 1923, with Clarence Williams at the piano, Bessie's first disk was "Downhearted Blues," a song written the previous year by one of Chicago's celebrated blues singers, Alberta Hunter, and her bandleader, Lovie Austin. Released without fanfare, the record outsold the top pop Columbia disk of the year by a ratio of eight to one, lifting Bessie overnight to the highest echelon of star singers.

The Empress of the Blues had been born in abject poverty in Chattanooga, Tennessee, where she had the good fortune, in her teens, to encounter Ma Rainey. Gertrude Rainey was the first blues singer to record for Paramount, to play theaters throughout the Midwest, and to appear in tent shows in the South. Credited with the authorship of one of the great blues, "See See Rider"—Big Bill Broonzy claims it was actually written by a bluesman of that name but credited to Ma Rainey because she was the first to record it—she was the star of the Rabbit Foot Minstrels.

Bessie's innate musicality and magnificent voice so impressed Ma Rainey that she persuaded the young, strapping girl to go on tour with the Minstrels. It was a valuable apprenticeship but not particularly rewarding financially. Until she hit pay dirt with her record of "Downhearted Blues," Bessie scrambled for a livelihood, singing in small-time tent shows like the Florida Cotton Blossoms and in honky-tonks and carnivals throughout the South.

Within a year after joining Columbia, she was a headliner on the top-ranking Negro vaudeville circuits—Milton Starr's and the Theatre Owners Booking Association. Toby, as the latter came to be called, had a reputation among black performers symbolized by its initials: TOBA ostensibly stood for "tough on black artists." During the period of her record renown, 1924–27, Bessie became the highest-paid black vaudeville star in the country, with a weekly draw as high as fifteen hundred dollars. In these years, her recording associates included many of the top jazz musicians in the country, among them Fletcher Henderson's Hot Six, Louis Armstrong, and James P. Johnson, later known as the father of the stride piano style and an outstanding songwriter-composer. What turned out to be her last recording date (November 24, 1933) before her accidental death involved a mixed group that included Frankie Newton on trumpet, Jack Teagarden on trombone, and, for one number, Benny Goodman on clarinet.

In the beginning, Bessie concentrated almost exclusively on country blues. Occasionally the language was so steeped in Negro jargon and local references that it could not possibly be understood by northern ofays. "Yellow Dog," for example, one of the best-selling blues of the day, contains inside references like "easy rider" (a male parasite or pimp), "on the hog" (broke and eating cheap), and "he's gone where the Southern cross' the Yellow Dog" (a place in Mississippi where the tracks of the Southern Railroad then crossed those of the Yazoo Delta Line, the Y.D., hence Yellow Dog). To black audiences, Bessie represented a kind of authority and power almost religious in nature. And she sang gospel songs like "On Revival Day" with a fervor and passion that foreshadowed Mahalia Jackson.

"She had a church deal mixed up in the blues," said New Orleans guitarist Danny Barker. "She dominated a stage. You didn't turn your head when she went on. You just watched Bessie. . . . If you had any church background, like people who came from the South as I did, you would recognize a similarity between what she was doing and what those preachers and evangelists did, and how they moved people."

On May 25, 1929, Bessie recorded one of the greatest sides of her career. Jimmie Cox's song, "Nobody Knows You When You're Down and Out," was not an exact portrayal of her situation, but Bessie had known hard times and by 1929 her career was on the downgrade.

After her initial acceptance, she had attempted to approach white listeners through such pop tunes as "After You're Gone," "Alexander's Ragtime Band," and "There'll Be a Hot Time in the Old Town Tonight." These recordings had not widened her audience and had, perhaps, even served to alienate some of her black following.

Moreover, the onset of the depression had brought a change in public taste, a change that temporarily weakened the appeal of the blues. During the dizzy prosperity of the twenties, people apparently had enjoyed crying in their beer. But as things really got bad, the blues seemed too depressing.

To these constricting social factors, Bessie contributed severe limitations of judgment and temperament. As her manager, Frank Walker had helped restrain Bessie's penchant for conspicuous spending, an almost inevitable concomitant of the rapid acquisition of money by the poor. He had made her put some of her earnings aside and even compelled her to buy a home. Bessie was not without gratitude. Walker was fond of telling the tale of how she had cancelled three weeks of bookings in the summer of 1926 and appeared without warning at his summer home in Long Beach. Walker's son Johnny, then two and a half years old, was seriously ill.

"I'm Bessie Smith," the Empress of the Blues said when Mrs. Walker opened the door. "You've got enough to do just taking care of your boy, so I thought I'd better come and take care of everything else." Over the protests of both Walkers, she washed, cleaned, shopped, and cooked until the boy recovered.

"I suppose that lots of people remember and think of Bessie," Walker has said, "as a rough-and-tumble sort of person.

Still, that wasn't the only side of her. They didn't know about things like her buying a rooming house for her friends to live in. . . . Yes, Bessie had a heart as big as all outdoors, and she gave all of her money away."

But, as happens rather frequently with performers, Bessie and/or her husband, a Philadelphia policeman, decided they could do without Walker's guidance and the slice he took of her earnings. Soon Bessie was alienating theater managers by irritating displays of temperament. A heavy drinker from her youth, she began indulging excessively, gave in to uncontrolled profanity, and got involved in a number of brawls. With the record market telescoping in the deepening depression, there was less call for Bessie Smith records after 1931.

The final session in 1933 was, in George Avakian's words, "a sentimental gesture sparked by John Hammond (an associate of Frank Walker's), who, like Walker, has never lost his enthusiasm for the greatest blues singer of them all." Formerly head of Columbia's jazz department, Avakian produced, edited, and annotated the invaluable four-LP compendium *The Bessie Smith Story*.

Shortly before her death on September 26, 1937, Bessie made a final New York appearance. It was at the Famous Door on Fifty-second street, then known to jazz fans everywhere as Swing Street, or just the Street. The Sunday afternoon jam session, as it was called, was sponsored by the United Hot Clubs of America.

"Symbolically," George Avakian writes in his liner notes to Volume I of *The Bessie Smith Story*, "she didn't even take off her cheap furs as she sang a few songs and returned immediately to the hit-and-miss gigs she was forced to play for a precarious living."

Writer Robert Paul Smith, who was present that cold February Sunday, reported in *The Record Changer*, "Bessie came in, she planted those two flat feet firmly on the floor, she did not shake her shoulders or snap her fingers. She just opened that great kisser and let the music come out."

Backed by Bunny Berigan's muted trumpet, she sang, according to guitarist Eddie Condon, who was part of the

Berigan combo, "Baby, Won't You Please Come Home?" "Mama's Got the Blues," "I'm Wild About That Thing," "The Gin House Blues," "Dirty No-Good Blues," and of course the song that had become her trademark, "Nobody Knows You When You're Down and Out."

In his autobiographical volume, *We Called It Music,* Condon reports that Mildred Bailey, the Rocking Chair Lady, was present and was invited to participate in the jam. But Mildred refused to sing and break the spell cast by the Empress of the Blues. (The same story has been told by others about Ella Fitzgerald.)

To George Avakian, Bessie's spell-casting appearance presaged increasing appreciation of her artistry by serious students of jazz and folk music. He could have added future performers to the list. The impact of the 160 sides she cut for Columbia and the extent of her influence are suggested by such recent albums as *Dinah Washington Sings Bessie Smith, The Legend of Bessie Smith* as sung by Ronnie Gilbert (one of the Weavers), and *LaVern Baker Sings Bessie Smith.*

"Bessie Smith was the greatest of them all," Alberta Hunter, co-writer of "Downhearted Blues," has said. "Even though she was raucous and loud, she had a sort of tear—no, not a tear, but there was a *misery* in what she did. It was as though there was something she had to get out."

Jazz reed man Mezz Mezzrow, viewing her from the man's angle, has said, "Bessie was a real woman, all woman, all the femaleness the world ever saw in one sweet package. She was tall and brown-skinned, with great big dimples creasing her cheeks, dripping good looks—just this side of voluptuous, buxom and massive, but stately, too, shapely as an hourglass, with a high-voltage magnet for a personality."

It may come as a surprise that in the twenties the blues was treated with the same contempt by whites, and even by urban middle-class Negroes, as hillbilly music was not too long ago, and more recently rock 'n' roll. Bessie Smith was the foremost of a group of singers who helped make the blues an in thing and paved the way for its use by white composers like Harold Arlen ("I Gotta Right to Sing the Blues" and "Stormy

Weather") and George Gershwin ("Blue Monday," "Rhapsody in Blue").

Novelist Carl Van Vechten tells of a party at his New York appartment in the twenties to which Bessie was brought by Porter Grainger, one of her recording accompanists.

"George Gershwin was there," Van Vechten recalls, "and Marguerite d'Alvarez and Constance Collier, and possibly Adele Astaire [all prominent performers of the day]. The drawing room was well filled with sophisticated listeners. Before she could sing, Bessie . . . with one gulp downed a glass holding nearly a pint [of straight gin]. Then, with a burning cigarette depending from one corner of her mouth, she got down to the blues, really down to 'em, with Porter at the piano. . . . It was the real thing—a woman cutting her heart open with a knife until it was exposed for us all to see, so that we suffered as she suffered, exposed with a rhythmic ferocity, indeed, which could hardly be borne."

In addition to Mamie and Bessie Smith, the outstanding proponents of the so-called classic blues included three other Smiths—Clara, Laura, and Trixie—all unrelated.

"Trixie's record of 'Freight Train Blues,' " pianist Sam Price has said, "is one of the greatest blues records ever made. Trixie had depth, real warmth and appeal. What was she like? She was just another woman called Smith—but she could sing like hell!"

So could Clara Smith, a Columbia artist who made an unforgettable version of Tom Delaney's great song, "Nobody Knows the Way I Feel This Morning," and who was advertised as "the World's Champion Moaner."

Ma Rainey, who discovered Bessie Smith, was born in Columbus, Georgia, in April 1896, and died there in 1939. A pudgy-faced woman, she had a bulging mouth of unevenly set teeth that gave her face a perpetual smile. Although she was short and squat and wore ankle-length dresses to make herself look taller, her voice was a deep contralto. A matronly bosom provided an ample sounding box. "Ma" was an appropriate nickname, though she may have acquired it due to

40

her affinity for young men. At eighteen Gertrude Pridgett, as she was christened, married Will Rainey when he came through Columbus with a traveling show. It was not a long-lived union, despite their working together.

The Georgia Jazz Band that appeared onstage with Ma was a Dixie-style combo of trumpet, trombone, sax, drums, and piano. At the eighty-eighter was Georgia Tom Dorsey, later recognized as one of the great writers of gospel songs. Wearing a necklace of twenty-dollar gold pieces, the Mother of the Blues, as she was called, would begin her act by emerging from an oversized phonograph. One of her most moving songs was the melancholy "Counting the Blues":

> Lord, going to sleep now for mama just got bad news,
> Lord, going to sleep now for mama just got bad news,
> To try to dream away my troubles, counting the blues.

But she also had a lively sense of humor, as in "Those Dogs of Mine": "Corns—corns—corns," read a realistic Paramount ad on her record, "she had to keep out of the light of the sun—had to walk on the shady side of the street. . . . Lawdy, those dogs of mine—they sure do worry me all the time!" The band that backed Ma on "Corn Field Blues," as the song was subtitled, was Lovie Austin and her Blue Serenaders. She was billed as Madame "Ma" Rainey in accordance with her desire to be addressed as Madame Rainey.

In an advertisement by Black Swan, whose logo read, "The Race's Own Record," Ida Cox was characterized as "the Uncrowned Queen of the Blues." Born in Knoxville, Tennessee, in 1889, where she died in 1968, Ida traveled from the age of fourteen with both the Rabbit Foot Minstrels and its major competitor, Silas Green's from New Orleans. She was married for a period to Jesse Crump of Paris, Texas, who was seventeen years younger and who served as her accompanist. On her Black Swan disks, she was backed by Lovie Austin, the Pruett Twins on banjo and guitar, or by her own Blues Serenaders.

Ida had much less voice and range than either Ma Rainey or Bessie Smith. But she left an indelible impression because of the depth of feeling with which she sang. Her admirers stress that she never sacrificed the true feeling of the blues to the trivialities of vaudeville showmanship. Just as Ma Rainey always seemed to be smiling and you could not escape Bessie's eyes, Ida Cox's natural mien was pensive, if not melancholy.

While most of the itinerant rural blues singers were male, the classic blues singers all seemed to be female. Lizzie Miles, born Elizabeth Mary Landreaux in New Orleans in 1895, first worked with King Oliver and other jazz pioneers and later made disks with Jelly Roll Morton and Clarence Williams.

Bertha "Chippie" Hill, born in Charleston, North Carolina, in 1905, made her debut in Harlem, sang and danced with Ma Rainey's troupe, and performed with King Oliver at the Palladium Dance Hall in Chicago. During 1925 and 1926 Bertha recorded with Louis Armstrong and other jazz greats, and made the first platter of one of the most recorded of all blues— Richard M. Jones's moving "Trouble in Mind." (Bertha, who participated in a memorial concert for Bessie Smith at New York's Town Hall in 1948, was herself killed in an auto accident two years later.)

Continuing the list of well-known female blues shouters of the classic blues era, there were Sara Martin, Alberta Hunter, who reportedly introduced the blues abroad in the twenties, Bricktop and Victoria Spivey. Bricktop became famous as the owner of a Paris nightspot, while Victoria Spivey, not to be confused with the nightspot owner of the same name, accounted for several of the most recorded blues of the era: "Dirty T B Blues," "Bloodhound Blues," and, of course, "Black Snake Blues."

Many historians and critics have tried to explain the female domination of classic blues as opposed to the male cast of rural or country blues. According to Wilfrid Mellers in *Music in a New Found Land,* "This was because the band-trained, town-dwelling male Negro had learned to speak through his 'horn'; but also because the deep resonance of the female Negro voice came to represent the mother-image, which seemed so significant to the rootless inhabitants of the big cities." The mama theory is interesting if entirely speculative. But the idea that all males were now instrumentalists, rather than vocalists, had no foundation in fact.

In *Blues People* LeRoi Jones comes fairly close to offering a tenable explanation for the preponderance of female performers in the classic blues era. He enumerates three factors: (1) the emergence of the Negro theater: "minstrelsy and vaudeville not only provided employment for a great many women blues singers but helped to develop the concept of the professional Negro female entertainer"; (2) "the reverence in which most of white society was held by Negroes gave to Negro entertainers an enormous amount of prestige"; (3) "the great swell of distaff protest regarding women's suffrage in the twenties" contributed to the emergence of white as well as Negro women as entertainers. "All these factors," Jones concludes, "came together to make the entertainment field a glamorous one for Negro women, providing an independence and importance not available in other areas open to them."

Unfortunately, Jones's analysis is more effective in suggesting why Negro women wanted to be entertainers than in explaining why there were so many. The latter factor was a matter of market demand, of buyer demand rather than the seller's desires. And here is where Jones did not dig deeply enough. Unquestionably, the rise of vaudeville as a major entertainment medium and the growth of Negro vaudeville chains were the basic factors, as Jones suggests. But we must go a step further and ask about the constituency of vaudeville audiences. When we realize that the audience was preponderantly male, the demand for female performers becomes inescapably clear.

A related point is made by Charles Keil in *Urban Blues*. "According to the American mores," he writes, "it is permissible for white men to be tantalized sexually by Negro women. A Negro man with sex appeal or singing songs with sexual overtones—blues or blues-based material—poses a threat and has only recently been permitted in white night clubs."

4

THE BLUES IS . . .

Although many Negroes, and particularly the religiously inclined, regarded the blues as "songs of the devil," it is as erroneous to think of them as sex or *blue* songs as it is to think of them as sad songs.

"To me, the blues are—well, almost religious," Alberta Hunter has said. "The blues are like spirituals, almost sacred. When we sing blues, we're singin' out our hearts, we're singin' out our feelings. Maybe we're hurt and just can't answer back, then we sing. . . ."

"Like the spirituals," W. C. Handy, Father of the Blues, has said, "the blues began with the Negro, it involves our history, where we came from and what we experienced. The blues came from the man farthest down. The blues came from nothingness, from want, from desire."

But the blues is broader than an expression of deprivation, economic or emotional. "Though the blues may frequently be associated with a state of depression," Paul Oliver writes in *The Meaning of the Blues*, "of lethargy or despair, it is not solely a physical or a mental state. It is not solely the endurance of suffering or a declaration of hopelessness; nor is it solely a means of ridding oneself of a mood. It is all of these and it is more. . . . Implicit in the term is the whole tragedy of the Negro race since Black Anthony Johnson, the first of the

20 odd Negroes to set foot on American soil, landed from a Dutch 'man of warre' at Jamestown in 1619."

Despite the validity of these observations, they all lack the historical perspective necessary to a full understanding of the sociology and the esthetics of the blues. The blues is a unique form and embodies a unique spectrum of feeling.

Richard Wright has characterized it in terms that sound contradictory: "The blues is a form of exuberantly melancholy folk song."

And Langston Hughes, in *Famous Negro Music Makers*, has written, "The blues are mostly very sad songs about being without love, without money or without a home. And yet almost always in the blues, there is some humorous twist of thought, in words that make people laugh. . . . The music is slow, often mournful, yet syncopated, with the kind of marching bass behind it that seems to say, 'In spite of fate, bad luck, these blues themselves, I'm going on! I'm going to get there.' "

Now, optimism in the face of adversity is possible at any time. But it became historically possible for the Negro only at a specific time, after the Civil War.

Before I develop this thought, let us take a look at the form as it crystallized—for the form itself carries the potential of ambivalence. Virtually all European musical forms are duple in character and operate with even-numbered formations. By contrast, the blues consists of a triadic arrangement. Lyrically, the first line is always repeated, creating an inevitable suspense, that opens the door to a third line with a turn, surprise, or punch in it.

Good morning, Mr. Blues, Mr. Blues, I come to talk with you,
Good morning, Mr. Blues, Mr. Blues, I come to talk with you,
Mr. Blues, I ain't doin' nothin' an' I would like to get a job from you.

The kicker can take many forms, and not all of them are blackouts. But it is apparent that the three-part form invites contrast, duality, ambivalence.

Whether one believes that this nonduple arrangement is African or not, there is an Afro element in the blues form. In classic blues, the first line occupies four musical measures.

Two of these are vocal, while the other two are frequently instrumental. This question-and-answer, solo-and-group style is followed in each of the other four-measure segments. In short, the twelve bars embody a call-and-response pattern, which we have come to know as indigenous to African chant and its derivative, the Afro-American ring shout.

Musically, the blues is built like Gregorian chant, on the three basic chords of the diatonic system. The first four bars are all on the tonic or I chord. The second four measures consist of two on the subdominant or fourth note of the scale and two on the tonic. The last four measures embody two on the dominant or fifth note of the scale and two returning to the tonic or I chord. To illustrate:

Bars											
1	2	3	4	5	6	7	8	9	10	11	12
Tonic (I)				Subdominant (IV)		Tonic (I)		Dominant (V)		Tonic (I)	
If you wanna go to Nash- ville and ain't got no fare				If you wanna go to Nash- ville and ain't got no fare				Cut your gal's throat and the judge will send you there.			

The so-called blues scale differs from the ordinary major scale in that the third and seventh notes are flatted. But blues singers and instrumentalists frequently flat, bend, alter, or smear other notes. It is believed that Negroes originally added the flatted notes because the scales they brought from Africa were pentatonic (consisting of five notes) rather than diatonic (consisting of eight notes). Flatting the third and seventh brought the European tempered scale closer to the African "whole note" scale. The significant point, however, is this: since flatted melody notes are played against the nonflatted notes in the chord or bass (E flat sounding against E natural), a large degree of tension is inherent in the blues.

Why did the blues develop only after the Civil War? In a large sense, the condition of the Negro did not change greatly (economically, socially, or politically) after the Emancipation Proclamation verbally eliminated slavery. But the verbalism itself created the anticipation, the hope, the dream of a condi-

46

tion of existence that once had not even seemed possible. When new constricting laws were enacted during the Reconstruction era, and the Ku Klux Klan rode through the night in white hoods and burned crosses, their purpose was to deprive the new citizen of something he allegedly had.

Before emancipation, the Negro sang spirituals that swathed a hard reality in the soft cotton of an imagined otherworld of peace and contentment. After emancipation, no longer a chattel, he stood in front of a door that opened out to better times in this world. The door was only slightly ajar. But it was there. The Negro still suffered, was still deprived. But he could hope!

"The most astonishing aspect of the blues," Richard Wright has noted, "is that though replete with a sense of defeat and down-heartedness, they are not intrinsically pessimistic; their burden of woe and melancholy is dialectically redeemed through sheer force of sensuality into an almost exultant affirmation of life, of love, of sex, of movement, of hope."

As I see it, the blues chronicle and psychologically embody four developments in the life of the Negro. First, they reflect the travail of the change from "we" and "us" to "I" and "me." The separation from the land to which he was attached as chattel, the removal from communal plantation life—to the Negro these represented as traumatic an experience as an adolescent's discovery of himself as an individual who dies by himself. This realization is what gives the blues their intensely personal and emotional quality.

Secondly, they reflect the change from the status of a faceless slave to the self-dependence and loneliness of the sharecropper or itinerant worker. Brutal and depressed as the life of the slave was, it did not involve starvation, or lack of shelter or clothing. The problem of satisfying these needs was now his and his alone.

Thirdly, the blues are the music and poetry of motion. The slave's existence was a static one. His movements were limited by the plantation. But the "free" man's life almost necessitated moving from one unproductive farm to another, from country to city, from one area to another. The Negro was not only

47

dispossessed. He was itinerant. No wonder, then, that the blues are so deeply imbued with the imagery of trains and highways and, inevitably, of prisons.

Finally, the blues chronicle the emotional travail of monogamy, a new experience in the life of the Afro-American. It is a well-known fact that many slaves, particularly the so-called field niggers, never knew who their fathers were. That was why slave families, and black families into much of the twentieth century, were headed by the mother. That was why, also, many slaves were known by the surname of their owner, who reportedly fathered not a few.

Masters feared strong family loyalties among their slaves and, after the embargo against importing new slaves in the 1830s, were more interested in having the women kept pregnant than in preserving monogamous relationships. The male stud became a recognized figure on many plantations. But with the coming of emancipation the possession or loss of a loved female could become a corrosive experience. Accordingly, in the words of a well-known Mayo Williams song, "The blues ain't nothin' but a woman cryin' for her man," and vice versa.

Taj Mahal, the contemporary bluesman, has said, "Blues, country blues, country western, and bluegrass are real music for the people. They say things in their music that they wish they could say in real life."

In short, the blues were the plaints, open and disguised, of a deprived people, without homes, without love, without money, without status, without identity—but, ironically, not without hope. Even if life offered little, there seemed to be an open road outside the door. And so there was melancholia but not without mirth, frustration but not without anticipation, despair but not without a tough determination, suffering but not without endurance. Out of these contrasts arose the ambivalence of the blues, their shifting major-minor tonality grandly reflecting the emotional ambiguity.

48

5

THE JAZZ
SINGERS

If any one date may be taken to mark the birth of jazz singing, an art closely allied to blues singing, it would be the February, 1926, Okeh record session at which Louis Armstrong and his Hot Five grooved a song called "Heebie Jeebies." It is not what Satchmo did with his horn but what he, perhaps accidentally, did with his chops that gives this session historical significance. The late Richard M. Jones, a mentor of Jelly Roll Morton, A & R'd the date.

"Jones always claimed," according to George M. Avakian, who assembled Columbia's archive collection *The Louis Armstrong Story,* "that Louis meant to sing the vocal twice through, but dropped the sheet music halfway and had to improvise monosyllables till he got straightened out."

Famed trombonist Kid Ory, who was one of the Hot Five sidemen, claims that "Louis forgot the lyrics, or at least pretended to."

In either event, what Satchmo sang soon came to be known as "scat singing," the substitution of nonsense syllables for intelligible words, the syllables being arranged tonally to imitate an instrument and rhythmically to swing.

There are historians who question the authenticity of these tales. And the truth is that Louis was indulging in scat singing before the "Heebie Jeebies" date. During 1925, when he worked with the Fletcher Henderson big band at Roseland Ballroom in Manhattan, he frequently participated in Thursday night jamborees at which visiting acts were invited to perform.

Richard Hadlock reports in *Jazz Masters of the Twenties*, "A great favorite on such occasions was 'Everybody Loves My Baby,' which Henderson soon recorded, complete with 'scat' (meaningless syllables) vocal breaks by Louis. It was his first recording as a singer, but it went largely unnoticed at the time." The importance of "Heebie Jeebies" is that the impromptu, or unrehearsed, scat vocal—a complete chorus—drew attention to this style of vocalizing.

Regardless of what date is taken as inaugurating jazz singing, scat singing embodies the essence of the style. The syllables do not, of course, have to be unintelligible. Jazz singers use words more frequently than scat singers. But whereas instrumental jazz has frequently been described as the use of an instrument as freely as if it were the voice, so jazz singing involves the rhythmic and tonal use of the voice as if it were an instrument. Like instrumental jazz, jazz singing must have a beat. It must swing, however subtly. And it must have the personalization and emotional expressiveness of improvised music.

Armstrong, the first jazz soloist to become a commanding world figure as an entertainer and show business personality, was the first of the jazz singers. The dividing line between blues and jazz singing is not a sharp one, since personalization, emotional intensity, and improvisational freedom are also earmarks of great blues singing.

In fact, Louis's vocal style was formed or influenced by the many recordings he made with classic blues singers of the twenties. His horn is to be heard on disks by Trixie Smith ("Railroad Blues"), Clara Smith, Alberta Hunter, Hociel Thomas, Maggie Jones ("Screamin' the Blues"), Sippie Wallace, Bertha "Chippie" Hill ("Trouble in Mind"), Ma Rainey ("See See Rider"), and even Bessie Smith, with whom he made eight sides in 1925, including "St. Louis Blues."

50

The difference between blues and jazz singing is partly a matter of audience but mostly of repertoire. Jazz singing came into existence, in short, when pop ballads and Broadway show tunes, attractive to white audiences, were reinterpreted by Negro artists.

Armstrong's first big pop hit did not come until 1929, when he was a featured player in *Hot Chocolates,* an all-Negro revue at the Hudson Theatre in New York City. Nightly, he stopped the show with his rendition of the Andy Razaf-Fats Waller evergreen "Ain't Misbehavin'." Later that year, he recorded the hit tune of *Blackbirds,* another all-Negro Broadway revue. "I Can't Give You Anything But Love, Baby" became the second in a long list of jazzily sung pop tunes that reached to 1964 when Satchmo made an award-winning disk of "Hello, Dolly."

In the years between 1929 and 1964, there have been many discussions as to the jazz content of Armstrong's gravel-voiced vocals. But regardless of how jazz critics evaluate "Ol' Man Mose," "You Rascal You," and the more recent vocal recordings, Satchmo's impact on the art of singing, jazz and pop, has been undeniable.

The impact of his jive vocals has been traced in the singing of such varied artists as Ella Fitzgerald, Cab Calloway, the Mills Brothers, Wingy Manone, and hoarse-voiced Louis Prima. But even the ballad singers have not escaped his influence. Echoes of Satchmo's phrasing and spacing are audible in the vocals of Ethel Waters, Lady Day, the Rocking Chair Lady, and even der Bingle.

"Of course, his voice is ugly," a British critic has said, "when measured against what Europe calls beautiful singing. But the expression which Armstrong puts into this voice, all the soul, heart and depth which swings along in every sound, makes it more beautiful than most of the technically perfect but cold and soulless singing in the white world today."

Lady Day, one of Satchmo's early successors, burst on the recording scene in the mid-thirties. Billie Holiday came to

Columbia Records via Baltimore, where she was born in 1915, and Harlem, where she learned as a waitress to pick up coins without the use of her hands or mouth. (Born Eleanor Fagan Gough, nicknamed Bill because of her tomboy ways and later Billie—her choice—because of her adoration of silent screen actress Billie Dove, she acquired her surname at the age of three when Clarence Holiday, her father, married her mother.) Her sordid childhood and adolescence, compounded of poverty, rape, hustling, pot, gin, and prostitution, left indelible marks that doubtless contributed to her death in 1959. But it also established an emotional frame of reference that made her one of the great ballad singers of our time.

In no small measure, the history of pop singing can be suggested by two names, Billie Holiday and Frank Sinatra. Before the Voice, there were tremendous singers in the minstrel tradition—Eddie Leonard, Joe Howard, young Eddie Cantor, and Al Jolson; evocative vaudevillians like Nora Bayes, Fanny Brice, and Belle Baker; appealing radio vocalists like the Street Singer, the Vagabond Lover, and the Groaner.

Singing was showmanship and movement. It was Joe Howard cakewalking and Al Jolson in blackface crying "Mammy" on bended knee. It was maudlin dramatics, soft-shoe dancing, clear diction, bel canto vocalization, and joyous excitement.

But it was not an art of intimacy—in the days before amplification, even Rudy Vallee had to use a megaphone to project in a club or theater. And it did not thrive on personal expressiveness or sexual warmth. Just as songwriting was then circumscribed by the euphemisms of Victorian morality—nature imagery a la the movie pan to the sea or sky was used to suggest intimacy—so most pop singers affected poses of nonchalance, ebullience, or gaiety, to suggest, but also to shield audiences from, the realities of epidermis.

The first pop singer who made a style of intimacy, desire, and sex was Francis Albert Sinatra. And who was the Voice's inspiration? "It was Billie Holiday," Sinatra has said, "whom I first heard in Fifty-second Street clubs in the early 1930s, who was and still remains the greatest single musical influence on me." And Frank adds, "With a few exceptions, every major pop singer in the United States during her generation has been touched in some way by her genius."

Billie Holiday said, "I don't think I'm singing. I feel like I am playing a horn. I try to improvise like Les Young, like Louis Armstrong, or anyone else I admire. What comes out is what I feel. I hate straight singing. I have to change a tune to my own way of doing it."

No more precise definition of jazz singing has ever been formulated. On another occasion, Billie said, "If you find a tune and it's got something to do with you, you don't have to evolve anything. You just feel it, and when you sing it, other people can feel something too."

Years later, in a somewhat more hip style, the Voice said: "When I sing, I believe. I'm honest. . . . You can be the most artistically perfect performer in the world, but an audience is like a broad—if you're indifferent, endsville."

Regardless of how banal or cliché the lyrics were, to Billie Holiday they were fragments of feeling. When she sang, she was not an entertainer or showwoman, but the blues singer of old reliving a painful or, on rare occasions, a happy moment.

Lady Day's was a love-starved world. "God Bless the Child," which she co-authored, suggests the hungers of her childhood. Torch ballads like "My Man," "I Cried for You," "Mean to Me," and "You Let Me Down" told of the tensions and tortures of her relations with men. And "Strange Fruit" was not only an indictment of lynching but indirectly a picture of Billie Holiday's suffering.

As Ralph Gleason of the *San Francisco Chronicle* put it, "She suffered from an incurable disease—being born black in a white society wherein she could never be but partially accepted."

In truth, Billie had the corrosive experience not only of being black in a white world (she was prevented from appearing on stage with the Artie Shaw band), but of being too white in a black world (she was forced to put on blackface in order to appear with the Count Basie band). Billie was always telling it like it was in her own life. In her songs, the bell never tolled for anyone but herself.

Lady Day may have lacked schooling. But she was not unaware of her own necromancy. "I've been told," she wrote in her autobiography *Lady Sings the Blues,* "that nobody sings the word 'hunger' like I do. Or the word 'love.' "

Billie's was a readily identifiable voice. She had a high-pitched hoarseness, a tightness of the vocal chords, that was a perfect sonic reflection of her turbulent existence. The sound she produced was inescapably tense, and even in the happy songs the timbre was searing. Of her appearance at Cafe Society Downtown in 1938—a high point in her brief, flaming career and an unforgettable experience for those who saw her— John Hammond has written, "Standing there with a spotlight on her great, sad, beautiful face, a white gardenia in her hair, she sang the songs, and the singers were never the same thereafter."

Cab Calloway, who first distinguished himself as a bandleader and more recently, since his role as Sportin' Life in Gershwin's *Porgy and Bess,* as a show singer, is of special interest because of his contribution to the black art of scat. In 1931 at the Cotton Club in Harlem, he introduced a novelty song, "Minnie the Moocher." It became so popular that he sang it in *The Big Broadcast of 1932,* one of many film musicals in which he appeared (*Stormy Weather,* for one). In fact, for a time the flamboyant singer was known as the "hi-do-ho man" after the nonsense syllables he employed in the crazy ditty.

Related to jive, a form of comic speech and double-talk also developed by black performers, scat was artfully practiced by Leo Watson and the Spirits of Rhythm and by Babs Gonzales in the bop era. There was also the team of Slim (Gaillard) and Slam (Stewart), who in '38 intrigued the public with a novelty known as "Flat Foot Floogie (With the Floy-Floy)."

Several years later, Slim Gaillard repeated his word necromancy in a zany song, "Cement Mixer (Put-ti, Put-ti)." This manipulation of language for its sounds and rhythms, practiced in our time by the Swingle Singers, has a strange way of enriching and augmenting the language. Certainly, jive, hipster talk, and hippie language have added much to our dictionaries.

Scat singing was carried to new heights in the 1940s by a girl who was discovered by bandleader Chick Webb at an amateur night at Harlem's Apollo Theatre. The hunchbacked drummer man took sixteen-year-old Ella Fitzgerald into his home and helped her develop into one of the venerated and long-lived voices in jazz.

The year that Ella won her amateur night trophy—a week's engagement at the Harlem "Palace" of black entertainers—was 1934. Thirty-five years later, her name still stood at the top of the marquee, in appearances at the Flamingo in Las Vegas, the Copa in New York, and the Cocoanut Grove in Hollywood—the rare exception of a jazz singer who managed to remain popular with the jet set as well as the expense-account crowd.

In part this is the result of extraordinary vocal equipment. Ella has a range, flexibility, and tonal richness that are the envy of many an instrumentalist. And she is, first, last, and foremost, an instrumental singer who pays limited attention to lyrics but can perform unique tricks of vocal magic with melody and rhythm. Possessed of an amazing ear, which gives her absolute sureness of pitch, she easily mastered the complexities of bop—and then proceeded to employ flatted fifths, whirlwind tempos and offbeat rhythms, making an irresistible tour de force of scat singing.

Her hold on the public inheres also in her sagacious handling of repertoire. In 1938 she had a pop record hit with Chick Webb in "A-tisket, A-tasket," a swinging nursery rhyme she concocted with Van Alexander, the band's arranger. Then for much of the two decades of her tenure at Decca Records, she recorded new songs on which her vocal skills were largely wasted. But that experience, and the European tours with Norman Granz's Jazz at the Philharmonic, helped her discover her special province. In show songs and standards—the works of Gershwin, Berlin, Cole Porter, Rodgers and Hart—she found material of a melodic and harmonic opulence that lent itself to her improvisational craft. They make up her programs in personal appearances and on a group of treasured Verve albums recorded with the swinging arrangements of Nelson Riddle.

"Take half a dozen Fitzgerald records," British critic Mike Butcher has observed, "and analyze them carefully. If you can find a single error of vocal technique or style, you are more critical than all the critics put together."

Another jazz singer who stepped into the limelight via an Apollo Theatre amateur night was Sarah Lois Vaughan, known more recently as Sassy or the the Divine Sarah. It happened in October, 1942, when, curiously, Ella Fitzgerald was the headliner on the vaudeville bill. Among those who heard Miss Vaughan during the week's booking that was her reward for winning on amateur night was Billy Eckstine.

Mr. B, as he was known after he became a matinee solo idol, was then singing and playing trombone with the band of Earl "Fatha" Hines, to whose attention he brought Sarah. A berth with the Hines band led to a stint with Eckstine when he stepped out and formed his own unit—made up, incidentally, of Charlie "Bird" Parker, Dizzy Gillespie, and other bop pioneers. After making records for several small labels, Sassy was signed by Musicraft, then seeking to become a major label.

In *A History of Jazz in America,* Barry Ulanov recalls how an executive of the company exclaimed at her first session, "Good God, she can't do that! Tell her to sing it straight. That stuff will never get anywhere. We'll lose our shirt."

The executive was right about the fate of his short-lived company. But "that stuff," and particularly a song called "Black Coffee," shook up the jazz world. Miss Vaughan's un-straight vocals soon brought her stardom on Fifty-second Street, the downtown outpost of the invading bopsters. Appearing at the Onyx that year and later at the Downbeat club, Miss Vaughan was paid a meager seventy-five dollars a week. A year later, she was receiving almost a thousand dollars a week.

Sassy's vocals have a polished and controlled quality that both reveals and conceals her early training. It comes as no surprise that she was a diligent student of the piano from the age of seven to fifteen and that she also studied organ. One little suspects that for some years she was a member of the choir of the Mount Zion Baptist Church of Newark, New Jersey, where she was born in 1924. But then, there are middle-class Negro churches where the frantics of storefront gospel singing are considered taboo. (Consider the controversial thesis that blues becomes jazz singing when the itinerant performer, agrarian or urban, settles down and becomes middle-class in outlook and repertoire.)

Through the years, the Divine Sarah has made only limited concessions to commercialism, pursuing instead the tough line of the jazz artist. But on several occasions she was fortunate enough to find smart, saucy songs like "Make Yourself Comfortable" and "Experience Unnecessary" that lent themselves to her bravura, suggestive style of singing.

The most successful of this period was a song I published in 1959, "Broken-Hearted Melody," a bossa-nova, instrumental type tune by Sherman Edwards, now known as the lyricist-composer of the Broadway hit musical *1776*, and Hal David, currently the collaborator of Burt Bacharach. Her record on Mercury became a near-million-copy seller and made the Top Ten.

Four years later, Miss Vaughan took a fetching harmonica instrumental by Jean "Toots" Thielmans and converted it into the beguiling jazz waltz "Bluesette." In these instances, as with Erroll Garner's "Misty," Sassy could approach the Easy Listening market without compromising her feeling for jazz.

Influenced by Sarah and idolizing Billie, Carmen McRae grew to maturity in the bop years. She made her debut as Carmen Clarke, being then married to drummer Kenny "Klook" Clarke of the experimental group at Minton's in Harlem where bop was born and where she served as intermission singer-pianist for several years. Although she worked with Benny Carter, Count Basie, and Mercer Ellington's band, she did not attract attention until she began making records for two offbeat labels, Stardust and Venus, in 1953.

57

The following year she was signed by Decca. Since then, she has produced a steady flow of albums on many different labels, including Mainstream, Kapp, and, most recently, Atlantic. Like most gifted jazz singers, she is a singer's singer. But she manages to command a sizable following in the country's expense-account clubs without deviating from her own thing.

Nancy Wilson is one of many fine singers—others are Lena Horne, Joe Williams, and Sammy Davis, Jr.—who walk the borderline between jazz and pop. Born in Chillicothe, Ohio, in 1937, Miss Wilson came to maturity in the rock era, but chose instead to follow the costly calling of the jazz singer.

Partly because of her physical attractiveness, a quality she shares with Lena, Abbey Lincoln, and other black jazz vocalists, she is in demand in the country's leading supper clubs. But she has not been as fortunate as Sassy was for a time in finding material that allows for her singular styling and still permits an appeal to a broad market. Attractive albums she made with Cannonball Adderley and George Shearing were what are known in the business as "turntable hits": people listen to them but do not buy. Recently, she has managed to reach a a larger audience. But, as the album titles indicate, *A Touch of Today, Tender Loving Care, Gentle Is My Love,* and *Today —My Way,* she is tackling material that already has audience acceptance and is attempting to sell it on her way of styling.

The problems posed by this concern with a large audience are most pathetically illustrated in the career of Fats Waller, a supremely gifted man. Composer of jazz pieces like "Squeeze Me" and "Jitterbug Waltz" and of impressionistic instrumental pieces like those in the *London Suite* (which he reportedly created in a British studio as he recorded them), Waller also left behind a legacy of memorable pop hits like "Honeysuckle Rose," "Ain't Misbehavin'," "Blue Turning Gray Over You," and "Keepin' Out of Mischief Now." All of these contain blue shadings and jazz rhythms that take them out of the area of conventional Tin Pan Alley tunes.

Waller also occupies an acknowledged place in the pantheon

of piano masters—more jazz than pop—a man who was taught stride piano by James P. Johnson and who was named by the great jazz virtuoso, Art Tatum, as his primary influence. Fats's special feeling for the organ, "the God box," as he called it, is well remembered by Count Basie, who once lay at his feet in the defunct Lincoln Theatre in Harlem to learn how to handle the pedal notes, and also by close friends who sometimes sat up all night in a hotel room to hear him play a Hammond given to him by the music firm of Lyon & Healy.

The organ was only one of the frustrations of Fats's life as time went on. An inspired and born clown, he could steal a movie scene, as he did in *Stormy Weather,* with one improvised line, "One never knows, do one?" With his derby hat cocked insouciantly over one ear and high spirits exploding at the keyboard, it was easy to overlook both his singing and playing.

Mezz Mezzrow, the well-known jazz clarinetist, who got to know him in the years when Fats was writing the score of *Connie's Hot Chocolates,* later said, "He was so magnetic, with such a robust personality, that you could never be sad in his presence." But Fats could be sad in your absence and drink like a man who could not reconcile his inner drives with the activities that brought him success, wealth, and audiences.

That he died at thirty-nine will perhaps come as no surprise. His death was, of course, accidental. Worn out from work and a trip to the Coast, he was returning east by train. He was suffering from pneumonia, but drinking so much that he was unaware of his condition. When the conductor came to wake him for breakfast one morning, he had been dead for several hours—as a consequence of heart failure, pneumonia, and alcoholism.

If people remember him at all, they doubtless think of him as a clowning piano player and novelty singer. But he was a gifted composer and, a serious student of the organ, who once forced RCA to let him record Bach (unreleased). If the projection of a song through one's personality, if its rhythmic reinterpretation to make it swing, if self-stylization—who can forget his recording of "I'm Gonna Sit Right Down and Write Myself a Letter"—are the earmarks of jazz singing, then Fats Waller was a fine jazz singer and pianist indeed.

Jazz singing requires vocal equipment and musicianship of a high order, higher than that necessary for effective pop singing. And yet the audience tends to be small, in-group, and superopinionated, provoking jazz singers and instrumentalists occasionally to reach for the wider market.

Even the genius of bop, Charlie "Bird" Parker, was not above recording well-known standards with strings. They did not bring the applause that he perhaps anticipated and that Billy Eckstine excited when he crossed over into pop. But for Fats Waller, success apparently posed graver dangers than the frustrations of living with small audiences. Would Waller have led a happier and better-adjusted existence if he had followed his inner desires instead of playing the clown? As he himself once said, "One never knows, do one?"

6

BLACK POP
AND THE
OREO SINGERS

Singing is a form of expression as well as self-expression, of communication as well as introspection. This observation provides a clue to the difference between pop and jazz singing. But repertoire and technique also figure. Jazz singers tend to be interested in more sophisticated, offbeat, and even esoteric material. They are so concerned with rhythmic pulse that they will manipulate note values in behalf of a swinging beat. And they feel free to alter melody and chord lines, and also lyrics, to achieve a more expressive reflection of their feelings.

All these are questions of degree. Without feeling and without a beat, pop singing becomes lifeless. But the pop singer is more of an *interpreter* and less of a creator than the jazz vocalist. And he is vitally concerned with entertaining and conquering an audience. The jazz artist who turns his back on an audience may be an extremist, but he serves to suggest the difference in approach.

The pivotal figure in the transition from blues-and-jazz to contemporary pop singing was a Nashville-born writer-performer who died even younger than Fats Waller. Leroy Carr was dead at thirty-six in 1935—a victim of nephritis, brought on by excessive drinking in which he reportedly indulged to deaden the pain of arthritis. During a brief seven-year career, Carr recorded one hundred blues and, in a sense, belongs with the singers of blues. But he was neither a rural shouter like Blind Lemon and Lightnin' Hopkins nor a classic blues stylist like Bessie Smith and Ma Rainey.

Possessed of a soft, mellow, caressing type of voice, he brought sophistication and tenderness to the blues. Forerunner of Josh White, Leon Bibb, and Harry Belafonte rather than Odetta, he helped prepare the way for two groups of vocalists: the white torch singers like Libby Holman ("Body and Soul"), young Dinah Shore ("Ah, the Apple Tree"), Helen Morgan ("Bill"), and Julie London ("Cry Me a River"), and the pop black singers like Billy Eckstine, Nat "King" Cole, Johnny Mathis, and Sam Cooke.

Carr moved to Chicago in 1928 and cut his first disk for Vocalion. "How Long, How Long Blues," which he wrote, was an instantaneous hit and has since been recorded by a long line of artists, virtually all of them black. Likewise with his other great blues hit, "In the Evening When the Sun Goes Down," written and recorded shortly before his death. Neither of these is a strict blues in form and both employ much more sophisticated chording than either rural or classic blues. Carr, who was a solid boogie-woogie pianist, was accompanied on most of his recordings by Scrapper Blackwell, whose single-string guitar style is regarded as a forerunner of Charlie Christian's artistry and innovations.

Big Bill Broonzy has told how he and other blues singers of the day used to pile in a car and drive from Chicago to Indianapolis, where Carr lived, to hear him play and sing some of his lesser-known songs, like "Six Cold Feet of Ground" and "Blues Before Sunrise." Despite his influence and renown among black artists, Carr lies buried in an unmarked grave in Floral Park, Indianapolis.

Young Ethel Waters was, like young Nat "King" Cole, a jazz singer. Jazz critics still characterize her phrasing and vibrato as "jazz-tinged." But she was one of the earliest black singers to invade and conquer the white pop market. As early as 1924 she made a best seller of "Dinah," later of "Memories of You," "You're Lucky to Me," and "Stormy Weather."

There was a period before these chart disks when she addressed herself largely to the Negro market, recording with Fletcher Henderson and other jazzmen. But she early displayed a theatrical flair that led to stage appearances in *Africana,* *Blackbirds of 1930, Rhapsody in Black,* the celebrated *Cabin in the Sky,* and the Irving Berlin hit revue *As Thousands Cheer.* In this Broadway musical, patterned after a newspaper, she made a splash with the song "Heat Wave" and nightly stopped the show with "Supper Time," a ballad about a southern Negro woman who learns that her husband has been lynched as she is setting the table for the evening meal. Into this song and others, poet Langston Hughes has said, "Ethel Waters could pour all of her own memories of grief, sorrow, loneliness, and make them unforgettable vignettes of great dramatic intensity."

Sweet Mama Stringbean, as she was billed for her debut in Baltimore, has recorded her memories in an autobiography written with Charles Samuels. *His Eye Is on the Sparrow,* a title that recalls the spiritual she sang in *The Member of the Wedding* on Broadway and on the screen, documents an early life that paralleled Billie Holiday's. The difference was that Ethel was tough enough to meet and overcome the challenge.

Born in 1900 in a rundown tenement in the slums of Chester, Pennsylvania, she knew neither affection nor care as a child and was surrounded by sordid and evil people. As she embarked on a singing career—for her debut she received eight dollars a week and her managers pocketed twenty-five—she had to fight constantly to prevent herself from being underpaid and cheated. Nevertheless, she forged her way to the top and had a long, distinguished career as a singer, actress, and film star. As her earnings rose, she began adopting needy youngsters and now has a family of twelve children. Despite her opulence, she has always said that "Stormy Weather" could have been the theme song of her life.

When Sarah Vaughan was once asked who had influenced her style, her quick answer was, "Eckstine, of course." Many analysts feel that the influence worked both ways. But Eckstine's could have been the more pervasive, since it was he who helped launch and advance Sarah's career. Eckstine, vocalist with Earl Hines in the late 1930s, and Hines's arranger-saxist Budd Johnson persuaded the Fatha to hire Sarah as well as altoist Charlie "Bird" Parker. Later, when Eckstine formed his own band, he took Sarah, Parker, Johnson, and Dizzy Gillespie with him.

Although the Hines band is regarded as a bop incubator, Eckstine's contribution to modern jazz is not to be minimized. From 1944 to 1947, when the band folded, Eckstine gave employment to a large number of jazzmen who developed into major figures. The long list included trumpeters Miles Davis and Kenny Dorham as well as Dizzy; saxists Gene Ammons, Dexter Gordon, and "Bird"; arranger Tadd Dameron; and drummer Art Blakey, whose Jazz Messengers brought the "funky" concept into jazz.

But Eckstine's contribution as a bandleader was submerged by his prominence as a pop vocalist, a development that peaked in his worldwide recognition as "Mr. B." Embarking on a solo career in 1948, Billy soon had the bobby-soxers swooning over his records of "My Foolish Heart" and "My Destiny."

In fact, when Mr. Swoonatra lost his voice during an engagement at the Copa in Manhattan, Mr. B, who was then appearing at the Paramount, was the only substitute acceptable to both Sinatra and the club management. It was the year (1950) of Billy's smash recording of "My Destiny," a disk with a low-voiced vibrato so pronounced that connoisseurs found it annoying, although youngsters thought it sexually exciting. A similar reaction greeted Eckstine's 1951 revival of the Bing Crosby hit of '31, "I Apologize."

An extremely handsome man, with blue eyes made luminescent by the café au lait color of his skin, Eckstine had early manifested his sexuality on a famed recording with the Earl Hines band. "Jelly, Jelly" was a blues, however, and it never emerged from black bedrooms. As his popularity with white audiences grew, and *Life* magazine ran a spread picturing him as the country's biggest male pop idol, Eckstine found himself the center of a racial controversy. The Negro community was less than pleased, a situation that had its ironic side considering the barriers black artists had to scale in order to penetrate white markets.

In the late forties and early fifties radio and TV were both guilty of the same kind of racism that made for black ghettos in major American cities. Between 1947 and 1955, only one Negro scored in *Cash Box*'s annual survey of the year's Ten Most Played Records. Nathaniel Coles, born in Montgomery, Alabama, in 1917, reared in Chicago, and better known as Nat "King" Cole, attained vocal stardom by way of an instrument and, not unlike Mr. B, after a career as a jazzman. From 1939 until the late forties, the King Cole Trio, with Oscar Moore on guitar and Wesley Prince on bass, appeared in a number of films and made records first for Decca and then for Capitol. On the latter label, it had a countrywide hit in Nat's own swinging composition, "Straighten Up and Fly Right." Four years later, in 1948–49, the trio became the first Negro jazz combo to have its own sponsored radio series.

Despite the jazz awards won by the trio and by Cole for his piano artistry and singing in *Down Beat, Metronome,* and *Esquire* polls, Nat's gravitation toward pop was almost inevitable. He sang with a clarity of diction rare even among white vocalists, and he had a feeling for pretty melodies that made him an outstanding balladeer. It took a curious song, "Nature Boy," with a then unpublicized arrangement by Nelson Riddle (later Sinatra's major sound architect), to indicate that Cole could go pop in a big way. The hit recording of "Mona Lisa," also with a Nelson Riddle score, which followed in 1949, established the Cole hegemony. His best-selling disk of the film song played no small part in making it the Academy Award song of 1950. The following year, Cole made a worldwide hit of the first teen-age ballad "Too Young," the only song in the twenty-three-year history of radio's famed "Hit Parade" to maintain the number-one spot for twelve consecutive weeks.

During the years of his popularity as a singing star, Cole unlike Harry Belafonte, Lena Horne, and other prominent Negro entertainers, displayed no *active* concern with the problems facing black people. He performed at benefits and made financial donations to Negro organizations. But he was not even a member of the NAACP, now criticized by many Negroes for excessive legalism and white middle-class leadership. Nevertheless, his "neutrality" did not prevent him from being attacked and mauled on a Birmingham, Alabama, stage in 1956 by a group of white supremacists. Afterward, Cole became a life member of the NAACP.

From the success of "Too Young" until his death of lung cancer in the early 1960s, Cole continued making pop hits of some of the most beautiful tunes of our time, among them "Pretend," "Answer Me, My Love," "A Blossom Fell," "Ramblin' Rose," and "Ballerina."

Only three other Negro male singers may be regarded as having moved in a big way from jazz to pop. (Jazz enthusiasts would hardly regard this as progress.) One was nurtured by Duke Ellington, a second by Count Basie, and the third by jazz dancing. Al Hibbler, who toured with Ellington from '43 into '51, was born blind in Little Rock, Arkansas, in 1915. A short stint with the rocking Kansas City band of Jay Mc-Shann preceded the Ellington association. Ellington decribed his style, in which he made extensive use of *portamento* (sliding from one note to another) and *melisma* (stretching one syllable over many notes), as "tonal pantomime."

It was not until '54 that a Decca recording of "He" drew attention to Hibbler as a pop singer. The following year, he established his preeminence as a pop vocalist with a best-selling record of "Unchained Melody." His handling of this ballad involved a degree of anguish heard only in some of Ray Charles's disks. Although he continued making records thereafter, in the sixties on Atlantic and Reprise, he was not able to repeat the phenomenal success of his mid-fifties disks.

Joe Williams, born Joseph Goreed in Cordele, Georgia, in 1918, served an extended apprenticeship with various jazz groups before he became associated with Count Basie. Brought up in Chicago, he worked with clarinetist Jimmie Noone, tenor saxist Coleman Hawkins's big band, Lionel Hampton, and Andy Kirk.

When the boogie-woogie revival was at its height in the early forties, he toured with pianists Albert Ammons and Pete Johnson. Although he worked with a Basie septet in Chicago in '50, he did not become the band's vocalist until later. In '52 the Basie-Williams collaboration transformed an old blues into a best-selling disk. Since then "Every Day I Have the Blues," written and sung originally by Memphis Slim (Peter Chatman), has remained a Williams trademark. A few years later, a hit recording of "All Right, Okay, You Win" added a new number to the requested repertoire of the man with the ebullient, metallic voice.

In personal appearances, Williams's repertoire tends to be more pop than blues or jazz. But his continuing popularity with jazz fans has made him a regular at annual meetings of the Newport Jazz Festival. Nevertheless, there are jazz critics, particularly *The New Yorker*'s Whitney Balliett, who have never thought of him as anything but "a loud imitation of a blues singer." Pure or impure, he brings to pop singing a rhythmic thrust with great kinesthetic impact.

The third singer in this group, Sammy Davis, Jr., has the least claim to jazz orientation. Part of the Will Mastin vaudeville trio from the time he was a child, he is an all-around showman whose talents include mimicry of a high order, superb clowning, and mastery of several instruments, as well as singing and dancing. His powers as a vocalist have grown through the years, enhanced rhythmically by his skill as a dancer.

When he was only six, he appeared in a film with Ethel Waters. In '56, as the star of the Broadway musical *Mr. Wonderful*, and again in '64, as the star of *Golden Boy*, he displayed his tremendous audience appeal and unabating promotional energy by keeping so-so shows going for long periods of time. When his best-selling autobiography, written in collaboration with Jane and Burt Boyar, appeared in '65, no one doubted the aptness of its title, *Yes I Can*.

The title of one of his most recent record hits is likewise a key to his impact as a human being and performer. When he sings "I Gotta Be Me," people believe it. For here is a Negro who converted to Judaism; who married a white,

Swedish film star, from whom he has since separated, asserting his indomitable independence; and whose career has continued climbing to new heights, despite an auto accident that left him with the sight of only one eye.

"Talk about handicaps," he said recently. "I'm a one-eyed Negro Jew."

Davis began recording in '49 on the Capitol label, shifted to Decca in '53, and switched to Reprise after his friend Sinatra founded that label. As a record maker, he first attracted notice in '55 with "Something's Gotta Give," made a hit of "Mr. Wonderful" in the following year, and in '61 helped "What Kind of Fool Am I" win a Grammy as Best Song of the Year. "I Gotta Be Me" demonstrates his unabating popularity and the power of his image.

Considering Davis's vocal equipment, his acceptance as a pop singer is a triumph of personality. Also, taking into account the obstacles he has had to overcome—and *Yes I Can* makes painfully clear that black entertainers do not escape offstage the indignities and cruelties visited upon ordinary blacks—his is a well-earned victory for a supremely talented man.

Davis's distaff mirror image is independent-minded Lena Horne, who has long felt ambivalent about the character of her appeal. Aware from the start that her beauty opened many doors closed to other Negroes, she could not help being excited about the good things it brought her, but she refused to be reconciled to the white man's interest in black sex.

In part, her appeal is the result of her arrogant and insouciant stance. She worked consciously to erect a barrier between herself and her preponderantly white audiences. (She, too, married white.)

"They are not getting *me*," she emphasizes in *Lena*, an autobiographical collaboration with *Life's* Richard Schickel, "someone they can touch and hurt—but just a singer."

Langston Hughes credits her, in his study of *Famous Negro Music Makers*, with "breaking the color bar in Hollywood and establishing a precedent for the presentation of Negro beauty and talent without resort to kitchen scenes." He fixes on the year 1942 and *Panama Hattie* as the startling film in which a Negro woman starred for the first time with white actors, "without benefit of apron or bandana." Two years earlier. Lena had become one of the few Negro vocalists to sing with an all-white name band, Charlie Barnet's.

For many years, she steadfastly refused to appear before segregated audiences and would not accept lucrative Miami offers so long as hotels refused admittance to Negro guests. And this bar applied even to the star performers. In '63 her recording of "Now"—protest lyrics written to the melody of the Israeli hora "Hava Nageela"—became a cause célèbre when the radio networks banned disk jockey plays.

Although she has performed in many MGM films under a long-term contract, among them *Cabin in the Sky, Stormy Weather,* and *Ziegfeld Follies,* and though she has starred on Broadway in *Jamaica* and other musicals, audiences think of her primarily as a singer and nightclub entertainer. Her independence of mind is typical of the jazz rather than the pop artist, but the bravura and impersonal style that make her a favorite of the chi chi crowd brings her down into the foothills where jazz and pop merge. As with Sammy Davis, Jr., the image of the woman frames and is greater than all her recordings. Unlike Davis, she has not had many best sellers. She remains today the spectacular figure of a beautiful black woman, tantalizing but distant, provocative but proud.

She is also realistic, if somewhat disillusioned, about her role in the struggle for black equality. She is aware that she was used as a symbol and "bilked by the previous generation's lies." And she adds, "The Negroes no longer need a handful of successful people to symbolize their hopes. They no longer need to live vicariously through us, for they are reaching out to take, en masse, what we were 'given,' in order to keep *them* still. History has passed us by—the generation of celebrity symbols."

In *Lena* she confesses that at first the realization that the "symbolic me" was no longer needed made her feel lonely and strange, and caused her to resent the younger generation responsible for the revolution. "However unhappy it made me," she admits, "it was an identity and sometimes a protection." But now she has accepted the situation and is satisfied that she is "free merely to be human, free to speak, frankly as an individual, not as an example, not as a 'credit' to my race."

Probably because the record-buying public is largely female, there are more successful male pop singers than female. Nevertheless, among top-notch black pop vocalists there are Dinah Washington, Della Reese, and Damita Jo. All three became interested in music as a result of singing in church. Della Reese, born Dellareese Taliaferro in Detroit in 1932, was singing in a choir at the age of six, performed with the Mahalia Jackson troupe during the summers of 1949 and '50, and while studying at Wayne University had her own gospel group.

Both Dinah Washington and Damita Jo had shorter careers in religious music. But Dinah, who was born Ruth Jones in Tuscaloosa, Alabama, in 1924 and raised in Chicago, played piano for her church choir. And Damita Jo's feeling for gospel music revealed itself in her first chart song on Mercury. "Love Has Laid Her Hands on Me" was a gospel song secularized by the substitution of the word *love* for Jesus.

Damita's most impressive and best-selling disk to date is her recent Okeh recording of the Rod McKuen-Jacques Brel song "If You Go Away (Ne Me Quitte Pas)." Here she displays a sense of dynamic contrast and dramatic projection that makes the record an intense emotional experience.

I first encountered the work of Jacques Brel in an off-Broadway revue, *O Oysters!*, at which time I bought every song of his that I could acquire. Before McKuen wrote the lyric recorded by Damito Jo, I had showed the song to countless white artists and lyricists, all of whom were profoundly moved by the Brel melody and words but shied away from it because of its somberness and intensity. It took a black artist to muster the depth of feeling the song demanded. After Damita Jo, many white artists, including some who had walked around it longingly but uneasily, summoned the courage to tackle it.

Della Reese has a big rather than an intense voice. It would be called a shout if it were not so polished. Starting on a rhythm-and-blues label (Jubilee) in the mid-fifties after a stint with the Erskine Hawkins band, she early made a dent in the pop market. An adaptation of "Musetta's Waltz" from *La Bohème* under the title "Don't You Know" yielded a disk that went high on pop charts and reached number one on R & B charts.

Della, however, is an artist whose work emphasizes the gap between a listening and a buying public. She has always had the former but generally lacked the latter. In the parlance of the business, a record has to grab a listener to produce the emotion that results in a sale.

When I was promoting the great hit "More" from the film *Mondo Cane*, Della became one of the first American vocalists to record it. But her popularity had slipped so badly by 1963 that I could not get her record played. This development could have been the result in part of Della's unwillingness to play the buddy-buddy game with disk jockeys, a gambit that involves occasional personal visits as well as unpaid performances at weekend hops run by the jockeys. It was also, perhaps, due to the material she recorded.

Possessed of a voice whose tone color reminds one of Sarah Vaughan—there's more chesty contralto in it—Della gravitated toward big musical ballads that tended to lock her out of the black market and did not make contact with teen-age rockers or middle-aged "easy listeners." An exception was the folk-type ballad "It Was A Very Good Year," an award winner for Sinatra and a hot record for Della in 1966. More recently, the expanding TV market for black artists has given her the showcase of a one-hour nightly show "Della," originating on Channel 9 in Hollywood.

The most interesting of the three females under consideration was Dinah Washington, whose successful career was brought to an abortive end by her accidental death in 1967. From an immersion in gospel music, the winning of an amateur contest in Chicago led her at eighteen to singing in a bar, and from 1943 to 1946 to a berth as band vocalist with Lionel

Hampton. In '47 she began cutting R & B disks for Mercury and quickly gained acceptance in the then segregated black market. By '50 Mercury was using her to cover pop hits for black buyers.

In this category, we find disks like "It Isn't Fair," the cover of a Don Cornell revival of a thirties song; "Cold, Cold Heart," the cover of the Tony Bennett pop cover of Hank Williams's country hit; and "Teach Me Tonight," the cover of best-selling pop records by the De Castro Sisters and Jo Stafford. In '52 she recorded "Wheel of Fortune," but Sunny Gale and Kay Starr grabbed the pop sales, just as the following year she cut "I Don't Hurt Anymore" but Hank Snow had a smash in the pop-country field.

Dinah's biggest years, when she finally broke into the pop market, came in 1959 and 1960. I may lay claim to playing a part in this development, since I brought "What a Difference a Day Made" to Clyde Otis, then the first and only black A & R executive in the business. On its release, Dinah's disk, with the tense of the verb altered to "makes," showed no signs of crawling out of the R & B market until I went on a long promotional road trip.

It was the first such trip I had made in a number of years—since it had then become accepted procedure in the business to hire territorial promoters—and, in retrospect, it was one of the last times that a music man could really promote a disk, that is, persuade disk jockeys to play a new record before it made trade paper charts. (The disappearance of name jockeys with the freedom to program their own shows, the emergences of the Top 40 type of programming, and, after the payola investigation of 1959, the use of station committees to make up play lists, all reduced or eliminated the chance of getting a new record plugged.)

As I traveled from city to city during the late spring, I was able to interest pop jockeys in Dinah's record, only to discover that executives of Mercury were later telephoning these jockeys to advise them that her record was not part of the company's spring promotion (pop) list. In one city where a Mercury executive reached me by long-distance phone, I was advised to go home and stop messing up the sales campaign.

"Dinah has always been a great R & B artist," said the executive, who shall remain nameless, "and she'll always sell her quota of ten thousand or more disks to her Negro followers. She never was a pop artist and you're wasting your time trying to move her into white markets."

Had anyone suggested that this was racist thinking, I am certain that the man in question would have given me a long list of black artists whom he recorded.

Several weeks later, when I had completed my tour, I stopped off in Miami for a brief rest and a visit to a disk jockey convention then in progress at the Hotel Americana. Over ten weeks of traveling seemed to have produced no appreciable reaction on pop charts. On the first evening of the convention, Mercury was the host of a patio cocktail party.

I had hardly entered the area near the pool when a Mercury executive greeted me excitedly. "Have you heard? Dinah's record just broke pop! We've shipped more than fifty thousand this week—and to distributors who never ordered her releases before!" I cannot refrain from reporting that the executive added, with typical humility, "How do you like the job we did on her record?" I will not repeat my comment.

By the time "What a Difference a Day Makes" had climbed to an award-winning position on pop charts, Dinah had a new pop revival in "Unforgettable." With Brook Benton, then riding high on pop charts, she soon cut two duets. Both "Baby (You Got What It Takes)" and "Rockin' Good Way (To Mess Around and Fall in Love)" were pop best sellers and vaulted to number one on R & B charts. So did "This Bitter Earth," an original by Clyde Otis, her A & R man, which she cut by herself.

Miss Washington combined the toughness of gospel shouting with the tenderness of superbly phrased, polished ballad singing. The Queen, as she liked to be called, is gone, but her records live on. And they should, because Dinah Washington was musical from the top of her clowning head to the bottom of the sleepless nights that led to her accidental death.

In the years before rhythm-and-blues artists were sucked into the pop market by the strong drafts of Rock, a certain number of male singers broke through. One of the first to penetrate the white record market was a chubby, shy man who combined blues feeling with an almost childlike sound.

Antoine "Fats" Domino, born (1928) in New Orleans in a family associated with early jazz, was beating the ivories in local bars at the age of ten. He was in his early twenties when his recordings on the West Coast's Imperial label began scoring with R & B buyers. "The Fat Man" was his first. By '52 he had a top R & B hit in "Goin' Home." Two years later, he made an initial dent in pop with "Ain't It a Shame." But it was not until the year of Elvis Presley's emergence that he became a pop favorite, without, incidentally, losing his black following. Two revivals were responsible: a pop ballad of the twenties, "My Blue Heaven," and a country ballad, "Blueberry Hill."

Accompanying himself on the piano, with a hop-hop-shuffle or a driving boogie beat, recording with the simplest and smallest of combos, generally creating his own material with Dave Bartholomew (the bandleader who interested Imperial Records in him), Fats eventually collected eighteen Gold Records.

Some of his best sellers also became hits for white teen-age artists. Pat Boone scored with "Ain't It a Shame," whose title he altered to "Ain't That a Shame," while Ricky Nelson had a chart record in "I'm Walkin'," both songs written by Fats and Bartholomew.

By the early sixties Domino's power as a record maker was gone. However, the current revival of R & B has made him an attraction on the white club and concert circuit as a pioneer rock 'n' roller doing his hits of the fifties. And in '68 Reprise Records brought him back into a studio and cut a new LP, *Fats Is Back*. It contains many of the hits that Fats wrote and that left unforgettable aural memories, like the beginning of "Ain't It a Shame": *You made* CHORD! CHORD! *me cry* CHORD! CHORD! *When you said* CHORD! CHORD! *goodbye.*

There are also some surprises in two Beatles songs, "Lady Madonna" and "Lovely Rita (Meter Maid)." But while it's Fats singing, and sounding as boyish, ebullient, and bluesy as he did at the height of the R & B era, curiously it's not Fats on piano. Except for "I'm Ready"—not the Willie Dixon-Muddy Waters haymaker of '54 but Fats's own hit of '59—a studio pianist and a New Orleans buddy polish the ivories—and manage to sound so much like Fats that the knowledgeable editor of the knowledgeable *Rolling Stone* was fooled.

Another New Orleans Negro whose career was launched by a West Coast label (Specialty) was Lloyd Price. In '52 he grabbed a large chunk of the black market with two of his own songs, "Ooh, Ooh, Ooh" and "Lawdy Miss Clawdy," the latter number-one best-selling R & B disk of the year. It was not until '58–'59, however, that he boomed into the pop market, and then only after he switched his record affiliation to an East Coast label, ABC Paramount. In rapid succession he had best sellers in "Stagger Lee," his own adaptation of an old blues, and "Personality" and "I'm Gonna Get Married," two originals he wrote with his manager, Harold Logan. Although all three were enormous R & B hits, each zooming to number one, and "Personality" finished as one of the 10 Most Played Disks of '59 (*Cash Box*), Price was not able to sustain his record popularity.

Short-lived, too, was the platter success of Roy Hamilton, who became interested in the ministry not long after he broke big on wax. A native of Leesburg, Georgia, he grew up in Jersey City, New Jersey, where he sang in church concerts.

Impressed by his singing ability, a Newark radio announcer, Bill Cook, brought him to the attention of Epic Records. Within a year after he began cutting for the Columbia subsidiary, he attracted white buyers with revivals of two of Rodgers and Hammerstein's big, dramatic ballads, "If I Loved You" and "You'll Never Walk Alone." The latter also proved extremely palatable to black buyers, who made it number one on R & B lists in '54.

His rangy, semioperatic, preacher-voiced baritone also gave competition to Al Hibbler on "Unchained Melody" and, in fact, outclassed the Hibbler version among black record purchasers. When Hamilton began recording again in the sixties, after a hiatus of several years, his disks were released by MGM, then by RCA Victor, and most recently by American Group Production of Memphis. At the time of his sudden death of a stroke in July, 1969, he had a new disk on the market, "Angelica."

There were black groups that made money in white markets before The Platters were formed in '55. During the forties both the Mills Brothers and the Ink Spots accounted for records that have become part of white America's standards. Both family groups, the Mills Brothers became known in the early thirties for their instrumental imitations, made smash pop hits of "Paper Doll" and the Johnny Mercer electrified version of "Glow Worm," and as late at 1951–1952 won a *Down Beat* award as a swinging vocal group.

Less jazz oriented, the Ink Spots made entertaining use of contrasting falsetto and deep bass voices—a device that became a staple of early rock 'n' roll disks—and created unforgettable hit recordings of "Into Each Life Some Rain Must Fall" (with Ella Fitzgerald in '44), the British ballad "The Gypsy" ('45), and "To Each His Own," which was also a best seller for Eddy Howard in '46. Neither of these groups was distinctively Negroid and their success was partly a triumph of fine showmanship.

The Platters, however, had an unmistakable R & B sound and were the first black group with that sound to climb to the top of the pop charts. The year was '55 and the songs were "The Great Pretender" and "Only You," both written by Buck Ram, their manager and record producer. Their achievement is noteworthy because they did not "whiten" their sound and were able to maintain a hold on the black listener as well as the white. In fact, both songs achieved top spots on R & B lists as well as pop. It was a sign of the times. Coinciding with the advent of Presley, the emergence of The Platters suggested that the musical scene was being desegregated with the advent of the rock 'n' roll generation.

The year after their smashing invasion of pop, The Platters began reinterpreting standards of the thirties and forties like "My Prayer" and "You'll Never Know." In '58 they revived the signature song of the Three Suns, "Twilight Time," one of whose co-writers was their manager, and also the Jerome Kern perennial, "Smoke Gets in Your Eyes."

It is reported that Kern's widow was so upset by The Platters' raucous harmonies that she phoned publisher Max Dreyfus to demand that he have the disk taken off the market. This he could not have done, since the copyright law provides that, once a song has been recorded and released for public performance, it can be recorded by anybody willing to pay the statutory royalty. Dreyfus was unsuccessful in calming Mrs. Kern until he casually mentioned the probable royalty to be derived the The Platters' disk. Then they agreed that tastes differ, and perhaps each generation should be permitted to reinterpret songs in ways that appealed to it.

With limited exceptions, record careers are notoriously short-lived. When a group comes up as explosively as The Platters did, they tend to pass their prime quickly. But that group has gone on making successful personal appearances all over the world. For some time, their act has included a medley in which they pay tribute to Motown Records, the Detroit-based firm responsible for The Supremes, the Temptations, and numerous other black stars.

There is a world of difference between these groups and The Platters, as much contrast in sound as in the temper of the times. But it seems pertinent to suggest that Motown owes The Platters a debt of gratitude, rather than vice versa. For they were the precursors and helped open the ears of white listeners to the black sounds of The Coasters, Gladys Knight & the Pips, the Four Tops, and all the driving R & B groups that now sell in white markets on their own terms. Except for

Nat Cole, Al Hibbler, and a few other black artists, they were virtually the only group to break the all-white monopoly hold on pop music.

How racist this scene was, and particularly in radio, may be gleaned from the following. In May '56 *Billboard* ran a list of what it called "All-Time Juke Box Favorites." There were 197 records on this list. How many were black? Just 13, or less than 7 percent. And the artists were the Ink Spots (3 records), the Mills Brothers (2), Nat "King" Cole (2), Louis Jordan ("Choo, Choo, Ch' Boogie"), Billy Eckstine ("I Apologize"), Cab Calloway ("Jumpin' Jive"), the Charms ("Hearts of Stone"), Al Hibbler, and Roy Hamilton, all one each.

In 1956 and 1957 two artists representing entirely different qualities than The Platters made a deep impact on white markets. Johnny Mathis and Harry Belafonte were delicate and tender balladeers, precise in their diction, musical in their deliveries, and literate in their choice of material.

"Wonderful, Wonderful," a song whose writing I prompted and whose rewriting was prompted by Mitch Miller, was representative of the type of pretty melody and lettered lyric that helped make a pop star of Mathis. In hits like "It's Not for Me to Say," "When Sunny Gets Blue," "Misty," and "Chances Are," he communicated tenderness and thoughtfulness. Not a rhythm singer and not a blues singer, he had a range and falsetto that made him sound almost feminine at times. He was a black singing white, a fact emphasized by his almost complete absence from R & B charts.

Like Mathis, Harry Belafonte continues to be a steady and a big album seller, with more than twenty LPs in RCA's active catalog, and a potent figure in personal appearances. (Even today he can play Los Angeles' cavernous Greek Theatre for three weeks to sellout crowds.) But, except for a period in 1957 when he crashed the pop scene with two hot calypso singles, "Banana Boat Song (Day O)" and "Mama Look A Boo Boo," he too has found no place on R & B charts.

Negro rejection is more difficult to understand in Belafonte's case, since he has long been an active and militant fighter in behalf of black rights. He has been outspoken and has taken chances when other Negro entertainers were content to stick to their singing. Not too long ago, when a TV producer raised questions about a sequence in which singer Petula Clark placed her hand on Harry's arm, it was Belafonte who made a public issue of the incident. Harry has also made a studied effort to perform root material in several albums of blues and Negro folk songs, and in his TV productions he has made extensive use of black-oriented scripts and black actors and singers.

Harry's marriage to a white woman did not sit well with Negroes, particularly since he divorced a black woman to achieve it. But he has also isolated himself from the black community by his singing style. Emphasizing qualities like elegance, artistry, and dignity, first introduced into the singing of the blues by Josh White, he has relied on his "white" handsomeness and sexy outfits to make himself physically appealing. In fact, he took Josh's open sports shirt and unbuttoned it to the navel. Beyond that, he has been concerned with poetic material, depth of expressiveness, and a contained intensity rather than the hot and aggressive exhibitionism of R & B styling. Think for a moment of James Brown, and it is clear that Belafonte is on the cool side of the singing spectrum.

In 1959 two black singers rose to prominence in the pop scene, each representative of a facet of black styling. Brook Benton popularized the type of boastful, self-satisfied masculinity projected in earlier songs like "I'm Ready" and "I'm Your Hoochie Coochie Man." Jackie Wilson popularized the style of ecstasy singing introduced by Little Richard and given flaming expression later by James Brown and Jimi Hendrix.

In his first year, Benton had three number-one disks on R & B charts that went Top Ten in pop. In both "It's Just a Matter of Time" and "Thank You, Pretty Baby," he projected the image of the black man-about-town, the former expressing a relaxed vengefulness and the latter a smug appreciation. The following year he once again demonstrated his combined pop and R & B power in three songs. Two songs, "Baby (You Got What It Takes)" and "Rockin' Good Way," were duets with Dinah Washington—the Queen could be as uppity as

79

Brook any day—while the third, "Kiddio," was a typical Benton solo venture. His record power lasted about five years, losing voltage steadily from '62, when he still made it with "Hotel Happiness," a song I published, and "Lie to Me," a song he wrote with Nashville's Margie Singleton.

Jackie Wilson's has been a longer-lived record talent. Although he first began recording in '57, *Billboard*'s "1969 Record Talent Edition" found him in the list of Top R & B Singles Artists. Quite a span. But Wilson has the high-pitched, choke quality of James Brown and he is able to handle gospel material with great excitement. He has a dissolute quality he can project on wax so that he sounds almost painfully ecstatic. This kind of showmanship brought him onto the floor of Manhattan's Copa as early as 1962.

It is not without interest that his early recordings were of songs written by a trio whose names are Tyran Carlo, Gwendolyn Gordy, and Berry Gordy, Jr. The last mentioned is, of course, the gent who built the General Motors of black pop recording, Motown Records, and its numerous subsidiaries and affiliates. However, Wilson's first really big disk on R & B charts was "You Better Know It," a song he co-authored and recorded in '59.

The following year, he cut "My Empty Arms," an adaptation of an aria from *Pagliacci*. Beyond affording an opportunity for a display of the dramatic reaches of his voice, it underlined his avid interest in the pop buyer. He did better with "A Woman, a Lover, a Friend" and "Doggin' Around," both number one in the R & B market. The latter, in fact, went pop and became a Gold Record. At last count, he had twenty active Brunswick LPs, with a recent album like *Higher and Higher* manifesting an attractive fusion of the Motown tambourine-tom-tom sound and gospel drive.

The year that Wilson and Benton zoomed up on the vocal horizon, Hank Ballard and the Midnighters recorded an original tune on the Federal label. Even though the group had had several big records, "The Twist," as it was called, did not make it with either black or white buyers. But the following year a former Philadelphia chicken plucker cut the tune on Parkway and bought himself a millon-copy seller.

Chubby Checker, who patterned his adopted name after Fats Domino, also racked up Gold Records in "Let's Twist Again" ('61) and "Limbo Rock" ('62), another variant on the same rhythmic beat. Although Chubby made other records, he never really scored again.

Inside the business, the envious said that he just fell into it. The reference was to the stir created by a nondescript Manhattan bar on West Forty-seventh Street known as the Peppermint Lounge. During 1960–61, high society, the jet set, and show biz luminaries, not to mention a curious and increasingly excited public, were all rushing to the lounge to watch youngsters doing a new dance, the twist. It was not new to black ghettos, where Negroes had for years been doing variants of it under such names as Ballin' the Jack and Messin' Around: "Twist around with all your might/Messin' round, they call it messin' round."

As everyone knows, the dance caught on, not only among teen-agers but among the middle and older generations, who found that it was simple, if not exhilarating, rhythmically to twist one's fanny. The combo playing at the Peppermint Lounge —Joey Dee and the Starliters—soon recorded a single called, naturally, "Peppermint Twist" and cashed in on the excitement with a Roulette LP of twists. But it was Chubby Checker who reaped the harvest and earned not only three Gold Records but the comfortable income emanating from performing and teaching the twist at swank hotels on the borscht circuit and in Miami.

Three black vocalists who broke the sound barrier in the sixties might be described as soulful but not Soul singers. I refer to Dionne Warwick, Lou Rawls, and O. C. Smith. Miss Warwick is an involved singer but not *possessed*. She does not lose herself in her material, as gospel singers do in moments of great stress and excitement.

Leonard Feather had it right when he observed, "Gospel

music is her heritage, not her bag." She is an inspired song-stress whose polished chirping is given a sharp, incisive edge by her gospel-blues background.

"I happened in a period," she told Feather, "when the Shirelles were the top female group, and Fabian was big, and there was a whole mess of very heavy rock people. It came almost as a relief to hear music—not that I feel I was the main instrument, but I happened to run into the greatest team of writers in the world."

The team was Burt Bacharach and Hal David, who produce her records as well as write her songs. Their first hit together, "Don't Make Me Over" in '62, was followed by "Walk On By," "What the World Needs Now Is Love" (a jazz waltz), "Alfie," theme of the film of the same name, "I Say a Little Prayer," "This Girl's in Love with You," a hit previously on Herb Alpert's "only" vocal disk, and other best sellers. Working with songs that were unorthodox in construction and form, with shifting meters and offbeat harmonic changes, she gave them the advantage of high musicianship and appealing, low-temperature delivery.

"Without seeming detached," Bacharach has said, "she has a certain coolness, a capacity for understatement. She is very normal, very appealing, and above all most honest as an artist and a person. She has remained totally unchanged by success."

Born Marie Dionne Warrick in December, 1940, in Orange, New Jersey, she became Warwick as the result of a spelling error on her initial Scepter disk, "Don't Make Me Over." While she was growing up, her mother managed and sang in a gospel group, the Drinkard Singers. Occasionally Dionne subbed for an absent or ailing member. Singing in the local church choir was a more regular activity for her and sister Dee Dee, now a hit maker in her own right on Mercury ("Foolish Fool").

For a time, the two sisters and a cousin had a teen trio whose style was suggested by the name they used, the Gospelaires. A scholarship at the Hartt College of Music in Hartford, Connecticut, opened the door to secular recording, which led to her meeting Bacharach and David.

"We met on a Drifters session," Bacharach recalls. "Dionne, Dee Dee, and a cousin were singing backgrounds (ooh's and aah's). The first thing I noticed was not how she sounded, but how she looked—the sneakers and dungarees, pigtails and those great cheekbones.

"A couple of months later, Hal and I needed demo records on two songs. Dionne was glad to make the money. We took the demos to Scepter, a record company that was pretty hot then with the Shirelles. They not only liked the songs but wanted the singer, too. They signed us to produce her records."

Once a high fashion model, Miss Warwick recently appeared in her first film. Flaring nostrils, high cheekbones, and an attractive overbite give her an exotically sexy quality that could lead to a movie career once her recording sales level off.

While Dionne Warwick comes from a comfortable, middle-class background, Lou Rawls knew slum deprivation in windy Chicago, memorialized in some of his spoken monologues on disk. Like a bluesman of old, he tells in "Dead End Street" of the cold nights when to go to sleep he had to get fully dressed. As in Dionne's case, Lou sang in his church choir, and after graduation from Chicago's Dunbar High School he joined the Pilgrim Travelers, a well-known male gospel group.

Although he hardly has the type of hoarse voice that one associates with blues singing, the blues are basic to his vocal work. His first Capitol album in '61, *Stormy Monday*, was a blues collection, as were *Black and Blues* and *Tobacco Road*, the succeeding LPs. His first hit single, five years in the coming, was a contemporary blues, "Love Is a Hurtin' Thing." But he is in many ways as much of a jazz singer as a bluesman, a fact evidenced by the appearance of his name in *Down Beat*'s Jazz Poll of '63.

He not only has a feeling for improvisation but sings with an inescapable, swinging dance beat. Jazz pianist Les McCann was his accompanist on his first album, and the big band of Onzy Matthews swung with him on *Black and Blues*. Although he has the impeccable diction of a pop singer, he spent many years playing what he calls "the chitlin' circuit."

As for radio, according to Rawls, "I never got played on the Top 40 stations because they said I was too, uh, well, not too limited but too black."

Rawls paid his dues in other ways, too. In periods when his career as a singer was not going anywhere, he studied at the Art Institute of Chicago and designed shoes for a footwear manufacturer. It is hardly surprising that he has a feeling for songs of deprivation—"Trouble Down Here Below," "You Can Bring Me All Your Heartaches," "Dead End Street." Also, that he occasionally turns to bitter songs like "Yes, It Hurts—Doesn't It" and acidly ironic ballads like "It's an Uphill Climb to the Bottom." Unlike Dionne Warwick, he has not been able to maintain the impetus that his two hit singles gave his record career in '66–'67, and by the end of '68 he was not to be found among Top R & B Singles or Album Artists.

One of the more recent black pop singers to emerge on the record scene is a thirty-two-year-old, Louisiana-born, ex-Basie vocalist who grew up in Los Angeles in a musically inclined family. Ocie Lee Smith, who goes by the name of O. C. Smith, was initally tutored by his mother. Jefferson High and Los Angeles City College afforded limited outlets for his vocalizing, but the U. S. Air Force provided the audience experience that made him interested in singing professionally.

A disparate trio of men paved the way for Smith's Columbia Records debut and his strike with "Son of Hickory Holler's Tramp." Ex-Tommy Dorsey arranger Sy Oliver heard him singing at a small New York club, the Baby Grand. The manager of the Rascals and American impresario of the Beatles, Sid Bernstein, to whom he was introduced by Oliver, took him to Count Basie. Not long afterward, he became a vocalist with Basie's band, succeeding Joe Williams, who had decided to go single-o. During a three-year stint with Basie, O. C. met Lee Magid, the manager of Della Reese and other black stars, who negotiated the Columbia contract for him.

Although success did not come quickly to O. C. Smith, it was not a tough climb, and he has a relaxed, easygoing disposition. "I've got no hang-ups about billing spots on a show," he said not long ago. "I've worked the Catskills, sung everything—ballads, up-tempo tunes, blues—and I've gained lots of valuable experience as soloist with Count Basie's band. I've played in rooms seating one hundred people, eighty of whom were tourists used to TV, with a minimum of applause. I knew these people were enjoying themselves and that they weren't used to beating their hands together. After all, who claps while watching the tube?"

As for his recording success, "I could have survived by working steadily in clubs without my big album *Hickory Holler Revisited* and my newest *For Once in My Life,* or my hit single. But with the help of these recordings I'm getting bigger and better personal appearance bookings."

Smith's development and direction are both suggested by the change in his booking at the Beverly Hills Century Plaza Hotel. When he first played there, in July of 1968, he sang in the Hong Kong Bar, an intimate, dimly lit spot that catered to lovers of Charlie Byrd and other jazz artists. But when he appeared at the hotel in April, 1969, he was booked into the large, swank, expense-account Westside Room.

Queried by John L. Scott of the *Los Angeles Times* as to what he was striving for, he replied simply, "A whole lot of money!"

Sam Cooke made a whole lot of money, possibly too much for his own stability. But he also exerted tremendous influence on many of the black singers of our time, particularly some of the soul singers. His style was, of course, decibels and frenzies removed from jubilant and ecstatic screamers like James Brown, Jimi Hendrix, and Otis Redding. He really had a crooner type of voice. But like Sinatra in the forties, he could command a degree of intimate sensuousness that brought female listeners to the edge of orgasm. His was the soft, tender, sweet, and soulful voice of a man in bed with a woman.

When he mooed "You Send Me," his debut million-copy record, he *sent* them. It may sound strange, but I maintain that Cooke added depth to soul singing. He vocalized with so much inner warmth and feeling that he moved soul singers to strive for something beyond surface values, beyond the vocal exhibitionism of gospel *possession.* The late Otis Redding, who idolized his records, was on the way to becoming the kind of soul artist who combined inner intensity with expressive force.

"It makes no difference what kind of song you sing," Cooke once said. "You must make your audience feel what you feel. Every song has a message, whether it is pop, rock 'n' roll, or spiritual. If you can't get this across to the listener, then you haven't done the job you are supposed to do as a performer. I learned this lesson at an early age in church. If you have ever attended Baptist services, you will know what I mean. You have to stir up the emotions of the congregation and literally lift them from their chairs. To do this, you have to muster up all the sincerity in your body and project it to every solitary person in the room. And this is precisely what I strive for every time I open my mouth to sing."

Cooke was remarkably successful in achieving this aim during a career that was brought to an early end by a white woman's gun in a motel room. His very first recording on Specialty, "I'll Come Running Back to You," made Top Ten on R & B charts. His second disk was "You Send Me" on Keen, a small label formed by an executive who left Specialty. After he switched to RCA Victor, he had one hit after another, including number-one disks in "Twistin' the Night Away" ('62) and "Another Saturday Night" ('63).

The Negro church was Cooke's training ground and teacher. One of eight children of a Chicago Baptist minister, he became a member of his father's choir, like the other children, as soon as he could vibrate a tonsil. By the time he was nine, he was part of a family vocal group (two brothers and two sisters) known as the Singing Children. They performed at Baptist church socials, passing the plate for free-will offerings.

During the years that he attended Chicago's Wendell Phillips High School, he and another brother sang with a group called the Highway Q.C.'s named after the Highway Baptist Church of Chicago. On his graduation, Cooke became affiliated with the Soul Stirrers, a gospel group for whom he wrote spirituals.

So steeped was Cooke in the gospel tradition that Specialty Records, with whom he made his first disks, did not want to cut pop songs with him, and even after he talked the company into it was reluctant to release them. The well-known taboo among Negroes against mixing sacred and secular material was the stumbling block. It led to Cooke's break with the label and brought a windfall to Keen Records when Bumps Blackwell, a Specialty record executive, formed the new label.

Things came so easily to Sam Cooke in his brief life that he was superconfident and, in a sense, courted disaster. Even before the casual rendezvous that brought an end to his life in 1964—no charge was filed against the woman—he was in an Arkansas automobile accident that nearly cost him his life and that blinded him for a time. His comment after he recovered: "The accident set me back for a while but God, in His infinite wisdom, saw fit to let me stay around a bit longer."

It was not for long. But in the time that remained, as in his earlier work, Cooke sang with warmth, vitality, and the insouciance, if not arrogance, of a hugely self-assured man. He had made it and he knew that he could make it—on several levels. In some ways, he harked back to the swaggering bucks of early blues and rhythm-and-blues, the sixty-minute, hoochie-coochie men who felt they had something the ladies could not do without. And, except for one dangerously destructive woman, ladies could not resist Sam Cooke's cocksureness. In his soul, he knew how to sock it to them, and he was not satisfied merely to express himself, but sought to elicit responses from those he entertained.

Into the '60s: The Oreo Singers

The term Oreo singer is of recent vintage, taking its origin from the chocolate cookie that has a white filling, and meaning a vocalist who is black on the outside and white inside. Although it is doubtless a pejorative term, I am using it merely as a descriptive one.

Two of the groups that fit this characterization are the Fifth Dimension and the Impressions. The former is a male-female quintet that came to public notice with "Up, Up and Away," the initial song hit of Oklahoma-Hollywood writer Jimmy Webb. Since that ballooning song that won four Grammy Awards in 1968, the group has had a number-one record in a medley from the hippie musical *Hair*—"Aquarius—Let the Sunshine In."

The three male members, whose ages run from twenty-nine (Billy Davis) to thirty-six (Ron Townson), came from the ghetto of St. Louis. Each migrated to Hollywood on his own, Ron, a former operatic tenor, to work with Nat "King" Cole's Merry Young Soul and Billy, a former sheet metal worker, to invade show biz. Lamonte McLemore, a former baseball player, had become a full-time fashion photographer and a part-time drummer with a jazz-rock combo. It was through McLemore that the group acquired its female members. One of his assignments was to photograph the winners of the Miss Bronze California Pagent. Marilyn McCoo was the '62 winner and Florence LaRue the '63 queen.

"Music is an international language," Ron Townson has said. "It means you're happy, and when you're really happy you should talk to everybody." That's what the group tries to do, seeking attractive songs, ear-catching arrangements, and a large, responsive audience, white as well as black.

Although they were turned down by the West Coast office of Motown when they first got together as the Versatiles, they acquired a manager in the Detroit company's office manager, who renamed them the Fifth Dimension and got them a contract with rock singer Johnny Rivers's Soul City Records label. *Time* has aptly characterized their live performances as projecting "a satin, silky, sexy kind of happiness." When they played Valparaiso University in Indiana shortly after "Up, Up and Away" had projected them into the big time, they were picketed by the Black Students Union.

Although Curtis Mayfield, lead singer and guitarist of the Impressions, has long been socially oriented in his work as a songwriter, it is doubtful that he would fare better with the Black Students Union. In "We're a Winner" he appeals to black pride and seeks to enhance black self-respect. But in "Mighty Mighty" he urges "spade and whitey" to realize that "we who stand divided . . . in stupidness we've been caught." And in his most recent song, "Choice of Colors," recorded by the

Impressions on Mayfields's own Curtom label, he addresses himself mainly to the black people and makes the suggestion that education, "love for our nation," and trust would go further in improving their lot than cussing and making a fuss.

"I'm just starting to get into the white bag," he said recently. And Richard Robinson, who has edited an attractive booklet about the group, states frankly that Mayfield feels audiences as an artist. Robinson notes that it has been difficult "slighted in spirit" by his inability to reach white pop trying to explain to Mayfield "that the pop audience must be told about him; presented with his music in the right album cover, theater and atmosphere; and generally led by the hand." Instead, according to Robinson, "like many black entertainers, Mayfield finds himself attempting to alter his music to please the white audience."

Nothing in Mayfield's background explains his determination to make it on the white man's terms at a time when soul singers have demonstrated that they can command acceptance on their own terms. Born in Cook County (Illinois) Hospital in June, 1942, he sang with his cousins in a group called the Northern Jubilees. It included Jerry Butler, who also attended the Traveling Soul Spiritualist Church of Chicago, where Mayfield's grandmother was the minister.

In tracing musical influences, Mayfield observes, "I loved music by gospel groups like the Soul Stirrers, whose lead singer was Sam Cooke, and the Dixie Hummingbirds. I heard strictly gospel music in those years. . . . After a while I heard a little bit of the Ravens and the Orioles and I can remember some songs by the Clovers. . . . Around 1955 I got into rhythm-and-blues and rock 'n' roll. I started to like all kinds of music, even classical, but especially loved The Coasters. We started a group called the Alphatones and learned all their songs. . . . The Chicago singing groups like the Spaniels ('You Painted Pictures') and the Dels really knocked me out, but I'd say The Coasters were my biggest inspiration."

After working together for three years, the Impressions approached various record companies. Vee Jay of Chicago released their first sides. One of the songs was "For Your Precious Love," Jerry Butler's launching pad. For a while thereafter, Mayfield worked as Butler's guitarist.

The first hit of the Impressions on ABC Paramount was "Gypsy Woman," a song Mayfield wrote for Dee Clark. He had previously co-authored "He Will Break Your Heart" and "Find Another Girl," two of Jerry Butler's big records. In 1964 the Impressions scored with "Keep on Pushing," a gospel tune that Mayfield revised. "I wrote it as a gospel tune," he explains, "and then I revised it for commercial purposes to cater to a wider public."

In 1969, the group left ABC Paramount and began recording for Curtom Records, the company that Mayfield owns. "I think ownership is very important for black people," Mayfield says, "simply because it tends to help make you an independent, an individual, and it is such a great inspiration for your own people to be part of a market that takes in great masses of financial, you know, dollars, and what have you. And you can show people, well, look, I can do it, too."

Richard Robinson characterizes Mayfield as "a socially important black man" because of his ownership, and notes that Curtom Records "is one of the handful of nationally important, black-controlled companies in the music business." He mentions as other examples Berry Gordy's huge Motown operation and the Isley brothers' recently established T-Neck Records. To these might be added Ray Charles's RPM operation, the James Brown Enterprises, B. B. Productions of B. B. King, and others. At his death Otis Redding was in the process of establishing an entertainment complex that was to embrace a recording company, publishing companies, and artist management a la the Motown combine. Just as the success of Atlantic Records was a spur to the establishment of other R & B labels in the forties and fifties, the sensational growth of Berry Gordy's operation moved other black writers and artists to become black capitalists.

Part II
RHYTHM-AND-BLUES

*I like low-down music, I like to barrelhouse
and get drunk too,
I like low-down music, I like to barrelhouse
and get drunk too,
I'm just a low-down man, always feelin' low-
down and blue.*

—TRADITIONAL

7

RHYTHM-AND-
BLUES IS . . .

It took three wars to urbanize the Negro and establish the black ghettos that pockmark major American cities today. The first war was to preserve the union, the second to make the world safe for democracy, and the third to end all wars. Whatever their success in achieving publicized aims, each of the wars created manpower shortages and employment opportunities that brought a population shift from farm to factory and from south to north. Accompanying the movement of black people during and after World War II was an urbanization of black folk music that transformed country and classic blues into rhythm-and-blues.

Basic to this musical development was the migration of southern bluesmen to areas where they could record. From Texas, Aaron T-Bone Walker and others traveled to Los Angeles, which also eventually attracted B. B. King *ex* Memphis. From Arkansas, Louis Jordan, and, from Kansas City, Joe Turner, moved by steps to New York. From the delta country of Mississippi, the most influential group—including Muddy Waters, Howlin' Wolf, Elmore James, and others—settled in Chicago.

Several other factors, however, entered into the rise, growth, and shape of R & B. Among these were the electrification of the guitar and later the organ and bass, the collapse of the big bands, black and white, and the emergence of numerous small, local record companies creating disks for black ghetto consumption.

In the forties records were not only becoming an increasingly popular form of home entertainment but were vital to the expanding coin machine industry that had made the jukebox a standard fixture in bars, clubs, brothels, and one-arm eateries. For this reason, we shall approach R & B by way of the many small companies that sprang up to produce "race" or "sepia" records, as they were then known.

During the twenties and thirties, Victor on its Bluebird label, American Recording Corporation on the Vocalion and Okeh labels, Gennett through its portable Electro-beam and Richmond, Indiana, Studio, and Brunswick all sent field units into the South to record the blues. Bluebird introduced Bukka White, whose major disks were cut for American Recording. Vocalion accounted for the all-important records of Robert Johnson, the short-lived Mississippi bluesman who greatly influenced Muddy Waters and Elmore James.

However, major documentation of the delta bottleneck or slide guitar style was the work of a subsidiary of the Wisconsin Chair Company of Grafton, Wisconsin, the enterprising Paramount label, whose Chicago and Grafton recording studios produced archive masters by Blind Lemon Jefferson, Charley Patton, Son House, and Skip James—in other words, the influentials of the "Yazoo-cotton" generation that fathered the postwar Chicago bluesmen. When the depression forced the curtailment of production, race or sepia records were eliminated by the majors as marginal lines, while marginal companies like Paramount and Gennett were forced to close their studios.

As the record business dug its way out of the economic holocaust and later out of the wartime stringencies and restrictions on production, one-man outfits, like Art Rupe's Specialty and Don Robey's Peacock label, and family-run companies, like the Bihari brothers' Modern and the Chess brothers' Aristocrat labels, came into being.

Because of the number of companies and artists involved, this survey will be limited to those that commanded the larger audiences, and specifically to those whose disks, style, and artistry helped spawn the artists of Rock and Soul.

In the West, the important R & B companies were and/or are Specialty, Aladdin, and Modern-Kent-Crown in Los Angeles and Peacock-Duke in Houston. In the Midwest, there were and still are two thriving diskeries: King-Federal-Bethlehem in Cincinnati and Chess-Checker-Cadet-Argo in Chicago. The East developed the largest concentration: in New Jersey—Savoy, Manor, and DeLuxe; in New York—Apollo, Herald, Jay-Gee, and Atlantic.

After the mid-fifties Philles became important in Los Angeles, Arhoolie-Blues Classics in Berkeley, California, Vee Jay in Chicago, Motown in Detroit, Stax-Volt in Memphis, Jamie-Guyden and Cameo-Parkway in Philadelphia, and Roulette, Jubilee, Amy-Mala-Bell, Scepter-Wand, Elektra, and Vanguard in New York.

To understand the nature of R & B, one must be aware of its audience, the climate of the times, and the status of its artists. Not all sectors of the Negro community were favorably disposed to it. Just as the blues were once frowned upon as "devil songs" by religious Negroes and dismissed as barbaric by middle-class Negroes, so with R & B. Don Robey of Peacock Records has pointed out that "in '49, R & B music was felt to be degrading and not to be heard by respectable people."

Accordingly, makers of R & B disks, as well as artists and songwriters, addressed themselves to ghetto dwellers for whom the home record player and local jukeboxes were major sources of entertainment. Inevitably, R & B tended to be loud and raucous, coarse if not vulgar, earthy if not erotic. By contrast with country, not classic blues, it was market-oriented and not primarily self-expressive. Besides, it was the ensemble work of professional singers and musicians, not of amateur solo creators or songsters, escapist rather than analytical, body and not head or heart music—in short, uninhibited and unpretentious entertainment.

Several factors operated to emphasize these characteristics. Although R & B was vocal, it was music for dancing, successor to the swinging jive of the big bands. The blues had also served as dance music at country barbecues, fish fries, picnics, and Saturday night parties. In fact, some bluesmen never thought of themselves primarily as singers.

"What we had in my coming-up days," country singer Mance Lipscomb has said, "was music for dancing and it was of different sorts." And Mack McCormick, the Texas blues collector to whom Lipscomb made this observation, adds, "To Mance, the ballad 'Ella Speed' is a breakdown; the work song 'Alabama Bound' is a cakewalk; the bawdy 'Bout a Spoonful' is a slow drag."

Whenever vocal music serves for dancing rather than listening or entertainment, sound tends to overpower sense. And so it was with much of R & B. Words were frequently employed and manipulated for their rhythmic properties, giving rise to the cry that R & B lyrics were incomprehensible.

Places where people dance are seldom noted for peace and quiet. A small combo, live or on a jukebox record, now had to produce the sound once delivered by an aggregation of fourteen or more musicians. Only electric amplification could compensate for the streamlining dictated by postwar economics. For that reason the electric guitar (part of some swing bands and used by some hillbilly artists in the thirties), later the electric organ, and, in the Soul era, the electric or Fender bass all came into their own. The tensions of life in the ghetto seemed to demand the shrillness, the distortion, the intensity, and the decibels of electricity.

Among bluesmen, T-Bone Walker claims priority in pioneering the use of the electric guitar. Taj Mahal, a contemporary bluesman, supports another candidate. "I think the first guy who really got into using the electricity of the electric guitar as a new instrument," he says, "was B. B. King. B. B. always wanted to play bottleneck guitar. He was a first cousin to Bukka White, who was a bottleneck guitarist. But B. B. could never learn. So he took advantage of electricity, distortion, feedback, overtone, and introduced a new style. He started the single-line style of blues. He's completely removed from the country corny bunch who used very small lines. B. B.

got into playing melodic passages, singing and backing up his voice."

Among many historians, Muddy Waters finds support as the man who "electrified" the postwar Chicago blues scene. "There is one man who holds an uncontested place at the very center," writes Barry Hansen, a knowledgeable and typical blues commentator. "The evolution of his band set the pace for the whole scene. . . . Muddy Waters, playing his old blues through an amp, found that he could still further increase the effectiveness of his slide sound"—produced by bottleneck fretting— "and enable people to hear many of the subtleties that were previously lost in a noisy room."

As a matter of time, Waters's influential disks antedated King's. His exciting "I Can't Be Satisfied" of 1948 preceded the Blues Boy's impact disk of "Three O'Clock Blues" by four years. Through T-Bone Walker, Muddy Waters, B. B. King, and a generation of bluesmen, the electric guitar became the style setter of R & B, as the bottleneck or slide guitar had defined the character of the delta blues era.

As dance music, R & B took off where swing left the beat. Technically, the swing beat is a four-to-the-bar pattern, with accents being rather evenly distributed on the four: 1,2,3,4. That's what one hears in Benny Goodman's "Stompin' at the Savoy," Glenn Miller's "In the Mood" and "Little Brown Jug," Tommy Dorsey's swinging "Marie," and all the hit numbers, slow or fast, of the 1936-to-1945 era.

It is heard also in the music of the men who originated swing—the black bands of Fletcher Henderson, Count Basie, Jimmie Lunceford, and the hundreds of territorial aggregations that played in the shadows of the white name bands. Black swing tended to embody an additional rhythmic factor. Extra stress on the second and fourth beats of a measure superimposed a two-beat feel on the chugging four. It was this afterbeat stress, previously heard in New Orleans and Dixieland jazz, that R & B took over.

Metrically, R & B owes an even greater debt to boogie-woogie, the black ghetto piano style that enjoyed a great vogue in the twenties, particularly at Harlem and Chicago raise-the-rent parties. A revival in the late thirties brought Meade Lux Lewis, Albert Ammons, Pete Johnson, and Jimmy Yancey out of menial jobs—Lewis was polishing cars, not the ivories, and Yancey was a grounds keeper for the Chicago White Sox—into urban nightclubs and onto records. By the early forties, Tin Pan Alley was turning out pop tunes with titles like "Boogie Woogie Bugle Boy," "Rhumboogie," and the biggest of the group, "Beat Me Daddy Eight to the Bar."

Boogie-woogie is, of course, an eight-to-the-bar pattern, as swing was metrically four to the bar: 1 and 2 and 3 and 4 and. By the mid-fifties a syncopated variant of 8/8, also used in boogie, took possession of R & B—and incidentally of early rock 'n' roll. Instead of spacing the eight notes evenly, the stress on the "ands" was lightened and their duration shortened: 1 . . . and 2 . . . and 3 . . . and 4 . . . and.

Here we have shuffle or stomp style, a rhythm audible in virtually all the early hits of Little Richard, Chuck Berry, and Fats Domino. "Tutti Frutti," "Mabelline," "Blueberry Hill" all exemplify the limping meter. (It's also the rhythm one hears on Bill Haley's "Rock Around the Clock," Elvis Presley's "Hound Dog" and "Don't be Cruel," and Paul Anka's "Diana.") Late examples are to be found in Wilson Pickett's "634-5789" and "The Midnight Hour."

R & B also brought the rise of a twelve-to-the-bar sound: 1 2 3, 1 2 3, 1 2 3, 1 2 3, in which the "1's" are accented. Whether you recognize the notation or not, you know the sound as the omnipresent, hammering, high-register piano triplets of early rock 'n' roll. It's also audible on Fats Domino's "Blueberry Hill," The Platters' disk of "The Great Pretender," and Dionne Warwick's debut disk "Don't Make Me Over," in which the melody becomes part of the figure. (In contemporary rock-and-soul, the 12/8 pattern has developed the added tension supplied by counting the four groups of eighth notes, but replacing the "2" note with a rest: 1-3, 1-3, 1-3, 1-3.)

Contributing to the use of these more complex rhythms is the flexibility afforded by the development of the electric bass. Once the bass looked like an oversized or bull violin and was known as the bass fiddle. Its main role then was to underline downbeats (1 and 3), afterbeats (2 and 4), or, as in swing, all four beats. It did so with a single plucked note, the first or fifth of the scale, or through the use of a walking figure, successive notes of the scale.

In the mid-fifties the electric bass was perfected by the Fender people—it is frequently known as a Fender bass even though other companies now manufacture it. The instrument looks like just another guitar but produces the deep, throbbing, roaring notes that give bottom and power to black and rock records. Paul McCartney of the Beatles plays the instrument and doubtless has had a great deal to do with its vogue and frontline position among rock groups. But it is also the pivot of Booker T. and the M.G.'s.

The heightened audibility and the melodic possibilities afforded by its reduced size have elevated the bass to a position of prominence in contemporary music. As repetitive horn riffs are basic to the Atlantic sound, electric bass riffs are the foundation of the Memphis sound. Along with the electric organ, the electric bass has greatly augmented the drive, dynamic range, and decibels of Soul.

But to return to the early days of R & B, one other instrument grew in stature along with the electric guitar. This was the tenor sax. The preference for the tenor is understandable, since the baritone sax is hardly as flexible an instrument and the alto is too sweet and high-pitched. After a time, the raucous, honking tenor became an earmark of the music.

"During the heyday of rhythm & blues," LeRoi Jones writes in *Blues People,* "blues-oriented instrumentalists, usually saxophone players, would vie to see who could screech, or moan, or shout the loudest and longest on their instruments. Men like Eddie 'Lockjaw' Davis, Illinois Jacquet, Willis 'Gatortail' Jackson, Big Jay McNeeley, Lynn Hope, and many others would have 'honking' contests and try to outshout and outstomp any other saxophonist who would dare challenge them. Finally, when most of the 'honkers,' as they were called, had reached a similar competence, the contests got more athletic. Jay McNeeley used to lie on his back and kick his feet in the air while honking one loud screeching note or a series of identical riffs."

The image of McNeeley on his back conjures up another, of a youngster giving vent to unendurable rage and frustration. And I believe there is something of this boil of emotion in R & B. As it was being fought, World War II aroused idealisms and hopes: the struggle to destroy those responsible for racial persecution in Germany and Italy, the slogans in behalf of the little people and gentle people, and the temporary unity symbolized by the raising of the flag at Iwo Jima.

But when Ira Hayes, one of the American soldiers who raised the flag, returned after the war, he was just an outcast Indian. Black people in the big urban centers likewise found that the end of the war did not mean an end to prejudice, discrimination, second-rate schools, and third-rate citizenship.

Black musicians, the second generation of schooled artists, once again found closed doors when they sought entry into symphony orchestras, recording studios, broadcasting house bands, and motion picture studio orchestras. Bop, "the modern malice," as an older group of Negro musicians damned it, was one expression of the anger, alienation, and resentment. On another and more primitive level, it was rhythm-and-blues.

But R & B was much more complex than this reference to frustration and bitterness would suggest. It was really less an overt expression of these tensions than a covert escape from them. There was neither social nor racial commentary in R & B. It was by and large a music of revelry—a music for dancing, drinking, whoring, and having a roughhouse of a sensual good time. It was fun music—the weary fun of a hardworking people for whom Saturday night was the only "get happy" night of the week.

In the years immediately following World War II, no black singer-instrumentalist was more successful in bodying forth the tough and pleasurable excitement of R & B—it was not yet known as that—than Louis Jordan and his Tympany Five. Hitting in 1945 with "Choo, Choo, Ch'Boogie" and "Caldonia

(What Makes Your Poor Head So Hard)," both million sellers of Decca breakable 78s, Jordan had a seven-year run of hit records. The year 1947 was particularly big, with disks like "Ain't Nobody Here But Us Chickens," "Reet, Petite and Gone," and "Open the Door, Richard."

Based on a comedy routine popularized in Negro vaudeville by Dusty Fletcher and John Mason in the thirties and forties, "Richard" was a best seller for Fletcher on National and for Count Basie on Victor. But Jordan was so popular that he could be counted on to lop off a significant slice of the market.

Considering the elements of self-caricature in his material, it is perhaps surprising that Jordan was popular among Negroes. The fact is that most of his records sold well enough among black buyers to give them a Top Ten position on R & B charts. But no black artist could sell over a million in the forties without commanding a sizable following among whites.

Jordan's appeal there was less as a singer-musician than as a sensational comic. While he played a searing sax, he brought the house down with his comedy patter and off-color lyrics. Unquestionably, he played into white prejudices regarding the "funny" customs, "colorful" modes, and "peculiar" outlook of Negroes. It is hard to miss these overtones even in song titles like "Ain't Nobody Here But Us Chickens," "Caldonia," and "Saturday Night Fish Fry"—the last mentioned went to number one on R & B charts in 1950.

"I identify myself with Louis Jordan more than any other artist," Chuck Berry has said. "I have a lot of flighty things like Louis had, comical things and natural things and not too heavy. . . . If I had only one artist to listen to through eternity, it would be Nat Cole. And if I had to work through eternity, it would be Louis Jordan!"

But Jordan was also a master of the blues, as was evident in records like "Daddy-O" of '48 and "Blue Light Boogie," another number-one R & B disk of '50. Doubtless this phase of his work was a carry-over from his early schooling in Brinkley, Arkansas, less than two hours from Memphis, and the time he spent as a jazz musician and singer with Chick Webb around 1937 and later with Earl Hines and Billy Eckstine.

So sensitive an analyst as bluesman Aaron T-Bone Walker has said, "Louis Jordan . . . plays good blues and he sings them like they were originally sung, too. Take his 'Outskirts of Town,' that's really fine old blues."

Soon, however, it became clear that Jordan was more interested in becoming a popular entertainer than an in-group jazz favorite or an ethnic bluesman. "Those guys," he said later, of the pioneering modern jazzmen with whom he worked, "except for Dizzy, who's the master, the king, they really wanted to play mostly for themselves. I wanted to play for the people."

As so he did, selling comedy rather than song and himself as an entertainer rather than the talented instrumentalist he was. I think of Jordan as a latter-day Fats Waller. But the gutsiness and drive of his Tympany Five, as well as his own propulsive boogie-blues style, made him a forerunner of the B. B. King-Muddy Waters-Chuck Berry generation of rhythm-and-bluesmen.

8

WEST COAST
R & B RECORD
COMPANIES

"Sepia" or "race" records, the "chitlin' circuit" (as Lou Rawls has termed theaters and clubs situated in black ghettos), a limited number of local radio stations and jukeboxes—these were the media that provided entertainment for black Americans and gave currency to rhythm-and-blues in the forties and fifties.

During the twenties and thirties, major as well as minor record companies had displayed an interest in blues talent. The classic era of the blues, at the pinnacle of which stood Bessie Smith of Columbia, had seen record men like Ralph Peer of the Victor Talking Machine Company and Frank Walker of Columbia scouting the Mississippi cotton fields, Alabama honky-tonks, Memphis medicine shows, New Orleans bayous, and Dallas tenderloins for indigenous black singers.

When the record business dug its way out of the economic doldrums, and later struggled under wartime stringencies and new restrictions on production, a curious thing happened. Only two of the so-called majors remained a force in the new blues market: Bluebird, through such artists as Arkansas-born Roosevelt Sykes, trumpeter Erskine Hawkins of Alabama, and Elvis Presley's idol—Arthur "Big Boy" Crudup; and the newly organized, aggressive Decca, through Louis Jordan,

Lucky Millinder, Lionel Hampton, Buddy Johnson, and Sister Rosetta Tharpe. A *Billboard* survey of Best-Selling R & B records between 1949 and 1953 revealed that, out of fifty disks, only two were released by majors. In short, black R & B power was in the hands of small, independent firms.

There are two possible explanations for this power shift. One is that the majors considered the black market too limited. The other is that black artists preferred to deal with small companies. In time, however, many of them had disillusioning experiences with the accounting procedures of the indies. Black artists were unanimous in claiming that they failed to receive a fair royalty accounting on their record sales. Many had to be content with, or came to prefer, outright payments. Some of the label owners were undoubtedly tough businessmen, while others were dedicated to and deeply involved with the music.

Art Rupe, who established the Specialty label in 1944–45, admits, "Some of this music moved me so much it brought tears to my eyes. I decided that this was what I wanted to do."

A graduate of UCLA from McKeesport, Pennsylvania, Rupe launched the label with an investment of six hundred dollars. A collector of blues and gospel disks, he loved to prowl Los Angeles' black ghetto. As he tells it, he discovered that "sure-fire sales would result from having 'boogie' in the title" of an instrumental. Having found a group called the Sepia Tones in an after-hours black club, he persuaded them to make a record for scale pay. He dubbed the instrumental "Boogie #1" and named his label Juke Box as a way of attracting the operators of coin machines.

With a sale of better than fifty thousand copies, he secured sufficient capital to record other artists. Soon he also had a partner in Eli Oberstein, then the all-powerful head of Victor Records. It was a short-lived association. When they split up, Oberstein kept the Juke Box label, while Rupe retained his masters, which he soon released on a new label, Specialty. He chose the name to emphasize that he was concentrating his recording efforts on blues and gospel. Among the black artists whose recording careers started or flourished on Specialty are Lloyd Price, Percy Mayfield, Guitar Slim, Larry Williams, Sam Cooke, and, of course, Little Richard.

One of Rupe's first finds was a man who came to audition a new song. He was so impressed with Percy Mayfield's demo of "Please Send Me Someone to Love" that he talked the young man into recording the song. The disk finished as one of the Top Ten R & B records of 1951.

"Percy is a poet," Rupe said recently. "He could have been as great as Langston Hughes. This was a socially significant song. The words were quite prophetic: 'If the world don't put an end to this damnable sin [meaning prejudice], hate will put the world in a flame.' "

The understated protest song, revived recently by B. B. King, emphasizes the double level on which much of Negro song operates. The field hollers and spirituals reportedly contained secret messages, like jive talk understandable only to the insider and comprehensible to others, like "the man," on an entirely different level.

Another Rupe find was Lloyd Price, whom he discovered on a trip to New Orleans.

"When I heard the first Fats Domino record," he recalls, "I really flipped. I had never been to New Orleans but I had heard that that's where it was at. A disk jockey named Okie Dokie interviewed me and I was deluged with people who wanted to audition. On the very last day, after a week of auditions, a young fellow showed up just as I was getting ready to leave. I thought he was going to cry when I said I just had time to hear one song. This sounds like a fairy tale. But he sang 'Lawdy Miss Clawdy.' He was so up-tight that he literally began to cry as he sang."

Canceling his plane reservation, Rupe remained to record seventeen-year-old Lloyd Price. Dave Bartholomew, Fats Domino's longtime collaborator, got the band together and Fats himself played piano on the side that outclassed his own "Goin' Home" to become the number-one R & B hit of 1952. In Rupe's view, "That period of 'Lawdy Miss Clawdy' was one of the first to bridge the gap between the Negro and white markets."

Larry Williams is not nearly as well known as Price, for whom he originally worked as a valet. But his influence on the Beatles is apparent in their recordings of "Slow Down," "Bad Boy," and "Dizzy Miss Lizzie"—all songs by Williams, with the last being a takeoff on "Lawdy Miss Clawdy."

When Price left Specialty, as Sam Cooke did at a later date, Rupe persuaded Williams, who could imitate Price's style, to become a recording artist. Williams's first disk was understandably a cover of his former boss' first release on ABC-Paramount, "Just Because." But Williams was soon recording his own songs, and in 1957 devoured a large slice of the R & B market with "Bony Moronie" and "Short, Fat Fannie," two delightfully humorous novelty songs.

Rupe claims that he always has dug gospel music more than R & B. It led him to record many local Negro choirs whose personnel included a surprising array of future black stars. Lou Rawls was part of the Chosen Gospel Singers. Sam Cooke was lead singer of the Soul Stirrers, with whom Rupe cut almost a hundred selections. For part of the six years in which Cooke led the Soul Stirrers, Johnnie Taylor, the new Stax-Volt star of 1968, also sang with the group.

No Specialty artist, however, was equal in impact to the Georgia singer Rupe began recording in 1955. His name was Richard Penniman, the shouter from Macon, Georgia, who became known as Little Richard. (His career will be sketched in full in chapter eleven.)

Another one-man western R & B operation is Peacock-Duke Records of Houston, still being run after two decades by its founder, Don Robey. Back in 1949 Robey owned a nightclub, the Bronze Peacock, into which he booked Gatemouth Brown, a singer whom he managed but who was recorded by Aladdin of Los Angeles. To bring audiences to the club, Robey asked Aladdin to release a new disk by Brown. But Aladdin delayed so long that Robey recorded Gatemouth himself and christened his new label after the club. Not unlike Rupe, whom he preceded in the recording business, Robey was interested in gospel music as well as the blues. It led to his early issuance of a recording of "Our Father" by the Five Blind Boys of Mississippi, a disk that continues to sell today.

Robey began recording Willie Mae Thornton of Montgomery, Alabama, even before she became known as Big Mama. Willie Mae acquired her colorful cognomen at the Apollo Theatre when she appeared on the bill with Little Esther.

"They put me on first," she told Ralph Gleason. "I wasn't out there to put no one off stage. I was out there to get known and I did! I didn't have no record and I was singing the Dominoes' hit, 'Have Mercy Baby.' They had to put the curtain down. Little Esther never got on that first show. That's when they put my name in lights [Big Mama Thornton and Little Esther] and Mr. Schiffman, the manager, came backstage hollerin' to Johnny Otis, who packaged the show. Poking me in the arms with his finger—it was sore for a week. 'You said you had a star and you got a star! That's your star! You got to put her on to close the show!' I traveled with Johnny Otis. But I went even further on my own after I recorded 'Hound Dog.' "

It was the same "Hound Dog" that became a nationwide noisemaker for Elvis Presley in 1956. But Big Mama's original version was cut in August, 1952, in Los Angeles. It was the same session on which Willie Mae memorialized the acquisition of her new name in the song, "They Call Me Big Mama." Although she was usually backed by a combo that included two brass, two saxes, four rhythm, and Johnny Otis on vibes, Big Mama cut her best-known record with rhythm only and made an R & B hit of it three years before Presley.

"But I didn't write it," she told Gleason. "Lieber and Stoller wrote it. [Johnny Otis was also listed as a co-writer on her disk though not on Presley's.] They were just a couple of kids then and they had this song written on the back of a brown paper bag. So I started to sing the words and put in some of my own. All that talkin' and hollerin'—that's my own. That song sold over two million copies. I never got what I should have. I got one check for five hundred dollars and I never seen another."

Like Cecil Gant with "I Wonder," Big Mama remained a

one-record artist, although she continued recording for Peacock into 1957. Then came a period of obscurity when she played drums and harp in small combos around the bay area of San Francisco and sang the blues she had first heard through Bessie Smith, Memphis Minnie, and Big Maceo.

"My singing comes from my experience," she has said. "My own experience. My own feeling. I got my feelin's for everything. I never had no one teach me nothin.' I never went to school for music or nothin.' I taught myself to sing and to blow harmonica and even to play drums by watchin' other people! I can't read music but I know what I'm singing! I don't sing like nobody but myself."

After appearing at the Monterey Jazz Festival in 1964, she went on a tour of Europe during which she rerecorded "Hound Dog" for Fontana in Hamburg, Germany. At about the same time, she cut an album for Arhoolie of Berkeley, California, in London, once again cutting "Hound Dog." An album she made for Arhoolie in San Francisco in 1966 found her in the company of James Cotton on harmonica, Otis Spann on piano, and Muddy Waters on guitar.

In 1952 Peacock Records purchased Duke Records, acquiring among other artists a young man from Memphis, Tennessee, whose name was John Marshall Alexander, Jr., and who streaked across skies to an early, sensational, and tragic end.

The year that Don Robey began recording Johnny Ace—as Alexander was known professionally—"My Song" became a number-one R & B hit. During the next two years, the twenty-four-year-old singer-pianist scored with "Cross My Heart," "The Clock," and "Please Forgive Me."

As the titles suggest, he was more of a black pop balladeer than a rhythm-and-bluesman and sang most of his tunes in a slow tempo reminiscent of Sinatra of the forties, whose meter was once described by a reviewer as *marche à la funèbre*.

Ace did not have a distinctive voice, and his songs and recordings were so starkly simple they seemed crude. But he had warmth and a tugging sense of youthful yearning, qualities that later contributed to the success of Johnny Mathis (who had greater range, dynamics, and musicianship) and Sam

Cooke (whose warmth was cuddly and sexy). Considering Ace's vocal limitations, he had perhaps gone as far as he could. But there was a legend in the making.

On Christmas eve in 1954, as a sellout crowd awaited his appearance at the Houston Civic Auditorium (on New Year's day, two years earlier, another audience had waited in vain at an Ohio theater for Hank Williams), word came that Ace had accidentally shot himself. "Foolishly" would be the more appropriate word, since he died while playing Russian roulette. The funeral eulogy was delivered by the Reverend Moore, formerly Gatemouth Moore, also a singer from Memphis.

"Pledging My Love," then a new release and now recognized as Ace's biggest song—it was written by Don Robey and Ferdinand Washington—climbed to the top posthumously. It won the deceased singer a number of awards, including *Billboard*'s coveted and rare Triple Crown. It was number-one R & B, number-one C & W, and number-one Pop, suggesting that the two regional tributaries were then beginning to flow into the mainstream of pop.

In 1949, before singing became his forte, Johnny Ace had played the piano in a Memphis band led by Adolph Duncan. The band's vocalist was a nineteen-year-old singer who came from Rosemark, Tennessee, a small town near Memphis. Robert Calvin Bland had grown up in Memphis, singing joyously in his church choir.

The sounds of many distinguished bluesmen were then to be heard in Memphis, including Howlin' Wolf (who was a local disk jockey and performer), T-Bone Walker, Roy Brown, Lowell Fulson, and B. B. King. Bland later credited one of the Dixie Hummingbirds, a famous gospel group, with influencing his phrasing. But the singer who left the deepest impression was the local disk jockey known as Blues Boy King. (Because of him, Robert Calvin Bland called himself Bobby "Blue" Bland.) For a time, in fact, Bland served as B. B.'s valet and chauffeur. He also drove for Roscoe Gordon, another Memphis bluesman who later recorded for Vee Jay Records. His contact with the two, both of whom were then recording for Modern Records of Los Angeles, led to an introduction to the Bihari brothers, for whom he cut his first released disk.

The contract Bland signed with Duke Records in 1954 has proved a long-lived relationship, as rare in the music business as Bland's staying power. Beginning with "I Smell Trouble" and "Farther Up the Road" in '55, he has cut numerous hits, including "Ain't That Lovin' You," "Turn on Your Love Light," and "Too Far Gone to Turn Around," and gospel-originated ballads like "Lead Me On," "These Hands (Small but Mighty)," and "Yield Not to Temptation." Bland has been a consistent seller rather than a sensational one, though he had top-rated disks in "I Pity the Fool" in '61 and "That's the Way Love Is" in '63. In 1961 he was also named number-one R & B Artist by *Cash Box* magazine.

Those who regard an artist's hold on the public as accidental would do well to examine Charles Keil's analysis of Bland's onstage show in *Urban Blues*. Keil demonstrates that Bland's program is engagingly crafted to evoke certain audience responses through the projection of an image. The image is an appealing combination of helplessness and self-assurance, a duality that "adds up . . . to charisma of a kind that may be peculiar to Negro culture."

Opening his program with a slow blues in a troubling vein, for instance, "The Feeling Is Gone," Bland delivers in a churchlike style marked by hoarse cries and melisma. An alternative starter is "Your Friends," a song that Bland concludes with a stutter—"a device used by preachers and bluesmen to convince an audience that they are trying to verbalize an emotion too big for words."

From this point on, Bland begins building an image of dependability with songs like "I'll Take Care of You" and "Call on Me." But as he concludes there is a turnaround and an emphasis on songs stressing his dependence. "Stormy Monday," the old blues popularized by T-Bone Walker, serves the purpose, with its recital of woes for each day of the week and the terminal cries of "Lord, have mercy, Lord, have mercy on me. . . ." Another effective clincher is "That's the

Way Love Is," with its sense of resignation and search for sympathy. In 1969 Bobby Bland's name was still to be found in *Billboard's* select list of Top R & B Singles Artists. It's the message that matters as well as the music.

In personal appearances Bland still looks like a slick black cat of the R & B era—gold-capped teeth in his smile, puffed pompadour of processed hair, pencil-line moustache, long, manicured fingernails, and custom-tailored clothes in color combinations running to the traditional pink-and-green and purple-and-lime, or the more sedate black-and-yellow. But recently Bland has eliminated the "Blue" from his billing.

"I am getting more air play on white radio stations," he explains, "since I dropped the name 'Blue.' " And he adds, "Take one of the songs I'm doing now—'Save Your Love for Me.' It's opened up different doors for me. With this kind of song, I can go to the Strip [Las Vegas] or places like that. For a long time, the public thought of me only as a blues singer. This song is giving me a different image." In short, rhythm-and-bluesman Bland is now intent on crossing into black pop.

The company that unintentionally prodded Robey into the disk business—Aladdin Records—is a family affair. Formed in July, 1945, as Philo Recording by the Mensers—Leo, Edward, and Ida—it became Aladdin in March, 1946. Initally jazz oriented, with artists like cool tenorman Lester Young and Basie vocalist Helen Humes, it recorded Nat "King" Cole before he went to Capitol.

In 1950 Lightnin' Hopkins shook up R & B charts with an Aladdin release of "Shotgun Blues." The following year, the Five Keys (later impressive on Capitol with "Close Your Eyes" and "Ling Ting Tong") made an auspicious beginning with "Glory of Love."

The name of Charles Brown is not nearly as well known as a number of other Browns, but between 1949 and 1951 he proved himself a powerhouse artist with R & B hits like "Trouble Blues" and Jessie Mae Robinson's "Black Night." The label's most important artist, however, was Amos Milburn, a bluesman from Houston, Texas, who went west with the many black people seeking jobs in California.

Between 1945 and 1949 Milburn recorded almost one hundred blues for Aladdin, achieving R & B chart songs in "Hold Me Baby" and "Chicken Shack Boogie." By 1949 Milburn was involved with urbanized blues and was recording songs like Jessie Mae Robinson's "Rooming House Boogie" and "Let's Rock Awhile"—the latter a precursor of "Rock Around the Clock."

In 1950, scoring a number-one R & B hit with "Bad, Bad Whiskey," he went on an alcoholic song binge that yielded best sellers in "One Scotch, One Bourbon, One Beer" by the talented writer Rudolph Toombs and "Let Me Go Home, Whiskey" by Shifte Henri. The latter was a thematic fore-runner of Jennie Lou Carson's "Let Me Go, Devil," a song I promoted as general professional manager of Hill and Range and had rewritten in 1954 as "Let Me Go, Lover." (With Mitch Miller's aid, it became the first song smash launched by a dramatic television show.)

After the rise of rock 'n' roll, Amos Milburn's career on wax lost impetus. Aladdin was successful for a time in maintaining its position with a duo known as Shirley and Lee, whose most important record was "Let the Good Times Roll" in 1956. But Aladdin lost its magic lamp after the mid-fifties when the genie seemed to move to the Midwest and East.

There were two other important family-run Coast labels— Modern, founded in March of 1945 by the Bihari brothers, and Black and White, launched by Mr. and Mrs. Paul Reiner in 1947. All the small independents have experienced difficulties in holding onto talent, and Modern had its ebb and flow of fortune. Among the artists who contributed to its growth in passing were Jimmy Witherspoon, a big-voiced bluesman (and jazz singer) from Gurdon, Arkansas; John Lee Hooker, the ethnic performer from Clarksdale, Mississippi, who scored with "Boogie Children" and "Crawlin' Snake Blues"; and Etta James, whose recording of "Wallflower (Dance with Me,

Henry)" prompted the white cover disk by Georgia Gibbs. In a sense, Modern needed no stable so long as it had B. B. King, who will be treated in a later chapter as one of the influentials, if not *the* major figure, of rhythm and blues.

Black and White's most important artist was Aaron T-Bone Walker of Linden, Texas, a small town near Dallas. Walker recorded for so many labels that he cannot really be associated with one. However, most of the companies were located on the West Coast and the song that became his trademark, "Stormy Monday," was recorded for Black and White in 1947. Walker's first recording was actually made for Capitol in the year of its founding (1942). A three-year hiatus led to Chicago, where he recorded briefly for Rhumboogie and Mercury. Returning to Hollywood in 1946, he cut about twenty sides for Black and White, a batch for Comet, and a dozen for Capitol. From April, 1950, for about three years, he recorded steadily for Imperial. Then the labels multiplied and included Atlantic in '55, Modern in '64, and Jet Stream of Pasadena, Texas, in '66.

Still active today, Walker, who has a widemouthed smile full of horse teeth, claims a number of firsts. In 1933 he joined the Count Biloski Band in Fort Worth Texas, thereby becoming the first Negro with an all-white band in the South. He also argues that he was the first man to put the blues on the Strip in Hollywood. This was in 1936–37. On a Trocadero bill that included Billy Daniels and Ethel Waters, he sang "In the Evening When the Sun Goes Down" and "T-Bone Blues."

But most significant is his claim that he was the first bluesman to use an electric guitar.

"It was kind of hard," he says, "getting used to because it had an echo sound. I would hit a string and hear the note behind me."

But he chose the electric because bands were always covering him over when he accompanied his singing on unamplified acoustic guitar. He dates his use back to 1935, before Charlie Christian introduced the electrified instrument in the Benny Goodman sextet and prompted its widespread use in the big

113

bands of the late thirties. Since B. B. King acknowledges T-Bone and his electrical arpeggios as an influence, Walker's contention of priority is doubtless well-founded.

Walker's career embodies a fifty-year history of the blues. Born in 1910, he was self-taught. Lead boy for Blind Lemon Jefferson for a time, he later accompanied Ida Cox and Ma Rainey. In 1939 and 1940 he played and sang with the Les Hite band. Thus by the time he began recording on his own he had worked with country blues, classic blues, and a territorial swing band. A Texas-style country bluesman had become an urban rhythm-and-bluesman. He cut more than twenty sides before he had his first hit in "Call It Stormy Monday," better known as "Stormy Monday" and actually titled, according to T-Bone, "Tuesday's Just As Bad."

Although he wrote more than forty songs, including "This Is a Mean Old World," "Hard, Hard Way to Go," and "Woman You Must Be Crazy," he never again had a bestseller approaching "Stormy Monday." In 1956 he rerecorded the song for Atlantic together with another of his trademark songs, "T-Bone Blues." But these had nostalgic value rather than impact. The current R & B revival has created an in-person demand for him, presaging his return to the record scene.

A West Coast label that had a short but notable existence was Swing Time, founded by Jack Lauderdale. During the six years from 1946 on, it achieved the distinction of issuing Ray Charles's first tentative and tender recordings. "Baby, Let Me Hold Your Hand," anticipating the title of the Beatles' first American smash, went to number one in 1951, while "Kiss Me Baby" made Top Ten the following year.

Swing Time's major contribution was the work of a bluesman from Tulsa, Oklahoma, Lowell Fulson or Fulsom. The Oklahoman was actually recorded in Oakland by Bob Geddins, who released the disks on his labels—Big Town and Gilt Edge—and leased them for almost simultaneous issuance on Swing Time. Of more than fifty sides, Fulson scored a smash in 1951 with "Blue Shadows" (revived ten years later by B. B. King) and racked up best sellers in "Old Time Shuffle" and Memphis Slim's "Everyday I Have the Blues."

Born in 1921 of an Oklahoma father who was part Indian, Fulson migrated in his teens to Texas, where he accompanied bluesman Texas Alexander, and, after service in the Navy, to Oakland, California. Here, the postwar prosperity of the ship-building insustry was attracting black migrants from the South-west, among them musicians like boogie pianist Pete Johnson, Kansas City blues shouter Joe Turner, and jazz pianist Jay McShann. Accompanied by McShann, and at other times by Lloyd Glenn, the genial-faced Fulson made the transition from rural Texas-style blues to urban California rhythm-and-blues.

Fulson's catalog is a large one. After Swing Time folded in 1952, he made a trip to New Orleans, where he recorded four sides for Aladdin. Returning to Los Angeles, he settled down to an association with Checker, though his rate of production dropped to roughly one disk each year. After 1964 he recorded in L. A., for Kent, a Modern subsidiary. Remaining close to his roots, Tulsa Red (as he called himself briefly) exhibited a strong feeling for songs of time, particularly night songs. "I Walked All Night," "Between Midnight and Day," "Rock-ing after Midnight," "Midnight Showers of Rain," and "Black Nights" all exemplify this preoccupation.

A representative collection of Fulson sides is to be found in the catalog of Arhoolie Records, the strange little company in Berkeley, California, that sprang into existence in the fall of 1960. Founded by Chris Strachwitz, an ex-schoolteacher of German origin, the company and its subsidiaries specialize in reissues. But it has produced its own recordings. And, although its initial interest was in root blues, it recently released a collection of *John Littlejohn's Chicago Blues Stars* cut in the Windy City. "I got started," Strachwitz explains, "by being a real insane fan of blues and other types of American music like R & B, which at the time was mainly blues, gospel, hillbilly, and New Orleans jazz. I started to collect records around 1951. Since then I have also become very fond of Mexican-Texas music, contemporary jazz, Cajun music, and just all the forms that flourish in this country." (An "arhoolie" is a field holler.)

It was Strachwitz's impulsive leanings as a collector that drove him to become a manufacturer and producer. Feeling that authentic blues were too difficult to obtain (in the early sixties, only Chess and Prestige had a slim representation), he went to Texas and, with the assistance of another collector, Mack McCormick, found Mance Lipscomb. The latter's first Arhoolie release was an unadorned vocal-guitar album in which the Texas Sharecropper and Songster performed fourteen root blues, among them "Rock Me All Night Long" and "Jack O'Diamonds is a Hard Card to Play." Since then Strachwitz has added three collections of Mance Lipscomb to his catalog. Also well represented is Lightnin' Sam Hopkins of Houston.

Although several collections of *Texas Blues* seem to give Arhoolie a western emphasis, the catalog includes Bukka White of Houstin, Mississippi, Willie Mae "Big Mama" Thornton of Montgomery, Alabama, Memphis Minnie of Algiers, Louisiana, and several volumes of Sonny Boy Williamson of Jackson, Tennessee. And now Strachwitz's documentation seems to be broadening to include postwar Chicago bluesmen like John Littlejohn Funchess.

Generally speaking, the development of R & B on the West Coast was the result of the postwar influx of black people from Texas, Oklahoma, and Arkansas into the factories, shipyards, and vineyards of California. Amos Milburn, Lowell Fulson, and T-Bone Walker represent an electrified, band-accompanied version of Texas blues—the difference between their urban existence and the cotton-growing world of Blind Lemon, Mance Lipscomb, and young Lightnin' Hopkins. Theirs is a music molded by resentment rather than resignation, written mostly by professional black songwriters, dedicated to revelry rather than rumination, and designed as a driving, screaming accompaniment for jitterbug, jive, and boogie dancing.

9

MIDWEST R & B
RECORD GIANTS

While the bluesmen who grew up west of the Mississippi River went west, those from the all-important Mississippi delta, Louisiana, and Alabama generally took the riverboat route north, eventually establishing Chicago as *the* postwar blues center of the world.

"The Illinois Central Railroad brought the blues to Chicago," says George Leaner, who opened the Groove Record Shop in the Chicago ghetto in the thirties. "With the thousands of laborers who came to work in the meat-packing plants and steel mills came Peatie Wheatstraw, Ollie Shepard, Blind Boy Fuller, Washboard Sam, Little Brother Montgomery, Blind Lemon, Memphis Minnie, and Rosita Howard." With these also came the largest group of influential bluesmen, including Muddy Waters and Chuck Berry.

Working with his sister and brother-in-law, Leaner founded One-Derful Records in 1946 after meeting Lester Melrose, a songwriter-producer for American Recording Corporation, and blues broker.

"In the beginning," Leaner explains, "artists didn't work directly with the record companies. They had brokers—people who handled all the paper work and details. I started recording blues artists upstairs over the Eli Pawn Shop in the thirty-four hundred block on South State Street. The big labels then were Exclusive, Modern, Aladdin, Specialty, and Supreme. These were basically West Coast labels. Blues was flowing into Los Angeles out of Texas.

"A number of circumstances led to the postwar blues explosion. When Cecil Gant's 'I Wonder' broke in '45, a number of refugees from Europe who had great ethnic knowledge saw the possibilities in blues, and the independent label was born. The emergence of BMI and the rapid growth of Negro radio in the late forties accelerated the blues movement."

Whether or not Leaner had them in mind, the Chess brothers, Leonard and Phil, came to the United States on Columbus Day in 1928 and settled on the South Side of Chicago. For a time they operated the Macomba Club at Thirty-ninth and Cottage Grove, where you could hear Billy Eckstine, Ella Fitzgerald, Lionel Hampton, Louis Armstrong, and other Negro entertainers perform jazz, blues, and pop.

Sometime in 1947, the Chess brothers noticed that talent scouts were interested in a young singer named Andrew Tibbs. "We decided to record him ourselves," Leonard Chess notes, "got hold of a studio, and cut 'Union Man Blues.' We also cut 'Bilbo's Dead' to commemorate the then recent death of the Mississippi governor."

Thus Aristocrat Records, the predecessor of Chess and its subsidiaries, was born. Though the Tibbs disk was the first, its catalog number was 1425, the address on South Karlov Avenue where the brothers had settled in Chicago as Russian immigrants.

Being located in a storefront office—like Chicago's storefront Negro churches—Aristocrat attracted talent off the street. One of the first to drop in was McKinley Morganfield, who soon became known as Muddy Waters. Another Aristocrat find was Robert Nighthawk of Helena, Arkansas, whose recording session was notable because it marked the beginning of Chess' long association with blues bassist-singer-writer Willie Dixon.

By the time he produced the Nighthawk session for Aristocrat, Dixon, who was born in Vicksburg, Mississippi, in 1915, had been prominent on the Chicago blues scene for a decade. On settling in the Windy City, he had pursued the curiously contrasting career of a heavyweight boxer. Big Willie was one player whose size literally dwarfed the older-type bass fiddle. But before the "Golden Boy" syndrome developed—he was an excellent bassist he became a member of the Five Breezes, a Chicago-based group that recorded for Bluebird. Later, he worked with the Four Jumps of Joy and in 1946, with the Big Three Trio, who played blues "for listening and dancing."

Pursuing a highly successful career as record producer, sideman, and songwriter, he became active as a performer again in the sixties when he teamed with Memphis Slim, also Pete Seeger, to record several albums for Verve and Folkways. His song credits include three of Muddy Waters's biggest hits ("I'm Ready," "Just Make Love to Me," and "I'm Your Hoochie Coochie Man"), Little Walter's "My Babe," and Sam Cooke's "Little Red Rooster."

Despite Dixon, Muddy Waters, and others, the Aristocrat label folded in two short years, leaving an invaluable documentation of early postwar Chicago blues. But out of the piles of unsold disks came Chess Records, its first single being an improvised instrumental by tenor saxist Gene Ammons—so big a seller that the fledgling label almost immediately acquired national distribution.

The Ammons hit side was "My Foolish Heart," then a massive seller for Billy Eckstine, with Junior Mance at the eighty-eight. Since the Chess Brothers had not yet built their own famous 2 X 4 studio, they cut at Bernie Clapper's Universal studios. But they were inventive even then and enhanced the original Ammons tenor by adding the hollow sound of a mike dangling in the studio toilet. They claim that this was the first echo chamber effect ever used on an American record.

Through the talents of Howlin' Wolf, Bo Diddley, Little Milton, Little Walter, and, of course, Chuck Berry and Muddy Waters, Chess developed into an R & B giant. Some of the early artists were drop-ins. Others were found by Leonard Chess in periodic swings through the South.

Carrying a heavy, two-piece Magnecord tape recorder in his car, he would record on location, frequently running a long extension cord from a bean or cotton field into an electrical

119

outlet in a farmhouse. Arthur "Big Boy" Crudup, whom Leonard found in Forrest, Mississippi, was recorded in this fashion. In Shreveport, Louisiana, on one of his trips, Chess was introduced to Ferdinand "Fats" Washington by disk jockey Stan the Record Man.

"Washington wanted to sell me a song for twenty-five dollars," Chess recalls. "I refused. I'd learned some hard lessons buying songs. If the song is good, a writer will sometime later say you approached him first. So I suggested Stan buy a piece. He did." Chess acquired the publishing rights and recorded the song, credited to Ferdinand Washington and Stan Lewis, with the Flamingos on his Checker label. Randy Wood covered it on Dot with Pat Boone and "I'll Be Home"—as it was called—became a million-record hit.

Howlin' Wolf was a field-trip find in 1948 in West Memphis, Arkansas, where Chess recorded two sides with a five-piece combo, including Ike Turner at the piano and James Cotton on harp. After a hiatus during which he recorded for Crown and RPM, Chester Burnett, as he had been christened in 1910 in Aberdeen, Mississippi, became a Chess regular. His first release, "Moanin' at Midnight" backed with "How Many More Tears," was a substantial seller in 1951.

A less sophisticated musician than Muddy Waters, the Wolf sings in a style reminiscent of the raucous field hollers. Some of the tracks in his album *Moanin' in the Moonlight* sound like songs that W. C. Handy could have heard in delta country around 1900, songs that the Father of the Blues described as "those over-and-over strains that seemed to have no very clear beginning and certainly no ending at all. . . ."

Born on a cotton plantation in the Mississippi delta, the Wolf became interested in music in his teens, but did not become a full-fledged singer until he was almost forty. "It was Charley Patton who got me started," he has said.

Patton was the oldest of the Mississippi group of slide or bottleneck guitarists that included Bukka White, Son House, Skip James, and Robert Johnson. Beginning in 1929 with "Pony Blues" (the Wolf's own first recorded song was "Saddle My Pony")—Patton recorded more than sixty sides for Paramount, half blues and half gospel. Patton's wife, Bertha Lee, recalls a day in Cleveland, Mississippi, when "Charley worked with him all day before Chester Burnett would leave him alone." Patton's heavy voice and power color Wolf's style.

Two other bluesmen from whom the Wolf learned were Robert Johnson (with whom he played until jealousy over a girl disrupted their friendship) and Rice Miller, the second Sonny Boy Williamson, who married the Wolf's sister. But the Wolf's boyhood idol, curiously, was a white singer brakeman from nearby Meridian, Mississippi, who became known as the Father of Country Music and whose forte was yodeling.

Young Chester Burnett tried hard to imitate tubercular Jimmie Rodgers, who was so popular in the late twenties and early thirties that southern general stores were accustomed to hearing farmers order, "Pound of butter, keg of nails, and the latest Jimmie Rodgers record." When he discovered that his voice was too heavy for "blues yodeling," Burnett took to growling, eventually adopting the name of Howlin' Wolf. Although he was known at times as Bull Cow and Foot, "I just stuck to the Wolf," he explains. "I could do no yodelin' so I turned to howlin'." The soubriquet is also strangely apropos to the vulpine features of Burnett's striking face and enormous head with the slotted eyes, high forehead, and massive jaw.

His first band, formed in the late forties while he was working on a plantation in West Memphis, Arkansas, was a country-style combo of two harmonicas and three guitars that included harpists James Cotton, then 13, and (Little) Junior Parker, in his early twenties. After a time, the Wolf became a blues disk jockey on West Memphis' station KWEM. It was pianist Ike Turner who interested the Biharis in recording the raucous growler on RPM Records.

The Wolf does not feel that his style has changed much since 1952, when he exchanged a Chicago slum apartment for a country cabin and began working at the Big Squeeze Club on the South Side or at Silvio's in the West Side ghetto. "Not much, really," he says, "but of course I did have to step with the tempo. I used to play very slow, but I had to come up with the tempo of today. I didn't know my positions when I

121

was playing those slow blues. But over the last few years I went to the Chicago Music School, and they taught me my positions."

The Wolf's candor about himself is matched by the tough realism of his outlook on the blues. "I just like the blues," he says, "because to me it sounds good. But blues is problems, and singing about them doesn't make things easier, I think. It just takes your mind off it."

With the revival of interest in the pioneers of R & B, a number of Howlin' Wolf songs have achieved new currency. His 1957 hit, "Sitting on Top of the World," has recently been cut by the Grateful Dead, Cream, and other rock groups. "Killing Floor," which he wrote and recorded in the sixties, appears as "Killing Ground" in a recent album by the Electric Flag, a rock blues band.

Although he distrusts record companies, the Wolf went back into the Chess studios early in 1969 and, not without reluctance, recorded to the accompaniment of a now-generation band. According to a Chess spokesman, the Wolf would "not perform until Phil Chess came in and gave him one of those I've-known-you-for-twenty-two-years looks." The spokesman admits that Burnett did "not dig the results, but maybe it'll get him a hit."

Younger than Howlin' Wolf and Muddy Waters—he was born Ellas McDaniel in McComb, Mississippi, in 1928—Bo Diddley has done much less recording than either of his Chess confreres. But the loud striped sports jackets and ties he wore represented a fresh brashness in the blues. In his first release on Checker, he announced "I'm a Man," and a new generation of black buyers echoed his sentiments by purchasing his record in prodigious quantities. Succeeding records, like "Bo Meets the Monster" and "Cops and Robbers," demonstrated that he was in tune with the gyrations of youngsters.

Although Leonard Chess claims that he gave McDaniel his soubriquet because of his skill as a storyteller, Bo Diddley was apparently a childhood nickname. Apart from the thematic relevance of his material, Bo's ebullience found rapport in the backing of a young vocal group, the Moonglows. The group's biggest recording was "Sincerely," an R & B hit on Chess that became a smash success for the McGuire Sisters on Coral. Co-writers of "Sincerely" were Harvey Fuqua, now a Motown executive, and Alan Freed, the Cleveland-New York disk jockey credited with coining the phrase rock 'n' roll, who was a casualty of the 1959 payola investigation.

Chess moved into the sixties with several new subsidiary labels and artists, and the purchase in 1963 of radio station WHFC, whose call letters were changed to WVON. The new artists include organist Dave "Baby" Cortez, who capitalized on the mounting interest in the electric organ as a solo instrument with "Happy Organ" ('59) and "Rinky Dink" ('62), and jazz-oriented Ramsey Lewis, whose trio scored with "The 'In' Crowd."

Most important of the new-generation artists is Etta James, a latter-day Dinah Washington, whose hold on record buyers is at a peak. Beginning in 1960 with blues ballads like "All I Could Do Was Cry" and "My Dearest Darling," Miss James demonstrated her vocal power with "Something's Got a Hold On Me" ('62) and "Pushover" ('63). In 1969 she was to be found in the company of *Billboard*'s top seven Female Artists.

The current excitement of the rock generation over the R & B pioneers has led Chess not only to reissue and repackage but to bring these figures into the studio for new sessions. *The Blues,* Vols. 1–5, on Argo, a Chess subsidiary, provide a rich sampling of the original recordings of the artists discussed as well as Little Walter, Little Milton, Washboard Sam, Rice Miller, John Lee Hooker, and other postwar Chicago rhythm-and-bluesmen. Chess has also recently released on a one-volume sampler, *Heavy Heads.* Incidentally, new albums by Muddy Waters and Howlin' Wolf, recorded in multitrack stereo and with souped-up electronics, have met with less than a favorable response both among the young people for whom they were intended and the artists themselves.

Vee Jay, a Chicago company founded in 1954 by Gary disk jockey Vivian Carter, led a short but exciting existence. Just about ten years later it was out of business. During its brief tenure, it proved successful in creating hits with well-known performers like Jay McShann and Roscoe Gordon, with newly formed groups like the El Dorados and the Dels, and with an ofay quartet that became one of the hottest record sellers of the sixties—the Four Seasons. Though white, the group exploited a device typical of black singing groups from the days of the Ink Spots: a high, humorous falsetto voice contrasting with a deep, deep basso, "Sherry" and "Big Girls Don't Cry," both number ones in 1962, started a long list of Gold Records and albums.

Another new group introduced on wax by Vee Jay was Gladys Knight and the Pips, a quartet that recently attained its majority on Motown's Soul label with "I Heard It Through the Grapevine." But even its first release on Vee Jay in 1961, "Every Beat of My Heart," was reportedly a million seller.

Gladys Knight, her brother Merald, and her cousins William Guest and Edward Pattern began singing together before they entered high school in Atlanta. Gladys had actually won first place on the Ted Mack Amateur Hour three times in a row shortly after she began primary school. Unwilling to thrust her into the world of show business before her education was completed, Gladys's mother allowed her to become the featured soloist of the choir at Mount Moriah Baptist Church. Harmonizing gospel hymns for Sunday services, the group assumed its present name when, as teen-agers, they began performing at school dances and entertainments.

Young Gladys has a vibrant voice with a sharp edge that cuts easily through the musical cloth of her own group and a rocking blues band. Guided by the savvy of Motown promotion, the youngsters have developed a highly polished and well-choreographed act that has played the Copacabana and appeared on the Ed Sullivan TV show. *Billboard*'s 1969 chart of Top R & B Singles Artists places the youthful group in the rare reaches of the number-ten spot.

Vee Jay's new talent also included Jimmy Reed of Leland, Mississippi, who cut his first sides in December, 1953, and by 1955 had a best seller in "You Don't Have to Go." In succeeding years, he developed a large following with ballads like "Ain't That Lovin' You, Baby" and "Bright Lights, Big City." On Vee Jay's demise, ABC Paramount's Bluesway label signed him.

The artist who has more than fulfilled his promise, after a sensational start at Vee Jay, is Jerry Butler. Born in Sunflower, Mississippi, Jerry was raised on Chicago's North Side, just a few blocks from the many clubs located on Rush Street. When his father passed away, leaving him, at fifteen, to support a family of three younger children, Jerry became a gospel singer. Despite the vocal talents he displayed in choirs at Olivette Institute, Wayne Baptist Church, and Mt. Sinai Baptist Church, he began studying with a Swiss chef to become a master chef and ice sculptor. After a time, he began singing at the Traveling Souls Spiritualist Church, where a meeting with songwriter Curtis Mayfield and Sam Goodin led to the formation of Jerry Butler and the Impressions.

Jerry Butler's first chart song on Vee Jay was "He Will Break Your Heart," a ballad he co-authored in 1960 with Mayfield. The following year, he attracted national notice with his version of the Academy Award-winning song "Moon River." Only Andy Williams's disk outsold his. Co-writer of "For Your Precious Love," he soon had best sellers in "I Stand Accused" and "Need to Belong." When Vee Jay went bankrupt he was signed by Mercury, where his recent recording of "Moody Woman" has helped to establish him as one of America's outstanding black pop vocalists.

For migrants from the Mississippi delta who followed the course of the Ohio River instead of continuing north to Chicago, the natural stopping place was Cincinnati. Here the late Syd Nathan, who became a record retailer after he left his father's furniture store, moved into a deserted icehouse in the early forties and founded the King dynasty. At first, probably because of the power of radio station WLW as a C & W outlet, Nathan made his mark with country artists. But by 1945 he had acquired a small stable of black artists, the most successful of whom was Bullmoose Jackson.

A Cleveland lad, Benjamin Clarence Jackson came out of the Lucky Millinder band, whose personnel provided the foundation for the King label. Millinder, who discovered Bullmoose when he was a member of the Harlem Hotshots, an early blues group, organized the Bearcats to back him. As a nickname, Bullmoose had more relevance to Jackson's physical makeup than to his voice, which was surprisingly high baritone.

Jackson became a record seller in 1946 by providing an answer to a Millinder chart climber, "Who Threw the Whiskey in the Well?" (Answer songs, rare in pop, are traditional in both the R & B and C & W fields.) In succeeding years, Bullmoose scored with "I Love You, Yes I Do" and "Little Girl, Don't Cry." But he was a natural comic and seemed to do best with novelties like "Sneaky Pete" and "I Want a Bow-Legged Woman."

Bullmoose has never confirmed that he once took a ride in a hearse that cost him thirty-eight dollars. But the Miami distributor of King Records claims that Jackson once passed out on his doorstep. Unable to move the man and anxious to close up shop, he phoned a funeral parlor. As he was being transported, Jackson awoke and, after some moments of uneasiness, realized that a practical joke was being played on him. It allegedly took thirty-eight dollars to make the hearse driver see the joke and take him back to his hotel.

From the Millinder band Nathan also took Wynonie "Blues" Harris, whose shouters in the late forties and early fifties included such suggestively titled songs as "Good Rockin' Tonight," "Lollypop Mama," "All She Wants to Do Is Rock," and "I Love My Baby's Pudding." (R & B writers expanded the blues tradition of employing items of food as sex imagery.)

Two other successful groups developed by Nathan are worthy of special consideration here. In 1951 the Dominoes, from whose personnel Clyde McPhatter and Jackie Wilson later emerged as star soloists, produced the spicy "60 Minute Man," a disk that sold a whopping two million copies. The following year, the Dominoes made number one with "Have Mercy Baby," prelude to a score of 1953 chart climbers, among them "I'd Be Satisfied."

The other hot combination was the Midnighters, led by songwriter Hank Ballard, who racked up two number-one disks in 1954, "Annie Had a Baby" and "Work with Me, Annie," a hard-to-understand sequence despite the euphemism "work."

126

Five years later, the Midnighters were still making fast-selling disks and were able to score, despite their comic propensities, with a ballad like "Teardrops on Your Letter," written by Henry Glover, King's A & R director and Millinder alumnus.

On the back of this recording was a jump tune by Ballard that drew no notice until 1961 and 1962, when it mushroomed into one of the biggest noisemakers of the era. Published by King's Lois Music, "The Twist" became a runaway hit for Chubby Checker on Parkway Records. (Associated by then with Roulette Records in New York, Glover produced records by Joey Dee, who led the combo at the Peppermint Lounge where the excitment about the dance erupted. Dee and Glover collaborated on "The Peppermint Twist.")

Before Ballard enjoyed the somewhat belated success of his "Twist," he came through in 1960 with two exciting fast-shuffle hits, "Finger-Poppin' Time" and "Let's Go, Let's Go, Let's Go." For a personal appearance in Dayton, Ohio, at the time, he collected more than one thousand a night for twenty successive nights. Six years later, in 1967, Dayton's interest was limited to a one-nighter for which he received about four hundred dollars. The difference is explained by the charts. As a writer in *Crawdaddy* nostalgically observed, "Without a hit, Hank has been forced to do the same routine for almost ten years now. . . ."

Three other King songwriter-instrumentalists who enjoyed a moment in the record sunlight—each briefer than Hank Ballard's—were Earl Bostic, an alto saxist from Oklahoma, Boyd Bennett, and Bill Doggett, a former arranger for the Ink Spots.

Bostic, who began his career as a jazz recording artist, made number one with an unforgettable throbbing R & B instrumental version of the Duke Ellington-Herb Jeffries hit "Flamingo." Boyd Bennett's "Seventeen" was a chart climber in 1955 for his Rockets, but a number-one disk for Perry Como's Fontane Sisters.

Bill Doggett, a rocking organist whose style was shaped by

Wild Bill Davis, whom he succeeded in Louis Jordan's Tympany Five, scored the biggest triumph of the three in the famous instrumental "Honky Tonk," credited to five writers, including Doggett and record producer Henry Glover. A two-side recording, it reportedly sold more than four million copies during 1956 and 1957. The only disks I can think of with comparable totals—and these were promoted and distributed by major diskeries—are Elvis Presley's "Heartbreak Hotel" and "Hound Dog" on RCA Victor, and the Beatles' first American smash, "I Want to Hold Your Hand" on Capitol.

In the career of Ivory Joe Hunter, a hugely talented songwriter-singer, King Records proved pivotal. Born in Kirbyville, Texas, in 1911, the seventh of thirteen children, he early manifested such musical talent that at the age of thirteen he was earning money professionally at local gigs, on the radio, and as a spiritual singer in church choirs. (He was known for a time as "Rambling Fingers.")

Although he was well loved throughout the Texas area, and particularly around Port Arthur, Houston, and Beaumont (where he had his own radio show on KFDM), he found it necessary to migrate to the West Coast to build his career. In 1944 he was able to attract attention with "Blues at Sunrise," a song he wrote and recorded on his own label, Ivory Records. The wartime shortage of materials forced him out of independent production, and he became a partner in the short-lived Pacific label of Berkeley. However, "Blues at Midnight" sold well enough in 1946 to interest Syd Nathan in signing him.

For three years King power helped put Ivory Joe on R & B best-selling lists with songs like "Don't Fall in Love with Me," "Pretty Mama Blues," "Landlord Blues," and Jenny Carson's country hit, "Jealous Heart." The biggest of his King chart climbers was "Guess Who." But none of these approached the impact of the first two disks he made in 1950 on MGM Records, "I Need You So" and "I Almost Lost My Mind." The latter tune became a Pat Boone smash, allowing Ivory Joe to make up in writer royalties what he lost on the sales of his own disk.

By 1956 the gifted writer had moved to Atlantic, where his

biggest song disk was the blues ballad, "Since I Met You Baby." In recent years Ivory Joe has recorded for Capitol and other labels, but has been unable to equal his achievement of the fifties.

Among the artists who recorded for King in passing was Memphis Slim, born in Memphis, Tennessee, in September, 1916, and christened Peter Chatman. Six feet, six inches tall, he is as potent a boogie-blues pianist as he is lanky. Writer of the great R & B standard, "Everyday I Have the Blues," Slim gave brief life to a Chicago label, Miracle, whose masters were taken over by King. With Miracle in 1949, Slim had "Angel Child" and "Blue and Lonesome," having previously scored with "Fool That I Am." Though the label was short-lived, Memphis Slim remains one of the longest-lived recording artists in the R & B field, and for most of his career without a really solid hit.

By way of indicating the peripatetic existence that performers lead, a capsule rundown of Memphis Slim's recording movements will prove illuminating. While Chicago was home ground, Slim made a trip to Cincinnati in 1949 to cut an album for King and a journey to Houston to cut unreleased sides for Peacock.

Remaining in Chicago during 1950 and 1951, he recorded for three different labels—Premium, Argo, and Mercury. Visits to Houston and Cleveland in 1952 yielded releases on Chess and, again, unreleased sides on Peacock. In 1953 he recorded for United Artists in Chicago, recutting "Blue and Lonesome."

After a hiatus of four years, he did a song for Vee Jay in Chicago in January, 1958. A year later, he had a release on United Artists of an April, 1959, concert at Carnegie Hall. In July, 1959, he recorded an album for Folkways in New York City. By the following month he was back in Chicago recording an album for Vee Jay. Before the year ended, he returned to New York to cut several albums with Willie Dixon for Folkways and Verve.

Now he began traveling and recording abroad. In July, 1960, he cut an album in London for Collector. The following month, he produced an LP for Storyville Records of Boston in Copenhagen. In October he was back in Chicago recording for Folkways and Xtra. Later that year, he went to New York, where he cut two albums for Bluesville and two for Candid.

The year 1961 found him in Chicago cutting for Strand of NYC, in London in April recording for Fontana, in Bayonne in May plattering for Agorilla, and in Copenhagen in June slicing for Storyville. The following October, he began cutting an album for Polydor in Bremen, which he completed in Paris. In October 1963 he recorded for Fontana in Bremen, and in November for Storyville in Copenhagen. Obviously it was motion and the enduring appeal of the blues that kept Memphis Slim alive on wax, since none of his albums racked up sufficient audience for the company to tie him down with a contract.

Quite a number of other black singers had their start on King. In a surprisingly long list, one finds the distinguished names of Otis Redding, Nina Simone, The Platters, Joe Tex, Little Esther, and Tiny Bradshaw. But Nathan was successful in bringing careers to fruition as well as launching them. The names of two artists stand out: James Brown, whose remarkable story will be covered in the Soul section of this book, and Little Willie John, whose career and life ended abortively.

Known best for his 1956 disk of "Fever," a smash two years later for Peggy Lee, and his 1958 hit, "Talk to Me, Talk to Me," Willie John went to prison in May, 1966, for manslaughter. He was in the Washington State Penitentiary in Walla Walla— the knifing had occurred in Seattle—when he died of pneumonia in June, 1968. James Brown, Soul Brother No. 1 has recently cut a memorial album, *Thinking About Little Willie John and a Few Nice Things,* whose contents include some of the songs popularized by the unfortunate bluesman.

"Talk to Me, Talk to Me, Talk to Me," in Little Willie John's treatment, may be heard in the Columbia *Anthology of Rhythm and Blues,* Vol. 1. To those who have not heard or do not remember the record, listening will be a startling experience, for there can be no question that Willie John owes a debt to Sam Cooke's warm, throaty, pleading ballad style. In fact, the lick that made "You Send Me" can be heard on this disk almost as Cooke sings it on his hit record. Columbia has also released another valuable anthology, *18 King Size Rhythm and Blues Hits*. This collection of King best sellers provides an informative compendium of nonsense riffs used by vocal groups of the fifties as rhythmic devices: "ah-oom, ah-oom" in the Midnighters' record of "Work with Me, Annie," "bup-bup-bup-BUP, bup-bup-bup-BUP" on The Platters' disk of "Only You," and "doo-wah, doo-wah" on the Charms' "Hearts of Stone." But the *pièce de résistance* of the collection is Lonnie Johnson's version of "Tomorrow Night," a bravura performance (and a hit), considering that the pioneer New Orleans bluesman was past seventy when he cut the ballad.

Once when I was talking with Syd Nathan, who presided over the King dynasty until his death in 1967, he said in his wheezing, asthmatic style, "It's no trick to find good performers." And, looking at me through the extremely thick lenses that greatly enlarged his eyes, he added, "The trick, my boy, is to find good writers who can perform. It's material, great songs, that make the difference."

Nathan was not only a good judge of record talent but a gifted songwriter himself. This facet of his work was known only to insiders, since for business reasons he seldom used his own name. His preference in pseudonyms, and he used many, was for female names. "Lois Mann"—his wife's maiden name and his favorite nom de plume—appears on "Signed, Sealed and Delivered," a Cowboy Copas hit; "Annie Had a Baby," the Midnighters' hit; "Sittin' on It All the Time," a Wynonie Harris hit; and "I Quit My Pretty Mama," an Ivory Joe best seller.

Moon Mullican scored with "Cherokee Boogie," a song he wrote with an unidentified William Chief Redbird. On rare occasions, Nathan's own name appeared on songs, for example, "New Pretty Blonde (New Jole Blon)" and "I Can't Go On Without You," both recorded by Moon Mullican.

Nathan's appreciation of the writer's contribution to the music scene manifested itself at the outset of his recording activity. As his first A & R producer, he appointed a member of the Lucky Millinder band, but only after he had ascertained that Henry Glover could write and arrange.

131

A schooled musician who was only a few credits from a Wayne University M.A. in music, Glover played with several black dance bands during the forties, including Buddy Johnson, Willie Bryant, and Tiny Bradshaw. He was co-author of most of the early Bullmoose Jackson songs and has a score of hits to his credit. His best-known song is "I'll Drown in My Own Tears," recorded by a long list of artists headed by Ray Charles. His association with King, begun in 1946 and interrupted by a sojourn from 1956 to 1962 with Roulette Records, continues to the present time.

Regarding the current invasion of the C & W field by black artists like Charles Pride and Joe Tex, Glover recently observed, "It's hardly a new development. And it wasn't new even when Ray Charles took the country road in the early sixties. Maybe because at King we worked with white country artists as well as black R & B performers, we constantly crossed boundary lines. Syd Nathan had me record blues with C & W singers like Cowboy Copas and Moon Mullican. And I did country songs with Wynonie Harris. In fact, 'Mr. Blues,' as he was called, had one of his biggest sellers covering a Hank Penny song, 'Bloodshot Eyes.' That was in the early fifties. And Bullmoose Jackson had a big disk on a country song called 'Why Don't You Haul Off and Love Me,' cut originally by Wayne Raney. And what about Ivory Joe Hunter doing Jenny Lou Carson's 'Jealous Heart' in 1949?"

Shortly after Syd Nathan's death, King Records was bought by Starday Records on the West Coast, which sold it recently to a conglomerate, Lin Broadcasting.

10

EAST COAST
R & B RECORD
SCENE

No study of the R & B scene, or for that matter of the classic blues era, is meaningful without reference to the Mother Church of black entertainment, the Apollo Theatre on West 125th Street in Harlem. There's the Howard Theatre in Washington, D. C., the Royal in Baltimore, the Uptown in Philadelphia, the Regal in Chicago, the Paradise in Detroit, and there are other well-known theaters in the black ghettos of American cities. But what the Palace on Broadway was to vaudeville in its heyday, the Apollo has been and is today to popular black entertainment.

Built in the early 1910s at about the same time as the Lafayette Theatre at 2227 Seventh Avenue, the Apollo was originally known as Hurtig & Seamon's, a burlesque house. In the twenties, as Harlem began to develop a large concentration of Negro residents and as interest in the classic blues singers mounted, H & S began booking Negro acts and mixed revues. It was renamed the Apollo after it was taken over in 1934 by Frank Schiffman, who had been operating the Lafayette and had made it into the top showcase for Negro jazz bands.

To compete with the Harlem Opera House, east of the Apollo on 125th Street, Schiffman began featuring Negro stage shows and name bands like Fletcher Henderson, Chick Webb, and Duke Ellington. The Schiffman family still runs the Apollo.

But the Harlem Opera House is gone, and the Lafayette and the Lincoln, another Harlem theater on 135th Street once owned by Schiffman, have been converted into black churches.

Three things give the Apollo special significance. First, it has followed a consistent policy of presenting only Negro entertainers. When an integrated duo like Billy Vera and Judy Clay are booked, only Judy appears. Secondly, the relationship between the Negro community and the theater is not unlike membership in a church. This is *their* theater—it has never been touched during Harlem riots—and all black performers are expected to show that they belong by playing it, particularly after they have hit the big time and can make a lot more money at downtown (white) theaters. Some years ago when Eartha Kitt was hitting the headlines in a sensational revue, Frank Schiffman's son Bobby, who does the booking, invited her to play the Apollo.

"At first I was afraid," she told me. "I had visions of my own people driving me off the stage. . . . I'll never forget the reception I got show after show. The very fact that I was there told them more than almost anything I could say. But I did usually make a curtain speech in which I would say, 'I didn't know whether you would receive me as a friend or just shut me out (because of what you've been reading about me in your own papers). But now that I see your faces and hear your applause, I don't even have to ask whether I am welcome—although I greatly feared that I was not.' The applause after that was always ear-shattering and so heartwarming!"

Then, adverting to Harry Belafonte's marriage to a white woman after divorcing a Negress, she added, "It had to look as if he were deserting the Negro people. . . . A man like Harry should come to Harlem and play the Apollo. It won't mean anything to him financially and it can't advance his career. But it would mean something to his people. . . ."

The third point of significance about the Apollo is its weekly Amateur Night. Wednesday is still the night, and anyone can appear merely by registering on Monday. The audience is tough and discerning. When performers don't produce a satisfactory routine, a female impersonator firing blank cartridges drives them offstage—unless the old-fashioned, hooked shepherd's pole coming out of the wings can yank them off. However, a performer who wins first place three weeks in a row, based on audience applause, receives a week's booking at the Apollo with union scale pay.

A partial list of the singers who got started this way includes Ella Fitzgerald, Billy Eckstine, Sarah Vaughan, Billie Holiday, Leslie Uggams, The Drifters, and Joe Tex. And these are only the headliners who have made it big. In entertainment biz, Wednesday remains the night when managers, bookers, and record men trek uptown to the Apollo for a black talent hunt.

It should be no surprise that one of the earliest independent labels founded in the forties in New York called itself Apollo Records. Although the company started in a Harlem music shop in 1943, its three white owners had no connection with the theater. Apollo's first big seller was not by a vocalist but by jazz saxist Coleman Hawkins. "Rainbow Mist" was its title.

By the early fifties Apollo had the Larks, with best sellers in "Eyesight to the Blind" and "Little Side Car." Bird names were then in, and the black vocal groups of the day included the Orioles, Cardinals, Swallows, Crows, Falcons, Robins, and Ravens, to name a few. Apollo's most impressive group was the Five Royales, who managed four hits in one year, two of which, "Baby, Don't Do It" and "Help Me, Somebody," finished among 1953's top best sellers.

Formed at about the same time as Apollo, Deluxe Records of Linden, New Jersey, was a family affair (the Brauns) whose artist roster included the Four Blues, the Southern Jubilee Quartet, and saxist Benny Carter. In 1946, when its catalog had grown to over a hundred titles, the Billy Eckstine band recorded for it. By the early fifties, it was a hot R & B label with chart makers in Roy Brown, Annie Laurie, and the Charms, still remembered for their record of "Hearts of Stone." The year 1950 was a particularly good one for Brown, whose many best sellers included "Hard Luck Blues."

Of four other R & B companies that came into existence in the forties, Manor and National have been absorbed by other labels, while Jubilee and Savoy still flourish under their

135

founders. Manor, a Newark, New Jersey, company, uncovered a noteworthy ballad singer in Savannah Churchill, originally from New Orleans but a Brooklynite after the age of six.

A choir singer during her growing years, Savannah recorded with jazz saxist Benny Carter before she ventured alone on Manor. Two of her most moving performances are found in "I Want to Be Loved (But by Only You)" and "Time Out for Tears" ('48). Boasting a timbral quality like Sarah Vaughan's, she spiced her style with an inner gospel intensity and a feeling for improvisation, evidenced by her use of jazz sidemen like Don Byas on tenor and J. J. Johnson on trombone.

With Herb Abramson, later one of the founders of Atlantic Records, as its A & R chief, National Records developed a roster that included boogie-woogie pianist Pete Johnson, blues shouter Joe Turner, and trombonist Billy Eckstine as he embarked on his solo singing career after years as a bandsman. Two of Eckstine's National best sellers were "Prisoner of Love" and "You Call It Madness (But I Call It Love)," both revivals of ballads associated with Russ Columbo, who used the latter as his theme. Columbo, one of the big three baritones of the crooner era—Vallee, Crosby, and Columbo—accidentally shot himself to death at the peak of his career.

National's most important R & B group was the Ravens, the vocal quartet credited with starting the fad for bird-named black singing groups. More musical and more polished than the Charms or the Larks, they were closer to the pop slickness of the Ink Spots than the raucousness of R & B. Their hit disks included "Write Me A Letter," a moving Howard Biggs ballad, and "I Don't Have to Ride No More." But the record that established them was "Ol' Man River." Their 1947 revivalist version of the *Show Boat* perennial, with deep bass lead and rolling Mills Brothers rhythm, opens Atlantic's eight-volume *History of Rhythm and Blues*.

Other bird groups that accounted for two of the best-known disks of the era were the Penguins, who made a memorable recording of Jesse Belvin's teen-age ballad "Earth Angel," and the Crows, who established themselves with "Gee." Both came during the "Sh-Boom" year, the former on the Dootune

136

label and the latter on Rama 5, later part of the Roulette record wheel.

Another impressive "bird" group of the time was the Orioles, originally known as the Vibranaires but renamed after the Baltimore oriole by a Baltimore songwriter, Deborah Chessler. Trundling the group up to New York, the enterprising Miss Chessler interested ex-bandleader Jerry Blaine, who had just started a label called Natural, in recording them.

When her song "It's Too Soon to Know" was released, it appeared on Jubilee, a new and still flourishing label launched by Blaine. The song was also recorded by Dinah Washington on Mercury and made such a strong impression in 1948 that it was revived ten years later by Pat Boone. The Orioles continued cutting chart climbers into the middle fifties, racking up their biggest disk in "Crying in the Chapel," a 1953 weeper that was recorded pop by June Valli and C & W by Rex Allen.

The catalog of Savoy Records of Newark, New Jersey, is large, compounded of jazz, gospel, and R & B, and is possibly the longest lived of all the independents. During its entire history, it has been the brainchild of one man, Herman Lubinsky, who is still active and says he founded the label in 1939.

Naming a disk by Bonnie Davis, "Don't Stop Now," as his first release, he boasts that he has garnered twenty Gold Records, all on gospel, and has the only gospel disk that sold a million, #14076 by James Cleveland.

Except for the majors, only Beacon, Continental, Keynote, and Musicraft were in business when Lubinsky opened his doors, and none of these is still active or in the hands of the original founder. Entering the jazz field in 1942, Lubinsky built a substantial catalog of bop, including archive recordings by Charlie "Bird" Parker and trumpeter Fats Navarro. By the late forties Savoy was making waves in the R & B field.

Two instrumentalists and three vocalists epitomize Savoy's contribution to this segment of the record industry. In 1949 both Paul Williams and Cecil "Big Jay" McNeely had instrumental rockers, the latter scoring with a honking tenor sax disk, "Deacon's Hop," and the former coming up with what became an exuberant R & B dance—"The Hucklebuck." *Billboard* rated the Williams platter as the number-one best seller of the year.

In the vocal area, Varetta Dillard scored her first chart climber with "Easy, Easy Baby" in 1952 and maintained a best-selling streak through 1954 with "Mercy Mr. Percy" and "Johnny Has Gone."

At about the same time, the label began releasing tough, hard-driving disks by Nappy Brown, whose "Don't Be Angry" was covered by the Crewcuts (shortly after their success with "Sh-Boom") and "Piddily Patter Patter" was covered by Patti Page (after I purchased the publishing rights from Savoy for E. B. Marks Music). Brown himself covered a 1954–55 country hit popularized by Hank Snow, except that he sang "I Don't Hurt Anymore" as "It Don't Hurt Anymore."

Savoy's most valuable vocal asset was a trio without a group name—Johnny Otis, Little Esther, and Mel Walker. In 1950 the trio accomplished the rare achievement of finishing the year with three of the ten best-selling R & B disks, "Double Crossing Blues," "Cupid's Boogie," and "Mistrustin' Blues." After Little Esther embarked on a solo career, Mel Walker continued cutting records with the Johnny Otis orchestra while the latter recorded instrumentals like "Harlem Nocturne."

Little Esther, who is a cross between Dinah Washington and Kay Starr, accounted in 1962 for one of the great standards of R & B and C & W music with her recording of "Release Me" on the Lenox label. After a hiatus, she began cutting again for Atlantic as Esther Phillips, but was unable to capture strong audience response to three superb albums.

Johnny Otis, who wrote all of Little Esther's smashes on Savoy, has continued to make his mark as a songwriter. In 1956 he was co-writer of "Wallflower," also known as "Dance with Me, Henry." He was responsible for at least an early version of "Hound Dog." In 1957 a group called the Fiestas scored with his black ballad, "So Fine." One of his biggest songs is the rhythm ballad that introduced Gladys Knight and the Pips to the record scene—"Every Beat of My Heart."

Until he recently revealed that he was white, he was regarded as one of a small group of black writers with remarkably consistent records as hit producers, a group that included the late Jesse Belvin, Jessie Mae Robinson, Rudolph Toombs, Winfield Scott, Rose Marie McCoy, Charles Singleton, Lincoln Chase, and the late Chuck Willis.

The fifties saw the emergence of a new group of eastern R & B labels, as well as renewed activity by the majors, who were unwilling to make a substantial investment but were not content to leave the field to the independents.

Having revived Okeh, Columbia moved into the fifties with Big Maybelle, a shouter in the Ma Rainey tradition (later on Savoy), and with Chuck Willis, the inspired songwriter of Atlanta, Georgia. Willis apparently had no roots in the black church, and his first professional assignment was as vocalist with Red McAllister's band. The sensitive ears of a Columbia scout led to his making records for Okeh in 1953. "Don't Deceive Me (Please Don't Go)" was more revealing of his unusual talent as a songwriter than as a singer. He did not make an impression as a record artist until he recorded his adaption of Ma Rainey's "See See Rider" in 1957, shortly before his death.

But he had been in demand as a songwriter before that time. In fact, in 1954 Ruth Brown attracted so much attention with her version of his "Oh, What a Dream" that Patti Page rushed in to make a cover record. The following year, the Five Keys' disk of his "Close Your Eyes" led to a cover by Steve and Eydie, just as the Cardinals' waxing of "The Door Is Still Open" prompted a recording by Don Cornell.

By 1956 Chuck Willis had moved to Atlantic, where his recording of his song "It's Too Late" won him a BMI Award. It was the first year that ASCAP's main competitor made awards in the R & B field. In the year of his death, Willis came into his own as a vocalist with "What Am I Living For," a song he did not write and possibly his biggest disk, and "(I Don't Want to) Hang Up My Rock and Roll Shoes," a song of his authorship. His passing in 1958 was dramatically announced by Dick Clark on the "American Bandstand" show. As a fitting testimony to his recording achievements Atlantic recently released a memorial album *I Remember Chuck Willis*.

RCA Victor also got into the act in the fifties, launching its Groove subsidiary, which was regrettably underfinanced and underpromoted. It moved Presley's idol, Arthur Crudup, from Bluebird to the new label, whose most successful releases came from Mickey & Sylvia and Piano Red. Willie Perryman, as Piano Red was christened, gave a fine account of his range as a boogie-blues pianist in eight years of recording—sessions that were held mostly in Atlanta and New York, and occasionally in Nashville. The smiling exuberance of Mickey & Sylvia produced a chart maker in 1957 in "Love Is Strange." (After Presley broke big, he financed sessions by Crudup that were released on the Fire label. The sides included "Rock Me Mama," cut in the forties on Bluebird.

Among the indie labels that emerged in the fifties, two of the more successful were Herald and Rama/Gee. Faye Adams, the major discovery of the former, made number one in 1953 with "Shake a Hand, Baby" and scored another hit the following year with "Hurts Me to My Heart." The Rama/Gee label first appeared on R & B charts in 1954 with the well-named Crows and "Gee." But it made its most exciting bid with the Teen Agers, a group that placed six young songs on the charts in 1956, including the number-one smash (and hardly a teenage song) "Why Do Fools Fall in Love?"

The oldest members of the quintet were baritone Joe Negroni and tenor Herman Santiago, each sixteen. Tenor Jimmy Merchant and bass Sherman Garnes were only fifteen at the time. The youngest, thirteen, was Frankie Lymon, the lead singer and the amazing writer of the chugging, up-tempo ballad. Born in Harlem in 1942 and a star in 1956, Lymon was dead in 1968 at the tender age of twenty-six.

Before he was out of public school, he played the Brooklyn Paramount and the London Palladium. He appeared on the Ed Sullivan TV show, then known as "Toast of the Town." In a movie titled *Rock, Rock, Rock,* produced by disk jockey Alan Freed, nabob of rock 'n' roll, Frankie Lymon and the Teen

Agers sang "Baby, Baby" and "I'm Not a Juvenile Delinquent." But in June, 1966, Lymon was arrested for possession of narcotics. The following year he wrote a magazine article describing how he kicked the habit. When he was found dead in the Harlem apartment of a friend where he was staying while on leave from the Army, a hypodermic needle rested near his inert body.

The late fifties saw the rise in Philadelphia of Cameo/Parkway Records, whose "Silhouette" by the Rays and "Butterfly" by Charlie Gracie made R & B charts in 1957. The most productive period of the labels founded by songwriter Bernie Lowe came in the early sixties, when Bobby Rydell, a teen-age superstar, made them hot. As a result, sales power was developed by the Dovells, the Orlons ("Wah-Watusi"), Dee Dee Sharp ("Gravy for My Mashed Potatoes"), and the Tymes ("So Much in Love"). But the real powerhouse artist was the former chicken plucker who devised his name out of admiration for Fats (Chubby) Domino (Checker) and whose record career virtually rose and set with the twist. The year 1969 found Chubby Checker attempting a comeback after a hasty retirement four years previously.

Another New York newcomer of the fifties was the Scepter label, formed in 1958. At first it released through Decca. In 1960, however, after the Shirelles had garnered a Gold Record on "Dedicated to the One I Love," Florence Greenberg, who founded the label and produced the group, ventured into full-scale production and promotion. The first release after Scepter became an independent was the Shirelles' "Tonight's the Night." It also earned a Gold Record.

It was a time of tough-sounding, sex-oriented girls' groups, black, white, and third world—the Ronettes with "Be My Baby" on Philles, the Crystals with "Da Doo Ron Ron," also on Phil Spector's Philles label, and the Shangri-Las with "Leader of the Pack" on Red Bird. (The last mentioned provoked a takeoff called "Leader of the Laundromat" by the Detergents.)

As the screechy Shirelles became the hottest girl quartet of the day, with hits like "Mama Said," "Baby, It's You," and "Foolish Little Girl," Scepter started a subsidiary label—Wand —and signed Chuck Jackson and the Isley Brothers. In 1962 the former hit with "Any Day Now" and "I Keep Forgettin'," while the brothers recorded their historic version of "Twist and Shout," one of the early Beatle best sellers.

In 1963 Scepter launched Dionne Warwick with "Don't Make Me Over," the first in a long list of hits that made her and songwriters Bacharach and David key figures of the rock revolution. That year Scepter issued the infectious "Louis Louie" by the Kingsmen, a record that was a long-lived turntable hit—extensive radio play but limited sales—and was covered subsequently by Paul Revere and the Raiders.

From "Twist and Shout" to "It's Your Thing" and "I Turned You On" in 1969, the Isley Brothers endured a seven-year dry spell. Not that they were inactive or unrepresented on wax. Three albums of their recordings appeared during this interval, one on United Artists in 1964 *(Twisting and Shouting)* and two on Tamla, a Motown subsidiary *(This Old Heart* in 1966 and *Soul on the Rocks* in 1968). But all of them lacked the magic and unaccountable ingredient that spells the difference between "dog" and "hit."

"It's Your Thing," their first hit in years—and really an overnight smash—was written, produced, and performed by the brothers—Kelly, Ronnie, and Rudolph. Once they had been four, but Vernon was killed in a car crash. There are two other Isley brothers, however, in the band with whom the three record; Ernest Isley arranges and plays many instruments while Marvin Isley plays bass.

"When we started singing," Kelly Isley has said, "we sang gospel. It never got recorded. But when we did start to record as R & B artists, the feeling of gospel music was still there. Even today, after all that time, the feeling is still with us. We couldn't get rid of it if we tried." He adds, "Our faith in God strengthened us to accomplish what we have, especially when our brother Vernon was killed."

Concerning their new venture—the brothers run T-Neck

Records, on which both their new hits were released—Kelly has this to say: "Until we owned our own record company, we had to stay in the particular bag that was selling at the time. Now we can do whatever we want, be it gospel, country-and-western, or rock. . . . It even gets to the kind of lyrics you write. If one thing is a hit and you're not in control, you wind up writing the same thing over again. We're writing what's happening now. We want people to catch what is going on."

11

THE FOREMOST
RHYTHM-
AND-BLUESMEN

Out of the din and drive of honking tenors, rousing boogie rhythms, roaring electric guitars, and raucous bomp-bomp vocal groups, four uniquely expressive rhythm-and-bluesmen emerged. B. B. King eventually became the most influential. Chuck Berry was easily the most commercial—a songwriter who perceptively sounded the themes of the first rock 'n' roll generation. Little Richard burst on the scene as the first of the frenzied singers, foreshadowing the rise of Soul.

Muddy Waters, earliest of the delta bluesmen to add big-city drive and electricity to country blues, walked out of the cold winds of the lakeshore city of Chicago into the storefront office of Aristocrat Records late in 1946. Working with Sunnyland Slim at the piano and Big Crawford on bass, he cut "Gypsy Woman" and "Little Anna Mae." Then early in 1948, with just Crawford on bass, he recorded "I Can't Be Satisfied (Looking for My Baby)" and "I Feel Like Going Home." His succeeding disk contained no hint of burgeoning happiness. "Train Fare Home" was backed with "Sittin' Here and Drinkin'." And Muddy was a country bluesman for whom the texture of his experiences, small and large, became the fabric of his song.

Years later, Muddy told Pete Welding, "Leonard Chess had a lady for a partner in Aristocrat. Chess didn't like my style of singing; he wondered who was going to buy that. The lady said, 'You'd be surprised.' Finally, though, he let me make a record. . . . Everybody's records came out before mine. Andrew Tibbs had two records out before me. . . . But when they released mine and it hit the ceiling, then Chess began to come close to me. . . .

"After the record hit ('I Can't Be Satisfied,' that is), I was building the group with Little Walter Jacobs (harmonica), Baby Face Leroy Foster (drums), Jimmy Rogers (guitar), and myself. Chess wouldn't upset things; he wouldn't mess with the harp or extra guitar. He wanted to keep the combination that had made the hit record—just Big Crawford's bass and my guitar."

And that's the way Muddy Waters made "Walkin' Blues" and "Rollin' Stone," the latter the side whose title became the name of one of the big British rock groups, and of a highly successful underground San Francisco periodical.

Waters had actually made his first recordings six years before he wandered into the Aristocrat office. Born McKinley Morganfield in 1915, he came from Rolling Fork, Mississippi, where his childhood nickname was Muddy Waters and where he early picked up the harp. He learned the guitar from a cotton-patch friend. However, as he recently told Don DeMicheal, "One night we went to one of these Saturday night fish fries and Son House was there playing. I was using the bottleneck because most of the delta people used this bottleneck-style thing. When I heard Son House I should have broken my bottleneck because this other cat hadn't learned me nothin'. Son House played this place for about four weeks. I was there every night closer to him than I am to your microphone. You couldn't get me out of that corner, listening to him, what he's doing." Muddy was then younger than Paul Butterfield was when, at eighteen, he sat in with him at a South Side Chicago club.

He was twenty-six when folklorists Alan Lomax and John Work found him in a cotton field on Howard Stovall's plantation and cut "Country Blues" and "I Be's Troubled" for the Library of Congress. These sides are available on Testament, as are the sides that Muddy cut in July and August of 1942 at Stovall's with the Son Simms Four. (Lomax and Work had actually come to Mississippi looking for Robert Johnson, who was dead.) Though not all of these early Waters sides are brooding blues, Pete Welding aptly characterizes them as "shot through with all the agonized tension, bitterness, stark power and raw passion of life lived at the brink of despair."

More than five years passed before Muddy cut a new batch of sides. By then he was settled in Chicago, where he first worked in a paper mill and later drove a truck. Titled "Jitterbug Blues," "Buryin' Ground Blues," and "Hard Day Blues," these 1947 records remain unissued by Columbia.

In this period Muddy worked with a trio of musicians who called themselves the Headcutters. With harpist Little Walter and guitarist Jimmy Rogers, he wandered around Chicago's ghetto at night, searching for spots where music was being played. "We called ourselves the Headcutters," he explains, " 'cause we'd go in and if we got a chance we were gonna burn 'em. . . . I'm not like that no more."

After he began playing regularly at Smitty's Corner (at Thirty-fifth and Indiana) and other bars, Waters's bandstand was always accessible to other musicians. That's how Chuck Berry got his start.

In 1950, after the Aristocrat label had been superseded by Chess, Muddy was able to record with harmonica giant Little Walter. Two years later, he completed his first sides with Otis Spann, the gifted blues pianist who was his half brother. Finally, in 1953, the Muddy Waters blues band was on wax: Little Walter (or Walter Horton) on harp, Spann on piano, Jimmy Rogers on second guitar, Elgar Edmonds on drums, and Big Crawford on bass. Two of their earliest sides which merit attention were "Mad Love (I Just Want You to Love Me)" and the exciting "I'm Your Hoochie Coochie Man."

By then it was clear that the Mississippi bottleneck style of Robert Johnson and Son House, on which Waters had been nurtured in his cotton-picking years, had undergone important modifications. Johnson's "Walkin' Blues," cut in San Antonio in 1936, is country blues. Waters's "Walkin' Blues," cut in

Son House

DON HUNSTEIN—COLUMBIA RECORDS

DON HUNSTEIN—COLUMBIA RECORDS

(Top) Marion Williams
(Bottom) Willie Mae Thornton

(Top) King Curtis
(Bottom) Sam & Dave

Bobby Bland   Wilson Pickett

Diana Ross and The Supremes

(Top) Martha Reeves and the Vandellas
(Bottom) Aretha Franklin

James Brown

(Top) Bo Diddley
(Bottom) Clara Ward

Muddy Waters

(Top) Chuck Berry
(Bottom) Fats Domino

Nina Simone

Stevie Wonder　　　　Otis Redding

Booker T. and the M.G.'s
with Carla Thomas and Steve Cropper

Ray Charles   Howlin' Wolf

Don Covay

B. B. King

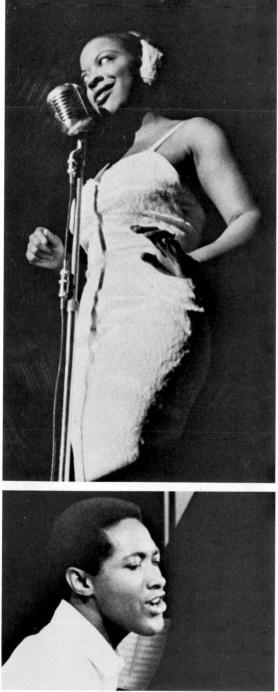

(Top) LaVern Baker
(Bottom) Sam Cooke

(Top) Little Richard
(Bottom) Brook Benton

(Top) Junior Wells

(Bottom) Marion Williams and Alex Bradford provide the gospel note in the musical history of early America *They Call it Folk Music*

(Top) The Coasters
(Bottom) The Drifters

Harry Belafonte and Miriam Makeba

Chicago in 1950, is rhythm-and-blues. To some extent, the difference between the two musical forms can be found in the varying efforts produced by acoustic and electric guitar, and between simple guitar accompaniment and driving combo accompaniment. It is also a manifestation of the disparity in tempo and tension between life in rural Mississippi and racist Chicago of the postwar years.

The moans, drones, and slides of delta styling acquire a new urgency against the roar of electrical amplification, and Waters's majestic voice responds with razor-edged power to the challenges of the instrument and the times. These are inner musical responses, not verbal notations. Like Robert Johnson, his sex-driven predecessor, Waters was a "hoochie-coochie" man whose songs were largely concerned with girls. He was always telling them, as he boasted on two of his hottest sides, "I'm Ready" and "Got My Mojo Working."

It is interesting to note that the sales of Muddy's disks do not really give a clue to his role in popularizing modern Chicago blues and influencing British rockers. For example, in 1951, while his "Long Distance Call" and "Louisiana Blues" made the Top Ten of R & B, another Chess artist, Jackie Brenston, had a number-one seller in "Rocket 88." The following year, when Waters again made the Top Ten with "She Moves Me," Willie Mabon reached number-one with "I Don't Know" while Little Walter, whose harp enhanced the Waters ensemble blues style, garnered two number-one disks in "Sad Hours" and "Juke."

Currently, Waters is enjoying a revival that has not only sent a new generation of record buyers—white as well as black—into stores but has opened the doors of clubs and concert halls previously closed to him. In an effort to capitalize on this burgeoning popularity, Chess recently brought Muddy back into a studio and recorded him with a late-sixties "electronic" blues band, replete with high-decibel amplification, feedback techniques, and machine-gun drumming. *Electric Mud,* as the album is engagingly called, is hardly representative of the style that made him a pivotal pioneer of R & B. For this, listeners must turn to old LPs like *The Best of Muddy Waters* and *Real Folk Blues*. Chess has also released two new albums in which four of its star rhythm-and-bluesmen—Muddy, Howlin' Wolf, Bo Diddley, and Little Walter—all do their thing together once again.

One has the feeling in listening to these records that either the material is unsatisfactory, the styles are dated, or (as seems most likely) their expressiveness is out of context. After all, the four men came out of the world of the forties and fifties, a wholly different universe of musical discourse.

Regarding his current popularity, Muddy told an American college audience, "I had to go to England to get here." This is a thought echoed by Bo Diddley, who recently remarked, "We all owe a debt to the Beatles. They started playing R & B with C & W rhythms and changes. It had to come from over there first for American kids to listen."

If the new recordings have not fulfilled the promise of excitement, a recent appearance of Muddy Waters in Chicago did.

It reminded one of Muddy's impact at Newport in 1960, an event happily enshrined in a Chess album. At the time of the Chicago concert, Muddy spent three nights recording a new LP with two white Chicago disciples—Paul Butterfield and Mike Bloomfield—each of whom has had or still has his own blue-eyed blues band. If the three succeed in capturing something of what they delivered at the Auditorium Theatre on April 24, 1969, *Fathers and Sons,* as it is titled, will be an album to remember.

Of the big record makers in the Chess-Checker-Cadet-Argo ménage, none was more successful as a songwriter and hit-maker than the young, wavy-haired man who wandered into their storefront office with a country-sounding song he called "Ida Red." Charles Edward Berry, better known as Chuck Berry, came from St. Louis, Missouri, where he was born in October, 1926, and where the influences were more pop and urban than those that formed Muddy Waters.

In fact, he recently told a college audience at Berkeley that his influences in guitar playing were Charlie Christian, guitarist for Benny Goodman, T-Bone Walker, and Carl Hoagan. "Much of my material begins with Carl Hoagan's familiar riff, like 'ba-doo-doo dah/ba-doo-doo dah'. . . . Jazz musicians? Well, would you call Les Paul a jazz musician. His 'How High the Moon' is just beautiful. . . ." As for singers, "One of my favorite singers—or rather I should say two—are Nat and Frank, in that respect, because I am moody and Nat sang moody music. . . ."

Although he displayed an interest in music in high school and at Poro College, mastering guitar, sax, and piano, Berry was headed for a career as a cosmetician when he spent a weekend in Chicago. Here, in a South Side club, he heard and was invited on the bandstand by Muddy Waters, who suggested that he go to see the Chess brothers.

Leonard Chess recalls that first meeting as follows: "Berry came in with a wire recorder and he played us this country music takeoff called 'Ida Red.' It had been turned down by Capitol and Mercury. We didn't like it as C & W, so we recut it in our little studio behind the office with two sidemen."

Acquiring a thumping afterbeat, "Ida Red" came out as the up-tempo R & B "Maybellene." The choice of the title, it is reported, had nothing to do with Berry's abortive career as a cosmetician. At the time, he had just finished cosmetology and was in practice six months when "Maybellene" broke.

"I didn't quit the cosmetic bit," he recalls, "until I got a contract for four hundred dollars. It pleased me and I sold my booth, and went on into music." "Maybellene" went on to become that rarity in music business—a *Billboard* Triple Crown: number one on the R & B chart, C & W, and Pop.

By 1956, the year in which he first did his famous duck waddle, Berry was in great demand for public appearances. Headlining Allen Freed's Easter show at the Brooklyn Paramount Theatre, he encountered a problem with clothes. "You could wear yellow suits, pink trousers, blue shoes—everybody was a plainclothesman," he says with a twinkle, "and I had to outfit the trio I brought from St. Louis. I always remember the suits cost me twenty-two dollars apiece. We had to buy shoes and everything. When we got to New York, the suits

—they were rayon—but looked like seersucker by the time we got there. We had one suit apiece. We didn't know we were supposed to change. So I actually did that duck walk to hide the wrinkles. I got an ovation, so I figured I pleased the audience, so I did it again and again."

After "Maybellene," a long succession of hits followed. They were songs that Berry wrote and recorded and that may be heard in the double album *Chuck Berry's Golden Decade*. A glance at the titles indicates a remarkably consistent record of best sellers from 1955 on. Many reached the top best-selling slot, and understandably so, considering the empathy he displayed with record-buying teen-agers in songs like "School Days," "Johnny B. Goode," "Almost Grown," "Sweet Little Sixteen," and "Rock and Roll Music." Berry could also write haunting blues ballads like "Wee Wee Hours."

His most original gift, however, was his wit, a quality in which he anticipated the Beatles, who revived "Rock and Roll Music" and his wittiest song, "Roll Over Beethoven." Humor and satire were rare in early rock 'n' roll but not in Chuck Berry, whose fund of good humor was so great that, like Terry Southern and the atom bomb, he could make discrimination sound idiotic instead of vicious.

Despite rocking backgrounds, Berry's vocal style is not black R & B but white rock 'n' roll. It is not merely that his diction has a pop clarity but that his delivery lacks black intensity. Berry's performance is a triumph of songwriting and showmanship over vocal style—and let's not minimize the effect of the combos that supplied the simple, visceral, hard-to-resist dance backgrounds.

It comes as no surprise, therefore, that the white, simplistic Beach Boys adapted the melody of Berry's "Sweet Sixteen" for one of their early hits, "Surfin' USA." The surfing sound was, after all, a white type of rock 'n' roll, and to the Bleach Boys, as they were sometimes derisively called, and to their followers, Berry's rock was more tractable than Muddy Waters's or Howlin' Wolf's.

That Berry's style also embodied elements of C & W is suggested by the recent success of country star Buck Owens in making a top best seller of "Johnny B. Goode." None of this is intended to minimize Berry's formidable contribution to the current rock scene. But it is noteworthy, and socially significant, that his impact and influence stem from his being a whiter shade of rhythm-and-blues—which, in a sense, is the essence of early rock 'n' roll.

In the true tradition of the blues, Berry talks with a down-to-earth candor—the present generation would use the phrase "no shit"—about his art and himself. "Would you have written those songs even if they hadn't paid you any money?" a Berkeley student asked him. He bluntly replied, "No, I wouldn't have had the time. The commercial value in songs is a great instigator."

Another student asked, "Do you think that music moves the country or does the country move the music?" He responded, "The dollar dictates what music is written. . . . Everybody knows about charts, at least the producers know about charts, and they wish for these things to be recorded in order that they can get sales, and everybody jumps on the bandwagon to record such. For instance, when the first psychedelic music came out, there were big sales on a couple of numbers. First thing you know, we had psychedelic music."

Still another student asked about his relationship with recording company executives and the effect the companies had on the artistic freedom of musicians. "Leonard Chess owns Chess Records," he replied. "He started out some years before I entered with the company. We have a *thing* together. We have had a thing together since the first time I walked into the studio. He said he saw beauty in my entrance. When I left to go to Mercury for—I might as well mention the amount because it's spent now—for one hundred and fifty thousand dollars, he said, 'Go, and I'll see you in three years,' which was my term at Mercury. Since I have been with Mercury things haven't been going too well. . . . I like little companies because there's a warmer relationship between the artist and the executive. I shall be going back soon to Chess Records. As of now, I'm on Mercury."

That was in May, 1969. By July, Mercury had a new

Chuck Berry album on the market. *Concerto in B Goode* was its title, inspired doubtless by Buck Owens's success with the song of the related title. The general consensus is that the old master has not lost his spark. The comic sensibility is there, the feeling for blues balladry remains, and the "Concerto," monopolizing one complete side of the LP, emphasizes that Chuck Berry has not lost his good-natured, bright-eyed zest for living. He is still master of the unpretentious, hard-driving type of body music that inflamed a generation tired of cliché thirty-two-bar ballads (so-called good music) and uninterested in cerebral jazz (bop and progressive jazz).

Out of Macon, Georgia, via Houston, Texas, onto the Specialty label of Los Angeles came Richard Penniman, projecting a still visible image of a performer drenched in hair-curling sweat. The shouter who became known as Little Richard popularized a new element in R & B—gospel frenzy —that has become the earmark of black music in the Soul era.

Penniman was under contract to the Peacock label in Houston when he sent Art Rupe, the owner of Specialty, a home-recorded tape.

"I could detect one little thing that sounded churchy," Rupe recalls, "very fervent, with that ow-ow that became his trademark."

Despite the amateur quality of the tape, Rupe and Bumps Blackwell, now Little Richard's manager and then Rupe's assistant, were so impressed that Specialty lent Penniman six hundred dollars to buy out his Peacock contract.

When Little Richard indicated a preference for Fats Domino's sound, Rupe decided to record him in New Orleans, where he had struck pay dirt with Lloyd Price and "Lawdy Miss Clawdy." Bumps Blackwell made the trip, returning with nine tracks instead of the planned eight. The ninth had started as an audition demo, consisting as it did of an inchoate story, some sexy references, and much explosive scatting: "Wop/bop-a-lou/bop-a-lop/bam-boom." But it became the sensational hit "Tutti Frutti," forerunner of a memorable list of up-tempo shuffle tunes.

152

Rupe explains, "Blackwell hadn't intended this song as a release because it had a lot of risqué, off-color words for those days and Bumps knew it wouldn't get played on the radio. A girl named Dorothy LaBostrie kept hanging around the studio to sell songs, and she revised the words, so we gave her a share of the credit."

Nineteen fifty-five was the "Tutti Frutti" year, presaging the appearance of Elvis Presley, who soon recorded many of Little Richard's hits. In 1956, when Elvis scored with "Heartbreak Hotel" and "Hound Dog," Richard had no fewer than four agitated rockers that climbed to number one on R & B charts: "Ready Teddy," "Rip It Up," "Slippin' and Slidin'," and "Long Tall Sally."

In a backward glance, it seems clear that boogie piano, exuberantly played by Little Richard, was the source of his music as gospel-shouting was the source of his style. The structure of his songs was based not on the blues—which relies on a steady, unchanging meter and a slower, reflective tempo—but on gospel singing, which does involve changing meters and driving rhythms. The songs mentioned begin with a freestyle, unaccompanied verse that builds up tension until Little Richard bursts forth in his howling, charging, shuffle-powered delivery.

"Long Tall Sally," originally known as "The Thing," was the biggest seller in Specialty's history. Recorded in New Orleans, it was rerecorded in Los Angeles, with Lee Allen playing a hot sax solo as he had done on the hit disk of "Tutti Frutti."

In 1957 Little Richard continued his amazing streak of best-selling songs and disks. The year's Top Ten R & B screamers included "Keep A-Knockin'," "Send Me Some Lovin'," and a brace of songs about "Jenny," "Miss Ann," and the luscious "Lucille." The fourth year of Little Richard's dynamic rise, 1958, was a strange one. He had a winner in "Good Golly, Miss Molly," then stopped recording.

Rupe explains the curious development as follows: "He began to get interested in the Seventh-Day Adventists. Joe Lutcher, one of our early Specialty artists, became a minister.

He felt his mission was to convert pop singers to the church, with this old superstition that it's evil to sing pop. He got to Little Richard. It was when the Sputnik went up in 1957 that Richard really decided to give up touring as well as recording. That's when he threw his jewelry off the boat in Australia. He thought that Sputnik was a sign from heaven, that this was it. He went and enrolled in a college in Alabama and started studying for the ministry."

But long before the present renascence of R & B, Little Richard returned to the music scene. At first, he would perform only outside the United States. When he began recording again, he insisted on cutting only gospel material. From Gone Records in New York, he went to Mercury, then to Atlantic, and back to Specialty when Rupe paid Atlantic a thousand dollars for his contract. The last disk released by Specialty before the company became inactive in 1963 was Little Richard's "Bama Lama Bama Loo," a record that was less than earthshaking. Typical of earlier Penniman hits, it indicated that the rock scene had developed beyond a point where it would accept Little Richard's crude combination of scat sounds and suggestive words.

Now that rock has passed out of its artsy, folksy, long-form, and poetry-deep stage, and there is a demand for the simple, exuberant body music of early rock 'n' roll, Little Richard is once again in great demand. At the same time as Specialty he reissued *Little Richard's Grooviest 17 Original Hits*, re-processed electronically for stereo, Okeh has cut a new album of the corybantic howler doing the same songs: *Little Richard's Greatest Hits*.

A comparison of the two suggests that the background accompaniment has changed more than Little Richard, whose voice has lost none of its tremendous vigor while his style retains a compulsive, high-voltage excitement.

In personal appearances, Little Richard's routine still includes frequent references to his beauty—"Put the sexy lights on me so they can see how pretty I am"—the use of "shut up" as punctuation, and repeated asides of "I'd rather do it myself." By comparison with most Motown artists, such as Ray Charles and Ike & Tina Turner, the shows of the King of Rock and Soul, as Penniman now bills himself, lack polish and style. He surpasses the others only in the elegance of his clothes—he apparently has an unlimited number of extremely expensive and exotic outfits—and in the sheer expenditure of energy, which drenches his massive mop of black hair and leaves his face looking as if it had been doused with oil.

In his personals, however, he displays a side of his vocal personality seldom heard on wax. Most of his records are up-tempo shouts, cut with a racing boogie shuffle. On stage he does a slow, intense version of Ray Charles's hit "I Can't Stop Loving You" that reveals him as one of the top soulful balladeers of today.

Bumps Blackwell, his manager, is not pleased with Little Richard's reception in the present R & B revival. While the Macon screamer played a six-week engagement at Las Vegas' Aladdin Hotel, the International—which opened with Barbara Streisand in the main room and Peggy Lee in its lounge—brought in Elvis Presley but was uninterested in Little Richard. "Take away the songs that Presley took from Richard," Blackwell argues, "and what's left?" There is the influence, of course, of Arthur "Big Boy" Crudup and there are the hit songs of Lieber and Stoller. But is is no secret that Penniman's hits and his style played an important role in shaping the career of Colonel Parker's charge. "Rip It Up," "Long Tall Sally," "Ready Teddy," and "Tutti Frutti" are among the Little Richard standards recorded by Elvis. Furthermore, Penniman's frenzied hoarseness is audible in the hipswiveler's early disks, as in those also of Jerry Lee Lewis.

In the period when Penniman had returned to the music scene but would perform only outside the United States, he once called Art Rupe from Hamburg, Germany. The head of Specialty became quite excited, thinking that Little Richard wanted to return to resume his recording career. "But he wanted to tell me about a group that was on the same bill with him," Rupe recalls. "Four guys who were singing and could imitate anybody. That was the Beatles and he wanted to know if I would be interested."

To this day, Paul McCartney does a remarkable imitation of Richard's hoarse howling. As a group, the Beatles reveal Richard's influence in their version of "Long Tall Sally," in their handling of "I'm Down," whose similarity to "Sally" is inescapable, and in their presentation of American rock 'n' roll songs like "Kansas City."

Perhaps the artist whom Little Richard most influenced was a Macon neighbor, the late Otis Redding, who grew up listening to him on his radio and idolizing him. In his first album, *Pain In My Heart*, Redding recorded Richard's "Lucille." On stage, Redding projected with the same power-house expenditure of energy. If Little Richard was not as sensual a singer as Redding, he was the pivotal figure in developing a phase of Soul that found rich expression in James Brown and Aretha Franklin.

The rhythm-and-bluesman whose reputation has escalated most in the current revival, and who is today regarded as the major master of modern blues, is Riley B. King. A man who began paying his dues when he was just a lad of nine, B. B. King, as he is better known, has independence of mind, great humility, and the remarkable facility, as a human being and a musician, to transform potentially destructive vicissitudes into victories.

Born on a delta plantation near Indianola, Mississippi, in 1925, he was living with his mother, who was separated from his father, when she died. He was just nine at the time. Instead of returning to his father, he went on living by himself and performed farm chores for the people who had employed his mother.

He received fifteen dollars a month and attended a one-room schoolhouse that was a five-mile hike from the farm. By the time he was twelve, he owned a mule and plough, and his education was limited to the months of cold and rain when the cotton crop did not require human ministration. "It was one of the happiest parts of my life," he told Stanley Dance of *Jazz* magazine. It was happy because he was accepted, not tolerated, cozened, or criticized but *accepted for what he was,* a circumstance that has concerned him all his life.

When he was fourteen his father found him and insisted on taking him back to the bosom of the family. Among his distant relatives was a sanctified preacher who used a guitar in his services. Visits of the preacher to his sister, B. B.'s aunt, led to an awakening of his interest in the instrument and to his purchase of his first guitar. "I never forget that red guitar with a round hole in it," he says. "It cost eight dollars."

At the outbreak of World War II, he took his basic training at Camp Shelby, was stationed briefly at Fort Benning in Georgia, and then was sent back to the cotton fields. As he explains it, plantation owners controlled the draft boards and managed to retain the services of their best workers, despite the war. He was a good tractor driver. The contribution of his army stint to his career: he started singing the blues.

On his return to plantation life, he faced a dilemma. He knew that there were fellows who made a living as blues singers. "But my people were very religious," he explains, "and I was afraid to sing the blues around the house. My aunt —I did a spiritual album for her a few years later— would get angry at anyone singing the blues."

B. B. was resourceful. On Saturday night, he would travel to a nearby town, park himself on a street corner, and sing for handouts. Sometimes he made three or four towns in a weekend and garnered twenty-five to thirty dollars in tips. It was more than he made in a week of cotton planting.

By the end of the war he was straining to make music his work. He had heard of W. C. Handy, Beale Street, and a cousin, Bukka White, who had settled in Memphis. He made the 130-mile trek northward and went to see Sonny Boy Williamson, whom he had met at plantation hall gambling-dances in Indianola. This was not the Sonny Boy Williamson who recorded for Bluebird, but the gifted harpist associated with "Eyesight to the Blind" and star from the late thirties of "King Biscuit Time," a daily radio show emanating from KFFA in Helena, Arkansas, and WROX in Clarksdale,

Mississippi. (Willie Rice Miller of Glendora, Mississippi, became known as Sonny Boy Williamson because one of the products advertised on "King Biscuit Time" was Sonny Boy White Corn Meal.)

Riley B. King also underwent a name change as a result of his radio work, though it was not as drastic as Rice Miller's. The radio association came indirectly as a result of the latter's presentation of King on his show and his generosity in recommending King for a job he could not take. The lady owner of the 16th Street Grille, a combination dance and gambling hall, was ready to hire B. B. King, but only with the proviso that he have a daily radio show on which he could advertise his appearances at the grill.

Approaching WDIA, since he could not appear on the same station as Sonny Boy, B. B. landed a ten-minute spot (without remuneration) on which he became known as the Pepticon Boy. (Pepticon was a new tonic seeking to compete with Hadacol.) Though owned by white southerners, WDIA was then the first, and possibly the only, radio station with Negro personnel. When one of the station's disk jockeys left, King became the replacement.

At the station's suggestion, he adopted the title of the Boy from Beale Street, which later became the Beale Street Blues Boy and led eventually to his being known as B. B. King. By the time he departed radio work, after three-and-a-half years, King was on the air every day for two hours and fifteen minutes. He still talks of WDIA, a 50,000-watter, as the Mother Station of the Negroes.

His affluence in this period came also from personal appearances and record sessions. The weekly stipend paid by the grill—sixty dollars plus room and board for five nights—was early supplemented by even more remunerative weekend dates. As his exposure and popularity on radio blossomed, the demand for personal appearances grew. Still in his early twenties, he had the most popular band in Memphis, a circumstance that brought the top musicians into his fold. He confesses that, while they liked the pay, they did not always enjoy working with him "because my timing was so bad. My beat was all right—I'd keep that—but I might play thirteen or fourteen bars on a twelve-bar blues! Counting the bars—that was out!"

This limitation was perhaps related to another that King turned to his advantage. "My coordination wasn't very good," he admits, "so trying to sing and play at the same time didn't get to me. . . . While I'm entertaining, while I'm trying to get my breath, or think of a new line to tell you, then the guitar takes over." In short, King found it necessary to depart from a style that had characterized delta blues for decades, a style in which the guitar served mainly as accompaniment and only occasionally as a responsive voice. Unable to sing and play at the same time, King developed a style that became the earmark of the new, urban blues. It was the single-note electric guitar style of Charlie Christian in jazz and of T-Bone Walker in the blues.

King early gave evidence of having big ears. As he grew up, he heard sounds he loved in Blind Lemon Jefferson and Samuel H. McQuery of the Fairfield Four, Big Maceo and Tampa Red. He liked country singers like Jimmie Rodgers and Gene Autry, and for a time idolized the Golden Gate Quartet. He admired jazz performers like Django Reinhardt and Phineas Newborn, who played piano on his first solo record dates in 1949, 1950, and 1951. Adopting the single-note style, he introduced into the blues some of the harmonic and rhythmic complexities of modern jazz.

Another limitation that B. B. transformed into an innovation was his inability to master bottleneck style. King loved the bright, vibratory, sustained sound that Bukka White and other delta guitarists were able to produce with metal bars, rings, tubes, or bottlenecks. "I could never use these," he acknowledges, "so I learned to trill my hands to sound somewhat like that. All this seemed to fit in with the soulful vibrato that Django Reinhardt had. Same with Elmore James; he used one of those things, you know. This sound always intrigued me." And B. B. adds, "Sounds are more important to me than trying to play a lot of notes."

Turning over his band to pianist Johnny Ace, King began his recording career with four sides for Bullet in 1949. The following year he switched to RPM, an association that lasted for twelve years. Despite the catholicity of his taste, his interest in innovation, and the diverse influences to which he reacted, he was first and foremost a blues singer and refused to switch despite the markets that remained closed to him until the middle sixties.

"One thing I always liked about you and Dinah Washington," he recently said to Jimmy Rushing. "You could leave the blues and switch over to ballads and standards, and sing them just as well. If I tried to sing a ballad, I'd be lost. So that's why I stay with the good old blues."

He confesses that as rock 'n' roll moved in he was subjected to pressure, some by whites, but mostly by Negroes. The latter wanted to know why he insisted on staying with something that was "still back *there*," in the days of Negro servitude. But to B. B., he was not singing of the past, unless it was his own.

"I remembered my childhood," he has said, "how things were with us then, the race problems and how bad it was in the thirties. . . . After that there was my life with modern people, and then there was the tragedies I experienced I could never talk to anybody about it, so it all just stayed with me. . . . And so the blues became a part of me right on from Blind Lemon Jefferson and Leroy Carr. . . . I heard Lonnie Johnson and I idolized him. . . ."

By 1952 the ears of bluesmen were standing up. "Three O'Clock Blues" and "You Know I Love You" demonstrated that B. B. could make records with popular appeal as well as power on R & B charts. A conga drum added a touch of Latin to "Please Love Me," Top Ten in 1953. In 1955 he cut "Everyday I Have the Blues" with a small combo and made the charts; but he cut it again in 1959, this time with a Kansas City-type big band, including seven brass and five reeds. By then he had begun using a streamlined electric bass instead of the bulbous string bass. Still adventuring musically, he cut an album of gospel songs in 1959, backed by a typical church rhythm section—organ, piano, drums, and tambourine—also the Charioteers vocal group.

As a singer, B. B.'s most expressive feature is his face. He moves little and uses few gestures, except occasionally a balled fist or a supplicating hand. But in emotional passages, when the lines are stretched by melisma, his brow is deeply furrowed, his cheekbones are puffed, and his closed eyes tense with pain.

B. B. calls his guitar Lucille, an appropriate choice by a singer-writer whose major subject is the trouble with women. He seldom uses a narrative approach but tends instead to focus on his reactions, his own feelings. He never takes the traditional pose of the black male as a fool worthy of sympathy or pity, an attitude manifest in the blues of Bobby Bland.

He possesses a fierce pride and, while he may plead, he demands respect and will not sacrifice his self-respect. Hurt, he asserts he is "Paying the Cost to Be the Boss." Uneasy, he orders his woman, "Don't open the door for nobody when you're home and you know you're all alone." Mistreated or fooled, he states, "That's Wrong, Little Mama," or "You Upset Me, Baby." He can also be ingratiatingly tender, as in "Sweet Little Angel," perhaps his best-known song.

In 1964, while he was on tour with the Jackie Wilson show and was traveling from New Orleans to Dallas, his truck skidded off the road and overturned. Of those in the car, two were uninjured, his alto saxist was shaken up, and he required forty stitches in his right arm just below the shoulder, twelve on his forearm, and seven above the right eye where a scar is still visible. After resting in a Shreveport hospital for a day, he rented another truck, made the trip to Dallas, and played five scheduled shows.

Nevertheless, after eighteen years of performing, he admits that when he goes out on stage he is "scared half to death. My knees rattle. Same thing in a club, although I'm more comfortable than in a theater." He is also still so self-conscious that he remains uneasy about being introduced socially as the "great B. B. King." He tells the story of how a friend once brought two girls over to meet him and made a rather high-flown introduction. Neither girl knew anything about music or blue singers, and one snidely asked why she should be impressed. B. B. King thought he would "go through the floor" in embarrassment.

King has no hesitation in admitting that when he first started making money he drank, gambled, and squandered much of it. He also went on buying sprees, feeling that he had never had enough clothes or "believe it or not, sweet potato pies. That lasted quite a long time, but now I have a Volkswagen at home and that's what I drive. Then, it had to be a Cadillac, and to me that proved I was popular." He admits that some of his ideas came from reading about Hollywood stars and how they attracted crowds. "I was a star," he says, "and I had to have everything that stars were supposed to have. I had it, everything except the courage, and I never did get that. Later I learned all this wasn't important and then I started to think about the comforts of the people who traveled with me."

In 1960 he had three records that displayed his appeal to record buyers: "Sweet Sixteen, Parts 1 and 2," "Got a Right to Love My Baby," and "Partin' Time." By this time, many of the Chicago bluesmen were sitting at his feet instead of Muddy Waters's, and new-generation performers like Buddy Guy, Junior Wells, Otis Rush, Albert King, Magic Sam, and Freddy King were studying his recordings and style. They were particularly interested in the inventive way that, being a bluesman, he used the guitar as another voice to amplify, comment on, and respond to his singing voice.

Nevertheless, B. B. was on the defensive about being a blues singer—and as recently as 1965.

"If Frank Sinatra can be top in his field and Nat Cole in his," he said, "why can't I be great in blues? Blues isn't dirty. It's American. . . . I would like to be called a singer and be given the same kind of respect for my style that Sinatra gets for his. . . . I'm a blues singer all right. But I don't mind being called a blues singer just so long as the tone of voice is right, you know. A lot of people say 'blues singer,' you know they're thinking of some ignorant lush moaning in a gutter some place. . . . There's no reason why a man can't sing blues as a profession and be a gentleman."

162

To the younger generation of record buyers, white as well as black, this seems self-evident. But obviously B. B. carries the scars of years when middle-class Negroes as well as whites had no use for bluesmen. "The middle-class Negro thought that the blues was holding them back," he recently told *Newsweek*.

Despite the regard in which he is held by modern bluesmen, his audience until 1966 was black, and he eked out an existence playing the "chitlin circuit" of ghetto clubs and theaters.

"I can still do a week of one-nighters," he said not long ago, "and not make what Ray Charles can working one place three nights a week." He adds, "But I get to good places now, where you're not scared of getting hurt. Sometimes, I'm bitter that we've been doing it for so long."

Even at the record end, his rewards were so slight and the income of the Modern-RPM-Kent-Crown complex so limited that in 1962 they parted company. He cut his first sides for ABC/Bluesway in March, 1962, and recorded more than fifty songs, traditional as well as modern blues, before he struck a best seller four years later with the two-sided "Don't Answer the Door." By that time his acceptance abroad and sponsorship by various British rock groups had led to an awakening of interest in him in his home country. B. B. King, *Live at the Regal*, recorded by ABC in 1964, is regarded as the most masterful documentation of his genius. Despite the anti-quated sound, youngsters are also buying *The Great B. B. King*, one of his early Crown LPs.

At the moment, his star is rising, with *Billboard* rating him as number twenty-seven among Top R & B Singles Artists in 1969. It is small reward for the man whose guitar style has the lean authority of a Louis Armstrong solo and who is credited with helping contemporary blues come of age.

B. B. King's limited acceptance through the fifties was hardly a singular phenomenon. Beginning in 1954 and continuing into 1955, the year of the coming of the Lord of Rock 'n' Roll, R & B artists kept losing hits to white pop artists who covered them.

A partial documentation of this development includes

"Sh-Boom"—Mercury's Crewcuts covered Atlantic's Chords. "Sincerely"—the McGuire Sisters covered the Moonglows. "Shake, Rattle and Roll"—Bill Haley covered Joe Turner. "Tweedle Dee"—Georgie Gibbs covered LaVern Baker. "Dance with Me, Henry"—Gibbs covered Etta James. "Seventeen"— Fontane Sisters covered Boyd Bennett. "Ko Ko Mo"—Perry Como covered Gene & Eunice. "Piddily Patter Patter"—Patti Page covered Nappy Brown.

Parenthetically, I might add, since I was personally involved in the first and last of these covers, that small record labels welcomed covers. The reason is simple. Owning the publication rights to the songs, they made up in song royalties and "sells" what they lost in record sales. Songwriters also benefited from covers. But black artists were the losers, even though cover disks generally spurred the sales of the original record. When the white public was ready to accept the black artist, as happened soon afterward, the cover failed to take the play away from the original.

Of course, when the rock 'n' roll wave developed tidal proportions, as it did beginning in 1956, it overwhelmed the whole generation of white cover artists and swept them out of the record market virtually overnight. A strange sidelight of the musical scene of this period is that white teen-age singers also began to penetrate deeply into the R & B market.

A survey of *Billboard*'s R & B chart for 1957 reveals that, of sixteen number-one disks, the white kids scored nine against seven for black artists. Presley had five number ones, while Jerry Lee Lewis, Paul Anka, Jimmie Rodgers, and Danny and the Juniors each had one. The following twelve months saw a continuation of this trend. However, by that time, both Pop and R & B charts had become integrated. Just as the white artists were scoring on black R & B charts, so Fats Domino, Chuck Berry, Sam Cooke, and The Coasters were making it on white Pop charts.

12

THE BIG THREE
OF R & B

A. Motown: The Detroit Sound

To black militants the full scale invasion and conquest of pop charts and markets by the Berry Gordy complex may be a doubtful accomplishment. But, viewed historically, the Motown achievement represents the culmination of twenty years of recording by R & B labels. Until Gordy arrived, black artists did the recording but white owners did the masterminding.

Much has been made of the British contribution to the elimination of racial musical barriers in this country. No one can question the vital role of the Beatles, Rolling Stones, and other English rock groups in the current R & B revival. But R & B began to interest white American record buyers shortly after the emergence of Elvis Presley.

By 1956, when white artists covered songs launched by black artists—for example, Sam Cooke's "You Send Me"—the youngsters were sticking with the original instead of, as in this case, buying the white copy by Teresa Brewer. And some time before the British invasion black artists had begun bustin' out all over our Pop charts. In August, 1962, for example, when *Cash Box* published its twentieth anniversary issue, there were thirteen black artists among the first fifty in its Top 100 chart. Five of these were among the first twenty.

Included in this group of Negro singers being bought by white youngsters were Little Eva on Dimension, Orlons on

Cameo, Isley Brothers on Wand, Chubby Checker on Parkway, Dee Dee Sharp on Cameo, Etta James on Argo, Shirelles on Scepter, Jerry Butler on Vee Jay, Timi Yuro on Liberty, Dave "Baby" Cortez on Chess, Sam Cooke on RCA, and Ray Charles on ABC-Paramount.

In short, the rockabilly wedding of C & W and R & B lit a small fire that smoldered until the wind blowing from overseas fanned it into a roaring blaze. There is a vast difference between the present revival of R & B and the rise of Motown, though both involve the flow of black artists and music into the main-stream of pop. R & B is ghetto music written and produced for the black market. Motown is black music—really gray—packaged for the white market.

Little has been printed about Berry Gordy's background, though much attention has been paid to the time he spent on the assembly lines of Detroit's automotive factories. (Motown is, of course, a contraction of motor town.) The fact is that Gordy was a not unsuccessful songwriter and struggling indie record producer for years before lightning struck. During 1958–59 he collaborated with his sister Gwen and Tyran Carlo to create three best sellers for another Detroit lad, singer Jackie Wilson. The songs were "Lonely Teardrops," "To Be Loved," and "I'll Be Satisfied."

During the same period Gordy met Smokey Robinson, lead singer of a group called The Miracles, which had been organized by Robinson when he was in his early teens. Gordy was so impressed by their sound that he borrowed seven hundred dollars from his family's credit union to record one of his own songs, "Way Over There," and a song by Smokey, "Mama Done Told Me." No one could have predicted on the basis of this disk that before long something known as the Motown or Detroit Sound would become a musical legend.

Only seven years later, the Motown conglomerate embraced four hugely successful companies: Jobete, the publishing oper-ation, whose contract writers include the hit team known inside the business as H-D-H, initials that stand for Holland, Dozier, and Holland; International Talent Management, superintend-ing the nonrecording activities—club, concert, film, theater, and

TV engagements—of the label's artists; Hitsville, USA, owner of the busy recording studios; and Motown Record Corporation, whose subsidiaries include five hot labels—Gordy, Tamla, Soul, VIP, and Motown.

The conglomerate occupies seven brick bungalows, situated on both sides of a tree-lined stretch of Woodward Avenue in an integrated, middle-class section of Detroit. Over a bungalow in which Gordy once lived as a youngster is a large sign identifying the location as Hitsville, USA. Not too long ago, the conglomerate's gross was estimated at twenty million dollars a year. Once Gordy defined the Motown Sound as "rats, roaches, struggle, talent, guts, and love." Recently, and not surprisingly, he has described it as "a happy sound, a big happy beat with a good strong bass. Tambourines give it a gospel flavor but it doesn't have so much of that now."

It was not until 1960 that The Miracles and Gordy had their first big hit. "Shop Around," a song by Berry and Smokey, went to number one on R & B charts and became Motown's first of many Gold Records. The following year, the Marvelettes also hit the top with "Please, Mr. Postman," included by the Beatles three years later in their first mammoth album.

By 1962 the number of breakout records for Gordy had multiplied impressively. At least seven, mostly by the Marvelettes, hit the Top Ten, while two disks, "Do You Love Me?" by the Contours and "You Beat Me to the Punch" by Mary Wells, climbed to number one. The following year saw a further multiplication of hit records. The Miracles scored number one with "You've Really Got a Hold on Me." But so did two new Motown artists. Little Stevie Wonder zoomed to the top with "Fingertips," as did Martha and the Vandellas with "Heat Wave."

Except for "Fingertips," which went to the top of Pop charts in 1963, Gordy's impact was in the R & B field. In 1964, however, when the Beatles, Rolling Stones, Animals, Peter and Gordon, Gerry and the Pacemakers, and the Dave Clark Five took over the Top 50 of American charts, Gordy's minions executed a major breakthrough.

Cash Box's anniversary issue in August, 1964, told an amazing story: Marvin Gaye was at the number thirty-five spot with "Try It Baby," The Miracles were higher with "I Like It Like That," and The Supremes with "Where Did Our Love Go?" glowed at number two. Farther down in the list were the Marvelettes with "You're My Remedy" and the Four Tops with "Baby, I Need Your Lovin'," which climbed to number one later in the year.

The years 1965 and 1966 were even more fantastic: the Motown companies accounted for 36 to 40 percent of all the hot disks, produced by the R & B labels.

Although the success of The Supremes seemed like an overnight occurrence, Diana Ross, Mary Wilson, and Florence Ballard (later replaced by Cindy Birdsong) served a reasonably long apprenticeship. Three skinny teen-agers living with large, poverty-stricken families in Detroit's Brewster Housing Project, they began singing together while they were still in elementary school. Diana Ross's memory of her growing years: "We were six kids, three girls, three boys. We slept in the same room, three in a bed, with a kerosene jar lighted to keep the chintzes away." Later she got a job after school at Hudson's department store as a busgirl. "I was the first colored girl in the cafeteria basement. Everybody came downstairs to stare."

Gordy auditioned them while they were still in school, but insisted that they complete their studies. Accordingly, they went on singing at class functions and local socials. Once they had put school behind them, they made their first recording. "I Want a Guy" backed with "Buttered Popcorn" hardly posed a threat to the Shirelles, then the top black female group. That year (1963) The Supremes cut eight other disks without making a splash in the market.

Then, in the spring of 1964, they were turned over to the songwriting-producing team of H-D-H. Within two years after scoring their first hit with H-D-H's "Where Did Our Love Go?" they had sold a total of nearly ten million disks, achieving Gold Records on "Baby Love," "Come See About Me," "Stop in the Name of Love," "Back in My Arms Again," "I Hear a Symphony," and "You Can't Hurry Love."

Interviewed about this time by Look magazine, Diana Ross,

whose voice is like a hoarse June Allyson's, said, "We've had six number-one hits in a row, but we're still treated like some ordinary rock 'n' roll group, except in clubs. On TV shows like Ed Sullivan's, we're pushed on and off the stage fast, as if we were nothin'. . . . On Hullabaloo they give me a cue card with a stupid speech to say. How dare they do that? I could be the mistress of ceremonies, but they never ask me. I see all these phonies . . . runnin' around actin' like big stars. I've got something they don't have and the kids know it. I'm for real, and every time I sing a song, it's part of my body. . . ."

Diana's body must be feline, since she purrs rather than sings, and her voice has a soft, almost childlike quality that suggests a cuddly kitten rather than a full-grown cat.

The phenomenal success of The Supremes helped to define, and doubtless to "broaden" or at least whiten, the Motown or Detroit Sound. The girls had an underlying feeling for gospel turns of harmony and call-and-response patterns as well as a vibrant beat that spoke to the feet. But they also had an inescapably girlish sound that was only tinted black, and their natural mode of expression was gentle and relaxed.

Actually, the Motown Sound is a more complex entity than any definition will comprehend, for the sound of The Miracles is quite different from that of The Supremes. It might be described as an admixture of R & B and pop. It uses black ingredients like gospel rhythms and harmonies, a pronounced afterbeat, and a swinging dance gait. But these are baked in an oven that is only moderately hot and the resulting biscuits are light and fluffy. It is hardly soul food, but rather a dish for which white listeners have acquired a taste and which attracts because of the freshness imparted by black flavoring.

Unquestionably, the most fervent fans of The Supremes are under thirty, and more likely under twenty. But the group's appearances at plush supper clubs and in concert halls demonstrate that their appeal extends to older audiences.

Another way of suggesting the character of the Motown Sound is to note that it is the product of black writers, producers, and singers working to the suave accompaniment of the

Detroit Symphony's string section, many of whose members play Motown record dates. The Detroit Sound is not nearly as black, gritty, loud, or intense as either the Memphis or the Atlantic Sound. Rhythmically, it is built on 8/8, or straight time, like most contemporary black music and rock, save that bass and snare drum together accent the odd-numbered eights, simulating an Indian tom-tom effect.

At one point, Mary Wilson, who sings low harmony in The Supremes, speculated, "Maybe the Motown Sound is just love and warmth. Like a family, we all work together, fight and kiss all day long." Hardly a definition. But the qualities of "love and warmth" are a far cry from the yearning and want in which the girls grew up (and which are a mark of the blues) and rather remote from the tensions, frustrations, and lustiness of urban life celebrated in rhythm-and-blues. Certainly much love and warmth can come from the satisfactions that earnings of $250,000 to $500,000 a year bring to each.

"The Supremes were our breakthrough," the head of Motown's record promo department told a *New York Times* reporter. "A few years back we couldn't make a WABC pick [being added to the list of records that disk jockeys play], because they'd say, 'That's a blues sound.' Used to be you had 'good' music, or popular music, and you had 'race' music. Then you had rock 'n' roll and rhythm-and-blues. Now, Motown's bridged the gap between pop and R & B."

The Supremes were the breakthrough, not only in white radio but in white clubs and theaters. Slender, youthful, ebullient, and blessed with gracefully contoured features, the girls quickly learned at Motown's charm school how to walk, talk, dress, and act in polite society. (The charm school, headed by Mrs. Harvey Fuqua, is known as the Special Projects Department.) International Talent Management helped them translate their aural appeal into visual impact, elaborating routines for their personal appearances and working out the attractive choreography for which all Motown acts are noted.

The results of the tutoring and many hours of rehearsal were apparent as soon as The Supremes began making appearances at New York's Copa, Hollywood's Cocoanut Grove, and other plush white clubs. At first, the audience was largely under twenty. But as the engagements continued the expense-account crowd came trooping in.

In the album area, the girls have pursued a parallel course. Early in their success, they demonstrated their versatility by doing an LP whose contents were suggested by the title *The Supremes Sing, Country, Western and Pop*. As their conquest of the white entertainment world assumed larger proportions, they cut an LP, *The Supremes at the Copa*. After a time, Motown released *The Supremes Sing Rodgers & Hart* and recently *Diana Ross and The Supremes Sing and Perform Funny Girl*.

From 1967 to 1968, the record appeal of the group suffered a serious setback. The story appears in comparative figures in year-end surveys: from number five in Top Singles, the group fell to number seventy-six; from number nine in Top Albums, they slipped to eighteen; where they had been rated in 1967 at number six and number four in R & B Singles and R & B Albums respectively, in 1968 they were not visible at all in the Top 50. Three explanations are worthy of consideration. Their hit cycle, short-lived with most artists, was over. Holland, Dozier, and Holland, who were at odds for a time with the Motown management, had written themselves out or were unable to function effectively in the controversial atmosphere. Or, as the market took a stronger soul and R & B cast, record buyers were moving toward the blacker end of the musical spectrum.

Having acquired a new set of producers in Berry Gordy, Jr., himself and H. Cosby, The Supremes made a better showing in 1969 than in '68.

In the summer of 1967, the billing of The Supremes was changed to Diana Ross and The Supremes, which signalized a belated recognition of the formidable contribution of her lead voice. About the same time, the male group on Tamla, a sister label, that was known as The Miracles became Smokey Robinson and The Miracles. Kickoff act for the Gordy empire, The Miracles had been in existence for about five years when Gordy became interested in them in 1958. William Smokey Robinson had organized them as a street-corner harmony quintet while he was attending Northern High School in Detroit. There were Ronnie White, Peter Moore, guitarist Marv Tarplin, Bobby Rogers, and his sister Claudette, now Mrs. Robinson—a group whose personnel has not changed.

"We've stayed together," Robinson has said—his friends call him "Smoke"—"because we legitimately love each other. . . . When you can no longer accept the fact that you're a human being and singing is just your job, and along with the glamour part of entertainment come the screams and the yells, then you're in trouble. . . ."

Apart from Robinson's tact and simple humanity, the group has been held together by Smokey's gift for writing songs, a talent that benefited, as Smokey is quick to acknowledge, from Gordy Berry's critical judgment. Robinson harks back to the audition at which another record man turned the group down in 1958 but Berry expressed an interest in his songs.

"I must have gone through sixty-eight of those songs," he recalls, "and on every one I'd say, 'What's wrong with this one?' and he'd say, 'Well, you left off this or you didn't complete your idea on that,' which really started me to think about songs and what they were. Gordy, man, that cat more than anyone else helped me get my things together."

After "Shop Around," the flow of hits from Smokey's pen —"I'll Be Doggone," "Ain't That Peculiar," "Going to a Go-Go,"—quickly established the preeminence of The Miracles among black singing groups. In "Tracks of My Tears," Robinson demonstrates his ability to take "The Great Pretender" theme and give it fresh intensity:

> Take a good look at my face
> You'll see my smile looks out of place
> If you look closer it's easy to trace
> The tracks of my tears.

Smokey's talents as a writer have earned him not only numerous BMI awards and records by other artists, but the admiration of Bob Dylan, who has called him "America's greatest living poet."

Despite his creativity, Smokey takes a hard, realistic approach to his craft and talent: "I've geared myself to radio time," he says. "The shorter a record is nowadays, the more it's gonna be played. This is a key thing in radio time, you dig? . . . But it's no hang-up because I'm going to work in it and say whatever I'm going to say in this time limit. . . . So we're just going to try to stay abreast of what's on the market. . . . The market, man, the market is people. It is the kids who are buying the records. These are the people you're trying to reach. I think that satisfying people is more important than self-satisfaction."

(The attractive girl appearing on the covers of early Miracles albums is Smokey's wife, Claudette, who is still to be heard with the group on disks but is no longer visible in personal appearances. The wife of Bobby Rogers, another member of The Miracles, is part of the Marvelettes, one of Motown's female groups. There is an inbreeding in the Motown family, and ten Gordys and in-laws are part of the complex.)

The year 1962 was a breakout one for many Motown artists. Four groups, the Marvelettes, the Contours, Gladys Knight & the Pips, and the Temptations, all contributed noisemakers, though not necessarily Top Ten disks. Of these, the Temptations have been the most successful, even though the present group has Dennis Edwards as a replacement for lead singer David Ruffin, now building a career on his own. Interestingly enough, in May '69 Ruffin had a Top Ten single in "My Whole World Ended" while the newly constituted Temptations had a Top Ten album in *Cloud Nine*.

Although the Temptations attracted attention in 1962 with "Paradise," a song by Berry Gordy, it was not until two years later that they made number one with "My Girl." The following year was their *annus mirabilis*, with three disks soaring to the top, "Ain't Too Proud to Beg," "Beauty Is Only Skin Deep," and "(I Know) I'm Losing You."

By this time the Temptations were known not only for their singing, but for dancing that brought standing ovations and for mimicry in which they imitated the Ink Spots, Mills Brothers, Four Freshmen, and other black and white groups.

173

"If two-a-day vaudeville ever comes back," a reviewer observed in 1967, "the Temptations are a good bet to top the bill at the Palace."

Incidentally, both in 1967 and 1968, *Billboard* named the group number one of all R & B album artists.

Dennis Edwards, newest member of the group, started at Motown with the Contours after a background of teen-age gospel singing with two Birmingham choirs, the Golden Wonders and the Revelation Wonders. The Contours were as short-lived as the Temptations have been long-lived, even though in 1962 they had a number-one hit in a Berry Gordy song, "Do You Love Me?" Their record stirred so much interest abroad that two years later the song was cut and revived by the Dave Clark Five. Best sellers through 1963 and 1964 did not prevent the Contours from disappearing from the recording scene.

Motown's pecking order has changed a great deal since the days when The Supremes were at the bottom. Two other girl groups have inevitably moved downward as the Diana Ross group rose. One of these, the Marvelettes, began, like the Supremes, as a school choir.

Gladys Horton, Katherine Anderson, and Wanda Rogers created such a sensation at Inkster High in a Detroit suburb that a teacher arranged an audition with Gordy. Their first release, "Please Mr. Postman"—number one in record time—presaged star status for the group, which has not been lacking in best-selling disks. But while they remain a force in the record market, stronger in the R & B area than in pop, they have been greatly overshadowed by The Supremes.

Martha Reeves and the Vandellas is another girls' trio that has remained somewhere below The Supremes' summit in the gray hills of Motown. Not unlike Diana Ross, who briefly took a job as an assistant secretary in Gordy's office (she was fired after two weeks), Martha Reeves worked at secretarial chores until an emergency recording situation permitted her to disclose and volunteer her talent as a singer.

A harassed record producer, William Stevenson, accepted the offer with the result that Gordy auditioned Martha and two classmates from her school glee club as they sang vocal backgrounds during a recording session. (Listen to their rocking chorus on Marvin Gaye's "Stubborn Kind of Fellow.")

Impressed by what he heard, Gordy scheduled a record date for the "new" trio. Their second release, in November '62, was the H-D-H hit, "Come and Get These Memories." H-D-H, whom Martha describes as "our songwriters—the Supremes kind of borrowed them for a while," also are responsible for the songs on hit disks from "Heat Wave" and "Quicksand" to "Jimmy Mack." Martha and first soprano Rosalind Ashford have remained with the group from the beginning, while Annette Sterling was succeeded by Betty Kelly and, more recently, by Martha's younger sister, Lois Reeves.

Early in 1969 the group made the Copa, where Martha Reeves told an interviewer, "We're not above the Apollo. We're just going into another field. We're widening the variety of our audiences." Martha feels that the Vandellas' audience has grown "because of the soul revolution. Now everyone wants to hear us. I think The Supremes opened a lot of doors. Their music is not as rhythm-and-bluesy as ours but people who dig them want to hear us, too."

As they travel the circuit of one-nighters and colleges, they carry their own trio. But when they return to Detroit for recording sessions, they use Motown's regular staff musicians: the redoubtable James Jamison on bass, Earl Van Dyke on piano, and Benny Benjamin on drums.

A late entry among Motown groups (1964), the Four Tops spun their way into the hit class with their first release, an H-D-H song, "Baby, I Need Your Loving." Lead singer Levi Stubbs, Jr., spokesman for the group, calls the ballad their national anthem. When they received the nod from Berry Gordy, they had been singing together for a ten-year period that took them back to their graduation from a Detroit high school.

Their most important influence was singer Billy Eckstine, with whom they worked for several years. Eckstine coached them not only in musical matters but in their demeanor offstage, and in their choice and upkeep of stage attire. Their second year of recording was a particularly rewarding one. Five Top Ten disks included number-one spinners in "I Can't Help Myself" and "Reach Out, I'll Be There," the latter an intense ballad with exciting call-and-response devices.

Like the Temptations, the Tops are a versatile group who dance as well as they sing. And like The Supremes, they have moved gracefully out of the R & B field and conquered the over-thirty crowd that frequents the Copa in New York City and the Diplomat in Miami. When the Beatles' manager, the late Brian Epstein, booked them for a London concert, he was compelled to schedule two additional performances to accommodate the overflow crowd from the first.

At the moment, it appears that the popularity of Levi Stubbs, Jr., Renaldo Benson, Lawrence Payton, and Abdul Fakir is growing, although year-end surveys showed some small drop in their sales from 1967 to 1968.

In 1962 Mary Wells looked like the up-and-coming queen of the Motown complex, with several disks riding the R & R turntables hard, including one, "You Beat Me to the Punch," that made number one. Somehow, after this promising beginning, she was unable to translate the promise into achievement.

On the other hand, Marvin Gaye has been growing steadily in stature. "Mr. Perfectionist," as he dubs himself, began by singing in the choir and playing organ in the Washington, D.C., church where his father was the minister. After graduating from high school, he toured the country as part of the Moonglows, acquiring a feeling of confidence and power before audiences that Berry Gordy sensed when he heard him at an informal Detroit party.

"Stubborn Kind of Fellow" and "Pride and Joy," best sellers in 1962–63, led to "Ain't That Peculiar," a number-one smash, and hits like "Little Darling" and "One More Heartache" in 1965–66. After a successful period of recording with Tami Terrell, at midyear '69 Gaye once again was in the enviable position of possessing a number-one R & B album, *M. P. G.*, and a number-one single, "Too Busy Thinking About My Baby." These were produced by Norman Whitfield, whose perceptive editing and booth work were also powering the work of the Temptations.

Blind since birth, Little Stevie Wonder was only thirteen when "Fingertips," extracted from a live performance at the Apollo Theatre, became the number-one hit both on R & B and Pop charts in 1963. Born Steveland Morris in Saginaw, Michigan, the third child in a family of six, he became a Detroit resident soon after his birth. Here, after a time, he struck up a friendship with the younger brother of Ronnie White, a member of The Miracles, who arranged for an audition by Berry Gordy. The year 1966 proved to be a bonanza, with high flyers in "Nothing's Too Good for My Baby," "A Place in the Sun," and "With a Child's Heart," and top-of-the-list disks in "Blowin' in the Wind" and "Up Tight."

At midyear '69 Stevie showed no diminution in his record power, as "My Cherie Amour" went soaring into the Top Ten both in Pop and R & B. Now in his twenties, Stevie has dropped the "Little" from his appellation. Not long ago he observed, "Consider all the great men of our day who come from under-privileged homes and you will find someone in their past who lent inspiration and encouragement at a time when they were needed most during adolescence. If a young person has someone who really cares—a parent, a relative, a clergyman, a teacher— and has a decent place to go and meet others of his age, he's well on the way to growing up with confidence in himself and his society."

Dedicated and talented though the family of Motown artists was, the conglomerate's phenomenal success required two other ingredients: songwriting and producing genius. In the early days, Smokey Robinson and Berry Gordy contributed both of these talents, as they still do. But a huge share of the credit in these departments must go to the three men frequently referred to as H-D-H, and bearing the names of Brian Holland, Lamont Dozier, and Eddie Holland. It would take more space than this study permits to list all their hits or all the artists who have recorded their hits. But in 1966 Jobete Music Company, Motown's publishing arm, boasted that it had received thirteen Citations of Achievement from BMI for hit songs, and an overwhelming number were from the pens of the three writer-producers.

Having launched The Supremes with "Where Did Our Love Go?" they kept the group high on best-selling lists with "Stop! In the Name of Love," "I Hear a Symphony," "Come See About Me," "Love Is Here and Now You're Gone," "Nothing But Heartaches"—to mention a few. The Four Tops enjoyed a similar run of successes with such H-D-H hits as "Baby, I Need Your Lovin'," "I Can't Help Myself" (number one), "It's the Same Old Song," and "Reach Out, I'll Be There" (number one). Marvin Gaye had a hit with "How Sweet It Is," the Contours with "Ain't Too Proud to Beg," the Marvelettes with "Please Mr. Postman" (number one), The Miracles with "Mickey's Monkey," and Martha and the Vandellas with "(Love Is Like a) Heat Wave" (number one) and "I'm Ready for Love."

Between 1961 and 1967, they received the unprecedented number of twenty-four BMI Songwriter Achievement Awards (these are given only to songs that go into the Top Ten on trade paper charts). Another figure that gives some measure of what their talents contributed to the coffers of Motown: from January 1, 1965, through June 30, 1968, they received salary, bonuses, and royalties aggregating $2,235,155.71.

The market thrust of Motown is the product of image as well as the genius and artistry of its creative talent. Anyone who doubts this has only to read letters received by *Soul* magazine when it became definitely known that Diana Ross was leaving The Supremes.

"So many times I had heard Diana say," one fan wrote, "that nothing would separate The Supremes. Regretfully, I hate to say how I lost faith in them. . . ."

And another, more analytical reader wrote, "There was unity in their trinity which was unique. The three little girls always together who rose from the ghetto to superstardom stood as an inspiration to us all."

But the unity in trinity was more than a Supremes image. When Berry Gordy's sister, a vice-president of Motown, died in 1965, the stars of the complex gave expression to their feelings of loss by singing at the services, and a memorial LP of songs, recorded at Detroit's Bethel AME Church, was released under the title *In Loving Memory*. To the recording, publishing, and listening worlds, Motown projected an image of a big happy family. Motown records seemed to have an effervescence and a togetherness that went beyond the mere music.

But fissures have been developing in the formidable facade. Diana Ross's departure from The Supremes and David Ruffin's exit from the Temptations at first seemed intrafamily changes, since both were to continue recording for Motown. But then in October, 1968, Motown and International Management Company filed suit, charging that two New York agents had conspired to destroy their contractual relationship with Ruffin. Months later, there were rumors that the Temptations themselves were seeking to sever their association with Motown.

All these developments are overshadowed by the controversy between Motown and the writing-producing team of Holland-Dozier-Holland. As of May, 1969, the trio were being legally restrained from performing their creative services pending the resolution of a four-million-dollar lawsuit in which Motown alleged breach of contract. Neither side has been willing to acknowledge the source of the conflict, though it seems apparent that questions of economics must have been involved.

Brian Holland has said, "We were negotiating for a better creative relationship. While negotiating with the company, there was a communications breakdown and they sued us."

Doubtless the suit will be settled out of court, and possibly H-D-H will return to write and produce for Motown. H-D-H were basically responsible for helping the company move out' of the R & B area into pop. Their concept of "soft rock 'n' roll," of blues with strings and modern harmonies—their style of mixing soul food with supper-club delicacies—resulted in a product that appealed to two worlds, black and white. The success of The Supremes was symbolical.

New producers and writers can be found to maintain the stability and speed of the Motown machine as it maneuvers over the bridge between pop and R & B. The rating of

Norman Whitfield, currently responsible for the continuing success of Marvin Gaye and the Temptations, has risen among Hot Producers from a number-seventeen rating in 1967 to the number-two position in '68, just as H-D-H fell from number two to number twenty-one. But the image of a family without conflict, of a segregated minority fighting joyously for its place in the sun, is gone. Motown has become a small mirror reflecting the fissures in the large world around it.

B. Stax: The Memphis Sound

When a journalist told Janis Joplin, formerly of Big Brother and the Holding Company, that he was going to write a little something for *Rolling Stone* about her new band's debut in Memphis, the girl who is regarded as the best white female blues singer of our time exclaimed: *"Rolling Stone?* They don't know what's happening. They're out in San Francisco feeling smug because they think they're where it's at. This is where it's at, Memphis!"

Although Memphis is the home of Sun Records, basically responsible for the development of rockabilly—white country boys singing black: Elvis Presley, Jerry Lee Lewis, Carl Perkins, Roy Orbison (a fusion of mountain C & W with urban R & B)—the Memphis Sound is today associated with another record company. Stax and its subsidiaries are much younger than Sun, having been launched as recently as 1959 by Jim Stewart and his sister, Estelle Axton. Stax is a combination of the first two letters of their surnames.

Asked to differentiate the Memphis Sound from the Detroit Sound, singer Carla Thomas said, "It's mostly the horns and guitar, a slurring brass and guitar that are dominant in the music. It's not like Detroit's Motown Sound where the drums and bass are important and it's beat, beat, beat, beat that counts." Miss Thomas, who was one of the first artists on the Stax label, has since become known as the Queen of the Memphis Sound.

Motown singer Martha Reeves offers a different interpretation: "Memphis has a bass drum and bass guitar beat. Motown is built from a bass sound but it takes in much more on the top.

There's a lot more elaboration in the Motown Sound. Also, Motown has a shuffle beat and the Memphis beat is different." "The Memphis Sound started in a church," says Booker T. Jones, gifted head of the famous M.G.'s, "in the Negro church in the South. The music was really soul-searching; it was enough to make the listener cry at times. We've retained the basic elements of this church music in the Memphis Sound."

What has been added? Jim Stewart states, "We keep abreast of changing trends at the same time that we remain close to the roots. . . . Today, people are seeking the truth . . . they are looking for reality . . . and this accounts for the popularity of the blues-oriented music of today."

In short, Stax represents a synthesis of past and present, the blues of yesterday with the harmonies of now and the rhythms of today. It's the Beale Street of W. C. Handy transformed into the launching pad of Elvis Presley and reconstructed as the rocket sites of Soul.

If Motown is the northern ghetto expanding into the white world of sleek automobiles and plush clubs, Stax is the Mississippi River overflowing the banks of the 1960s. Inescapably, the Memphis Sound has more grit, gravel, and mud in it than the Detroit Sound.

Like Motown from its start until recently, Stax projects the image of a happy, working family. "I think we have the best marriage of people alive today," guitarist Steve Cropper told Jann Wenner of *Rolling Stone*, "to work basically 365 days a year with the same thought in mind, and this includes the president, vice-president, the secretaries, the musicians. . . . I know of no other company in the world or no other group of people working around music that have this sort of marriage, that every day is for today and that everybody lives for tomorrow to make Stax a better company. . . ."

Commenting on how the death of Otis Redding had affected the Stax family, drummer Al Jackson explained, "What Steve is saying is that we realized we could never replace Otis, so we spend all the time we can really trying to make a William Bell, trying to make a Johnnie Taylor, to take up the slack and all that we lost in Otis and, I must say, the Bar-Kays."

From the start, the Stax family was an integrated one, and the emphasis in its image was on not only the harmonious family but the harmoniously *integrated* one. Although Stax is owned by a white, his closest associate has always been a black, now the company's executive vice-president and possibly the first Negro to hold such a post below the Mason-Dixon line. The house band has also been integrated.

After Jim Stewart's sister mortgaged her home to raise twenty-five hundred dollars for an Ampex recorder, they moved their recording studios and offices into the deserted site of a former vaudeville-movie house. (The marquee of what was once the Capitol Theatre now carries the legend "Soulsville/ USA," contrasting with Motown's "Hitsville/USA.") It was in the heart of blacktown.

"Had we been located in any environment," Stewart has said, "other than at 926 East McLemore Street, we wouldn't be the same Stax Records at all. In our case, black and white has equaled nothing but success. If we've done more, we've shown the world that people of different colors, origins, and convictions can be as one, working together toward the same goal. Because we've learned how to live and work together at Stax Records, we've reaped the material benefits. But most of all, we've acquired peace of mind. When hate and resentment break out all over the nation, we pull our blinds and display a sign that reads, 'Look What We've Done—TOGETHER.' "

Stewart acknowledges that the tenor of his social consciousness "is a result of the relationship Al Bell [his executive vice-president] and I have established."

Although Booker T. and the M.G.'s did not produce their first Gold Record until three years after Stax started—the million-copy-seller "Green Onions" came in the spring of 1962 —everything at Stax starts with this remarkable group. Organist Booker T. and drummer Al Jackson, Jr., are black, while guitarist Steve Cropper and bassist Donald "Duck" Dunn are white.

This relaxed mixed marriage of southerners is the key to the Memphis Sound, a contemporary interplay of black blues and white country producing country Soul. M.G. stands for Memphis Group, an appropriate designation since all except Steve are Memphis-born and he, though born in Willow Springs, Missouri, came to Memphis before he was ten.

Booker T. Jones was twenty-five on November 12, 1969. But he already has a motion picture score to his credit—the black remake of *The Informer* by Jules Dassin known as *Up Tight*. He was not eighteen when the M.G.'s cut "Green Onions," credited to the group as it was then constituted, with Lewis Steinberg instead of Donald Dunn.

Playing organ professionally from the time he graduated from elementary school, he joined Stax almost at its founding. As he progressed through Booker T. Washington High School in Memphis, he earned fifteen dollars a day as a part-time member of the studio's backup band. Two years after he became a name artist, he enrolled at Indiana University in Bloomington and earned a B.A. in music. Although he majored in trombone, he has a prodigious mastery of instruments. On Rufus Thomas's disk of " 'Cause I Love You," he played baritone sax, on William Bell's "Tribute to a King," guitar, and on a Sam and Dave session, tuba.

Except for bassist Donald "Duck" Dunn, who is self-taught, the M.G.'s are educated men and/or musicians. Steve Cropper spent two years studying mechanical engineering at Memphis State University, and drummer Al Jackson, Jr., a teen-age member of his father's sixteen-piece orchestra, was a student at A.M. & N. College at Pine Bluff, Arkansas. Cropper, now A & R chief at Stax, slowly achieved recognition that moved his name from in-group adulation to across-the-seas praise.

Apart from his superlative work as Stax's resident guitarist, Cropper has written many hit tunes, including Eddie Floyd's "Knock on Wood" and Wilson Pickett's "634-5789" and "Midnight Hour."

Commenting on the source of his songs, Cropper told *Rolling Stone*, "I would say fifty percent to seventy-five percent of all songs we cut come from a conversation. They don't come out of Dave Porter going home and sweating, staying up until three in the morning. . . . It comes natural. . . . We'll all be talking . . . and somebody will say something and everybody will turn around because everybody's always looking for titles . . . like Al said he was talking to Otis [Redding]. . . ."

Jackson had told the story of Redding's song "Respect": "I can remember a conversation that Otis and I had about life. We were speaking about life in general, the ups and downs . . . I said, 'What you are griping about, you're on the road all the time, all you can look for is a little respect when you come home.' He wrote the tune from our conversation. We laughed about it quite a few times. In fact, Otis laughed about it all the way to the bank. But I think Aretha Franklin did a beautiful job on it. . . ."

Of his drumming, Jackson has said perceptively, "I believe in solid rhythm whether I'm playing four-four accented or two-four accented. It's syncopated rhythm with the bass drum, and less emphasis on the left stick. . . . It's a different groove from the Motown beat. They have one set of rhythm patterns and they change the bass rhythms. I dig their sound but they use the stomp rhythm practically in everything. The records they do are made from the switchboard and ours are natural. . . . They use echo and we don't. We cut our drums flat.

"I don't use any muffling or anything. I just play the way I feel. I play with the butt end of my left stick. I developed that from playing hard on gigs. . . . It sounds crisp because it's cut flat and no echo. The Telefunken mikes are set up to get the natural sound of the drums, and we don't cover it up with conga, bongos, tambourines, and all the creative rhythm. That's Motown's thing. It's just not our bag."

Bassist "Duck" Dunn may be self-taught, but his musical insights are educated. "In country-and-western," he has said, "bass players usually play two and four [the so-called after-beats of a measure]. In R & B you've got to play a definite line and color it here and there. You've got to color it because even if you have a gassy line going, it's got to get monotonous."

What makes the M.G.'s so tremendous as performers is not the unquestioned talent of each, but the way they mesh.

"If you could watch us in a session," Booker has said, "you'd see what I mean. When there's an accent on a bar or something, we just have to look at each other. We spend so much time together that we have this great feel. It's a real tight unit."

Steve Cropper picks up on the phrase "Stax classic." "By its being a classic," he told Jann Wenner, "it just means one thing: there were more people involved than just a writer, a producer, a singer, or any particular musicians or engineer . . . like 'Midnight Hour' came in basically different from the way the record came out. It came in with rhythm changes, it came in with a melody, but it came out with a distinct bass line, a distinct guitar part, a distinct drum rhythm. Beautiful horn lines . . . most of them written on the session."

Even though they constantly work with "head arrangements," that is, they create backgrounds for singers in the process of recording, the M.G.'s do as little overdubbing as possible. They prefer to do another take in order to keep the natural feeling.

Contrasting the Detroit and Memphis sounds, *Record Mirror*, a British trade paper, has observed, "The Motown Sound is like computerized music in that everything is worked out before a session take place and a lot of overdubbing is used. Whereas the Stax musicians control their music, they are 'live' on a session. They 'feel' a session and therefore believe that the Stax Sound has more 'heart' and more 'soul' than the music Motown produces."

Not long after the M.G.'s received a RIAA certified Gold Record for "Green Onions"—it did not pass the million mark until 1967—they displaced superstar Herb Alpert and the Tijuana Brass as the Top Instrumental Group in *Billboard*'s 1967 poll. In February, 1968, they became the first mixed combo to entertain in Nashville at the annual awards dinner of NARAS.

By that time their list of hit instrumentals had grown considerably and included such well-known titles as "Tic Tac Toe," "Chinese Checkers," "Soul Dressing," "Hip Hug Her," "Soul Limbo," "Hang 'em High," and, most recently, "Time Is Tight." The last mentioned is from the film soundtrack of *Up Tight*, on which Booker T., instead of using a large studio orchestra, employed only the four members of the M.G.'s.

185

Shortly after ex-bookkeeper, ex-bank teller, ex-country fiddler Jim Stewart opened his doors in Memphis' black ghetto, Rufus Thomas, a disk jockey at WDIA, and his daughter wandered in and asked to make a record together. It was April, 1959, and Stax was then known as Satellite Records.

"In May, 1960," Stewart reports, "we brought out 'Cause I Love You' by the Thomases. It sold about fifteen thousand copies locally, and to us that was like having a million seller. Atlantic Records of New York came to us and we worked out a deal nationwide, and the record went about thirty-five thousand."

It was at this time that Stewart discovered there was a Satellite company in California—and the Stax handle was born. (But the Satellite Record Shop adjoining the Stax office and studio is still owned and run by Mrs. Axton, cofounder of Stax.)

Rufus Thomas, like two of the M.G.'s a graduate of Booker T. Washington High in Memphis, began in show biz as a black comic. He became a singer by accident when Georgia Dixon, a well-known blues singer, offered him a spot in her show. Two years after Satellite released the father-and-daughter disk, Thomas became a nationally known rock 'n' roll star (at forty-five) as the creator of the dance known as "the dog."

Singing one night at a ballroom in Millington, Tennessee, about fourteen miles from Memphis, Thomas noticed a girl dancing like a dog standing on its hind legs.

"She really turned it on me," he recalls. "I gave the bass player a different beat. The band picked it up from him. The drummer just stumbled onto the break. I did twelve bars of 'Do the Dog,' then twelve bars of 'Do the Hound Dog,' then 'Do the Bird Dog' and any other kind of dog we could think of. At the end we all started barking." Before long, Stax had released a single with "The Dog" as the "B" (back) side of a blues. It quickly became the "A" side and sold steadily for two years, stirring Thomas to try a follow-up, "Can Your Dog Do the Monkey?", in which he combined two post-twist dances. Other memorable Thomas disks include "Walkin' the Dog,"

"The World Is Round (But It's Crooked Just the Same)," and "Greasy Spoon."

Daughter Carla was born in December, 1942, and at the age of eight began singing over station WDIA as part of a local group, Teen Towers. A saucer-eyed girl who looks friendly but admits that she is a snob, Carla was only eighteen when she wrote and recorded "Gee Whiz! (Look at His Eyes)." Released on Atlantic in 1961, it was a fast seller and became Stax's first Gold Record. Eight years later, when Carla was touring Germany, one of the papers summarized her performance in the phrase *Carla ist Gold wert,* a statement that really is worth its weight in gold in any language.

In the intervening years, Carla not only produced some hot disks, among them "I'll Bring It Home to You" and "B-A-B-Y," but earned her bachelor's degree in English at Tennessee A. & I. State University. She also began work for her master's degree in English literature at Howard University in Washington, D.C. Those who knew her on either campus found it hard to reconcile her sound on disks with her normal demeanor. Carla Thomas, the student, was quiet and reflective. The Queen of the Memphis Sound—a title she acquired as a result of making an album *The King and Queen* with the late Otis Redding—had spunk and sass.

Stax producers are not satisfied that they have given attractive play to Carla's silken sass. They have long suspected that Memphis rhythm was too strong and dense for her voice. In the process of making "Picking Up the Pieces," producers David Porter and Isaac Hayes flew a basic track up to Detroit, where they overdubbed voices, strings, and rhythm at a local studio—not Motown, they emphasize, though they were not surprised to find that all Detroit studios seemed to have the Motown Sound.

Lighter and texturally less dense than the Memphis Sound, the pop Detroit Sound allowed Carla's voice to front the disk as it never had before. (It was appropriate that Carla should be chosen for this experiment, since her record of "Gee Whiz" had first brought Stax into pop. In Booker T.'s view, it was

"Green Onions" that thereafter established Stax as a new force in the world of pop.)

Isaac Hayes and Dave Porter are resident writer-producers at Stax. Bearded, bespectacled, and nearly bald, Hayes dreamed of being a singer from his student days at Memphis' Manassas High. Then, he had a group called the Teen Tones, sang with a gospel group, the Morning Stars, and with a rock-and-rhythm group, the Ambassadors.

"Well, one day," as Ike tells it, "a singer, Jeb Stuart, called me and wanted me to play the piano for him. I couldn't play but I needed the money . . . so I began playing simple things with him and got by. Guess I musta had an ear for it." After Ike began hanging around the Stax studio, Jim Stewart began using him occasionally when resident pianist Booker T. was away at college.

Partner Dave Porter has said, "I was born in Memphis. It was just my mother and a bunch of kids. I ran around barefoot and we were so poor it hurt. I lived in the neighborhood of Stax since its inception. I was one of the first artists on the label, with a record that didn't do anything, a corny R & B thing called 'Old Gray Mare.' Ike came in on a few sessions, and when we talked we found many similarities in our thoughts. Before I came to Stax, I was working across the street in a grocery store pushing carts, and at night I sang in nightclubs."

Hayes tells it like this: "I've been in Memphis since I was seven. Was raised by my grandparents—never knew my mother or father—in Covington, Tennessee, where they worked as sharecroppers. I used to work in a meat-packing plant. But when I got laid off, I joined a band and decided to stick with it till I made it. Came to Stax three or four times with bands and vocal groups, trying to sell records. I played saxophone."

The collaboration started with a long list of flops. Eventually, around 1966, they came up with "Hold On, I'm Coming" and "Soul Man," both smash hits for Sam & Dave. Both have a vivid memory of how the former was written.

"I came up with the introduction," Hayes told Jim Delehant of *Hit Parader*. "Took the horn line from another instrumental

188

I had been working on. When we got into the melody, we hit a block and decided to hold it until a later date. Then one night we started to work on it again."

Porter continues the narrative: "I went into the rest room and was gone a few minutes. Hayes kept calling me. I yelled, 'Hold on, man I'm coming.' I swear, right then I broke out of the rest room, shouting, 'I got it!' When I told Hayes the title, he had the perfect thing for it on the piano. We had the whole song in five minutes."

Once the song was finished, the next step was to see how it could be made to fit Sam & Dave. "We tailor-make songs for a particular person," Dave Porter explained. "First we saw if the melody line fit. We compared other tapes we did with them. We threw in little phrases they could use on the side. Once they get the song down, they naturally inject their own interpretation. Also we kept the message in mind. If words started to throw us off, we'd look at the title, 'Hold On, I'm Coming.' It was a rescue song. We followed that all the way through."

Ike plays piano on all the records he and Dave produce. "I'm on quite a few others," he adds. "Wilson Pickett cut '99½' and '634-5789' down here and I played on those. I'm on Albert King's records. I also play piano and organ with the Mar-Keys. Booker T. usually plays organ on all records but sometimes we switch. Booker's playing is slower and smoother than mine."

Both Porter and Hayes attribute Memphis' growth as a musical center to its being integrated. "It's a mixture of people giving their ideas," Dave says, "and molding them into one individuality. Hayes and I even study country-and-western tunes because we have discovered some of the greatest lyrics in the world come from there. We might take a country line and put it into an R & B bag but we get our definition out of the line."

(In the early fifties, Sam Phillips had launched Memphis' Sun Records, feeling, as he recently told journalist Stanley Booth, "that if a person could get a combination of Negro spirituals, rhythm-and-blues, and hillbilly or country music—

not just an imitation but with feeling and fervor and soul, like the Negro singers have, and the true country singers, too—well, I could really do something." Memphis was obviously the place to get the combination, as Phillips's discovery of Presley and the other rockabilly artists proved.)

Ike Hayes pursued Porter's thought. "There is no race problem in Memphis. It's a tight harmony really." Queried as to whether the Mississippi River had something to do with the talent coming out of Memphis, Ike commented, "I've gotten a lot of inspiration from it myself. Every summer I used to go down and sit in the park overlooking the river. I've read a lot of history and I can just feel all my Negro heritage there. The riverboats, singing, sunsets, and all the history. I can't really explain the feeling you get late in the evening. That may have something to do with it. Memphis once was a town that exported cotton. There was an awful lot of singing. That influenced Handy and everybody else."

Molded in brass and holding a trumpet, the figure of W. C. Handy stands today in Handy Park near Beale Street—unfortunately, directly in front of a public lavatory. The source of some of Handy's blues, Beale Street was the post-Civil War mecca of freed slaves from the neighboring states of Mississippi, Arkansas, and Missouri. It also attracted musical talent from New Orleans and St. Louis via highway (routes 49, 51, and 61) and railroads (Texas & Pacific, Illinois Central, and Louisville-Nashville), all of which converged on Memphis.

After World War II, B. B. King, who had never been out of Mississippi, went north to Memphis because he had heard of Handy and because his cousin Bukka White, also a Mississippian, had settled there. When B. B. became a disk jockey on Memphis' radio station WDIA, it was the only station with Negro personnel. Known then as the Mother Station of the Negroes, it remains today "America's only 50,000-watt Negro radio station."

As to the meaning of Soul, Ike said, "It's a feeling—an expression from someone who has been under pressure of some kind. . . . It's an expression that reaches another person, and they can really feel what you feel while you're singing it, or painting it, or writing it, or whichever way you communicate it. Anyway, you reach the people—and they can feel it just the way you do at the time you're feeling it—that's Soul."

A more earthy concept of Soul appears in their song "Soul Man":

> I was brought up on a side street
> I learned how to love before I could eat
> I was educated to good stock
> When I start lovin', oh, I can't stop
> I'm a soul man, I'm a soul man, I'm a soul man,
>   yeah, I'm a soul man.

Sam & Dave, for whom this was a Gold Record in 1967, had become a team six years earlier. Samuel David Moore, son of a Miami Baptist deacon, met Dave Prater, a laborer's son from Ocilla, Georgia, while he was performing at a club in Miami. Prater was then working as a short-order cook and baker's assistant. Soon after they joined forces, they began billing themselves as "Double Dynamite."

Their first recording for Stax in 1965, "It Was So Nice While It Lasted," did not explode. But the following year they had one chart climber after another. First there was "You Don't Know Like I Know," then "Said I Wasn't Gonna Tell Nobody," and finally the electrifying "Hold On, I'm Coming," the disk that rocketed to number one.

Because they began making records only after years of club work, Sam & Dave are potent visual performers. "Of all the R & B cats," *Time* wrote not long ago, "nobody steams up a place like Sam & Dave. . . . Weaving and dancing, they gyrate through enough acrobatics to wear out more than 100 costumes a year. Their voices—Sam's higher and more cutting, Dave's huskier and darker-toned—blend robustly in mournful, harmonized wails or fervent gospel-style shouts. And their listeners respond like converts at a revival meeting." On their best recordings, Sam & Dave are able to convey aurally a large measure of the exuberance and fantastic expenditure of energy that make them "double dynamite" on stage.

One of the newest Stax artists to break into the charmed

circle of Gold Record winners is a young man of whom Ike Hayes said, "With Sam & Dave we have to create excitement in the material. With Johnnie Taylor—that's the new star's name—the material has to be more subtle." And Dave Porter adds, "Johnnie is selling one-hundred-percent message. He's capable of getting any message over."

Taylor's first hit (1969) was also the fastest-selling record in the history of Stax. In just five weeks, "Who's Making Love?" aggregated sales large enough to earn him a Gold Record. Overnight success it was. But Taylor had paid his dues. Born in Crawfordsville, West Memphis, Arkansas, in 1937, the son of a minister, he was singing in a church choir at six. On his radio he loved to listen to Sonny Boy Williamson and Junior Parker.

When he was fifteen he left Arkansas and took a job in a Cleveland chemical plant, singing with a gospel group in his spare time. In Chicago, his next stop, he became associated with the Five Echoes, a group that recorded for Vee Jay and that filled out the bill on tours with the Spaniels, the Flamingos, Moonglows, and Billy Ward and the Dominoes.

During the decade in which he lived in Chicago, he also became part of the Soul Stirrers on the recommendation of Sam Cooke, whom he replaced. The Stirrers were an important gospel group that traveled with Mahalia Jackson and made appearances at places like Carnegie Hall and Madison Square Garden. From Chicago, he migrated to Kansas City and then to Los Angeles, where he lived for three years. When he made an attempt to go it alone in 1960, Sam Cooke got him onto his Sar label. His first album on Stax was titled *Wanted:One Soul Singer*. He had the sound but needed the right song.

The opening screech of "Who's Making Love?" instantly brings to mind James Brown. Taylor can match the intense expressiveness of any of the ecstasy singers. But "Poor Make Believer" on Side 2 of the album suggests that Sam Cooke was as potent an influence as Taylor's years of gospel shouting. Taylor has the sweetness and intonation of Cooke, perhaps with a thicker strain of hoarseness.

"When I joined the Soul Stirrers," he explains, "they

needed a voice just like Sam's. I really had to work at changing." His present attitude: "Please don't bag me as a blues singer. Bobby Bland and B. B. King [two of his favorite bluesmen] are always telling me to stick with the blues. They tell me that's what I do best. But blues is too limited and I don't want to limit my career."

The career of Eddie Floyd, who made the Top Ten in 1966 for the first time, developed along lines that parallel Johnnie Taylor, beginning with a gospel group in Montgomery, Alabama. For a time he worked with the Falcons, a group that included Wilson Pickett, for whom Eddie later wrote "634–5789."

Floyd's gospel moorings are evident in songs like "Someone's Watching Over You," recorded by Atlantic's Solomon Burke, and "Comfort Me," a Carla Thomas disk. His first stint for Stax in 1962 was as a writer-producer. With Al Bell, now executive vice-president of Stax and then a Washington, D.C., disk jockey, he produced Carla's disk of "Comfort Me."

Idolizing singer Johnny Ace, Floyd hungered for the chance to record rather than supervising others. After he joined the Stax family in 1965, his first solo release was "Things Get Better." They had to—and they did with "Knock on Wood," a song he wrote with Steve Cropper.

His more recent song, "A Saturday Night," benefits greatly from his experience as a producer and hints at the many influences on his work. To make the record, he explains, "I got the spiritual group, the Dixie Nightingales, to do the harmony part. I got the bass line from one of those 'doo-wop' groups. Then I got the guitar idea from Hank Ballard and the Midnighters. I think it was 'There's a Thrill on the Hill.' You know that old tinny guitar. Then I put in the shuffle beat, as in Wilson Pickett's disk of '634–5789.' "

One of the more recent additions to the Stax family is a bluesman of the early fifties who languished for audience and acceptance until he began recording in Memphis in 1966. Now bluesmoppets searching the mud bayous for a soul guru "have finally found him," according to rock critic Richard Goldstein, "in Albert King. Thanks to their ardor, Albert has busted out of the pop ghetto and now he plays to reverent audiences wherever he ventures into the Day-Glo realm of hip rock."

The deification was a long time coming to B. B. King's half brother, who was born in the heart of the Mississippi delta country in Indianola in April, 1923. The fatherless family of thirteen moved about a good deal, and Albert early earned his livelihood at hard man's labor. As soon as he was strong enough, he left farm work to operate heavy construction equipment.

"Actually I'm a bulldozer operator," he has said. "I traveled all through Mississippi, Arkansas, and Tennessee and a lot of other places on construction. I was a mechanic for four years. I was a short-order cook and truck driver." And, with a candor rare in show biz circles, he told Jim Delehant of *Hit Parader*, "Sometimes I think I'd like to go back to driving a bulldozer. This music can get awful boring. You can't rest when you want to and you can't stop when you get ready. There's always somebody that's got to see you. You can't say no because they get mad."

To purists who hear in this less than the monolithic dedication that they associate with blues gods and ethnic performers, learning of the diverse influences to which Albert King admits will likewise be something of a shock. By his own admission, he early listened to the Mills Brothers and the Golden Gate Quartet.

"I was particularly crazy," he says, "about Woody Herman's band. He had 'Blue Flame' and 'Uptown Blues.' Then there were the Dorsey brothers. I was crazy about their band because they could play 'Jumpin' at the Woodside.' Boogie-woogie piano was real big then and I loved it. . . ."

And to the consternation of folk fanatics, who view country bluesmen as if they lived in a vacuum devoid of all impurities, he savored and liked country music, or, rather, western swing. Once when he was working as a chauffeur, he stopped off in El Paso.

"We worked on a ranch there that must have been a hundred miles long," he recalls. "The owner put on a party and barbecue, and they had Bob Wills and the Texas Playboys perform for dance music. . . . It was jitterbug music. All the teenagers really went for it. . . . Shuffle rhythm grew out of boogie-woogie when some dude got the idea he could play the same walking time on the piano. . . . The Bob Wills band could play that stuff better than anybody I've ever heard. He could even do it with violins. . . ."

King also listened to rock 'n' roll, or what sounded like it. "The first time I ever ran into it," he says, "was in the 1940s in a little Virginia town. I heard Fats Domino's band and Ray Charles. This was long before they were popular." And doubtless some time before they played rock, a development of the mid-fifties.

Despite these diverse sounds, many of which he liked, King was and is a delta bluesman. He had taught himself to play guitar by listening to records, mostly those of T-Bone Walker and Blind Lemon Jefferson. It is said that his first instrument was an ingenious device consisting of whisk broom wires strung from nails in the floor to nails in a wall. He learned to fret, like most country bluesmen from Bukka White to John Lee Hooker, with the broken neck of a bottle.

He did not see an electric guitar until he was seventeen and had saved enough money to travel into Memphis to catch the Dorsey band. King bought his first electric some years later when he was working in Little Rock, Arkansas. Now he owns four electrics: a big, powerful Showman amplifier for gigs, an Epiphone, a Gibson V-shaped flyer, and, for recording, "a little bitty Fender amp, about as big as the biggest clock radio."

Regardless of which he plays, at least one reviewer (Albert Goldman) has described King's impact as follows: "Squeezed from tough, dirty Delta roots, filtered through taut metal mesh and boiled down to an attar of acerbity, King's music cuts like fretted steel, burns like dry ice and thrills like an electric needle in a nerve. A fusion of the ancient Mississippi 'bottleneck' style and the sighing, swooning, 'psychedelic' sound of the Hawaiian steel guitar, King's blue note is so 'nasty', so cruelly inciting, that after a quarter of an hour under its spell, one itches for a bottle to break and a face to cut."

Even if one makes allowance for the neon-bright rhetoric, it is hard to avoid the conclusion that King is a bluesman of rare power.

Contrary to Goldman's assertion that King's first efforts at recording were "a big batch" of blues for Bobbin Records in St. Louis in 1956, Albert made his first records in Chicago almost three years earlier (December, 1953) and he cut only two sides for the Parrot label. The "big batch" he did cut for Bobbin in St. Louis was made, not in 1956, but over a three-year period in 1959, 1960, and 1961–62. These were less than world-shaking. Nor did King stir listeners greatly with seven sides he cut for King Records around 1962 and four sides he made in 1965 in East St. Louis for Coun-tree Records.

In Goldman's view, the sides King cut for Stax in 1966 are "a true country sound undefiled by commercialism." How do we reconcile this assertion with Goldman's comment that "I Love Lucy"—a single that made the charts—"seems at first listening not much better than the novelty numbers that once were ground out by the white Tin Pan Alley: a love song about a girl who turns out to be a guitar"? And is "I Love Lucy" an uncommercial title? Moreover, what does Goldman mean by his statement that King's guitar playing "sets a new standard for purity of style" when he himself had earlier noted that King's blues were a fusion of two styles? What we encounter here is that ridiculous concern of fanatics for a purism that neither has historical or esthetic validity nor is meaningful to performers, folk, pop, rock, or soul.

If we believe that, in music, feeling is the essence of greatness of performance, then it is clear that performers alter with time and changes in their own situations. What moved Albert King as an adolescent or as an artist hungering for an audience probably would not stir him at a time when he had large-scale acceptance. And what excited him in the R & B fifties may have had no impact on him in the soulful sixties.

Speaking about the blues, Albert King has said, "What most people don't understand is that it has no color. It's just a musical language that man uses to express his inner self. . . . You might call the blues a problem song." And he adds sagely, "The old blues made sense in their day but the problems today are different."

King's impact today is the result, not of his ethnic purity, but of his ability, as Pete Johnson noted in the *Los Angeles Times,* to bring "the traditional irony . . . pathos and comedy of the blues into a mid-20th century setting."

Take as an instance King's recording of "Laundromat Blues," the first side he cut for Stax in 1966. Infidelity is the theme, as it has been of hundreds of blues. But the lady's doin' her dirt in a very contemporary setting—the laundromat. In another blues, he updates traditional imagery. "I want to be your personal manager, baby," he sings. "I want to do everything for you/If you sign my contract, baby/All your worries are through."

One can reject this as commercialism or dismiss it as impure revisionism. But Albert King has had the experience of personal managers that promised everything. It's not Blind Lemon Jefferson's bag. Additionally, the updating that is expressive of his own feelings makes them meaningful to today's audience. Then why, except for a dreary dogmatism dear to the hearts of purists, should Albert King sing his blues the way they were sung in the twenties?

His achievement is aptly described by Al Bell, Stax's exec VP. "Albert King has taken one extreme," he has said, "the gutbucket blues in its rural form, transposed all elements except its reality, and added a touch of urbanism. Thus his style becomes contemporary and communicable. Those who enjoyed the naked blues twenty years ago still appreciate Albert King. In addition to his faithful followers of yesteryear, Albert has become a top artist because of the new breed, the hippies and the Europeans. To them, Albert is the father of modern blues."

As Atlantic Records was bought by Warner Bros.-Seven Arts, so in 1968 Stax/Volt was purchased by Paramount Pictures, which in turn became part of the Gulf and Western conglomerate. During '68 Stax expanded from a mere production studio (whose disks were manufactured, promoted, and released by Atlantic Records) into a full-fledged record manufacturer. Doubtless the celerity with which Johnnie Taylor's recording of "Who's Making Love?" racked up phenomenal sales was in part due to Stax's new control of its product. In the same period, Stax acquired and released its first motion picture sound track, the score written by Booker T. for *Up Tight*. It happened to be a Paramount picture.

Whether the vast expansion, including the formation of a new subsidiary, Hip Records, will result in a dilution or transformation of the Memphis Sound is a matter for speculation. Certainly the character of one new artist group recently added to the family does not suggest any change of direction or style.

The Staple Singers have been characterized as "the first family of gospel." Contrasting them with other gospel commandos of the Lord who "overwhelm their audience by force or volume and insistently spiralling rhythms," critic Nat Hentoff observes that they are "softer in texture but burn more deeply and for a longer time. Rather than exploding in tambourine-whacking euphoria, they are introspective, so much so that a listener gets the impression he's overhearing a family service."

And that's actually the way the Staple Singers began. The quartet is a family group, consisting of Roebuck "Pop" Staple, daughters Cleothe and Mavis, and son Purvis. As Cleo tells it, "A man to whom pop had lent some money left his guitar as security and never claimed it. So in the evening after work, pop would get us all together and we'd sing hymns and spirituals. It was his favorite form of relaxation."

"It was all for fun," brother Purvis states. "Until one day somebody got sick and they called up and asked if we'd fill in for 'em at church. We did it and the congregation kept shouting for more. After that, we did some other churches and then weekend jobs in South Bend and Gary, Indiana."

Eventually, the group cut a single for United Records, "Sit Down Servant," and then one for Vee Jay, "Cloudy Day." From 1962 on, the Staple Singers began to garner awards from *Down Beat*, the *Chicago Courier*, and elsewhere. In recent years, more and more interest has focused on the voice of Mavis, who has succeeded Pop as lead singer and whose contralto range extends from near-baritone to high soprano. More than one critic has compared her vocal thrust and emotional expressiveness with those of Aretha Franklin.

"We're trying to carry a freedom message," Purvis Staple said recently. "We're relating the black experience. The white man can't relate to the black experience 'cause he hasn't had it, and now we're trying to give it to him. One reason we changed our way of singing from straight gospel to this new style is 'cause we want to reach more people—we want them to know what we're singing about. And it's for sure we couldn't have gotten to all the concert halls we've played so far as a pure gospel group."

The new style, typed "soul folk," has given their first album on Stax its title, *Soul Folk in Action*. The producer is M.G. guitarist Steve Cropper. Out of it came the exciting single "Long Walk to D.C.," with instrumental background by Booker T. and the M.G.'s. Like Albert King, the Staple Singers are unconcerned with *purity*. They sing and record in order to communicate. To do so, they must deal with contemporary problems in contemporary terms. Gospel purity, like ethnic purity, can only result in a dedicated alienation and isolation.

Significant as the Stax/Volt contribution has been, the Memphis Sound encompasses more than its family of record makers. Although Sam Phillips, the founder of Sun Records, is no longer active as a record producer, his studio operates full time and he remains the acknowledged father of the Memphis record industry, today estimated to be a fifty-million-dollar enterprise.

Among those who cut up this pie are Joe Cuoghi, a former grocer who admittedly cannot carry a tune but who runs Hi Records; Rudolph "Doc" Russell, a successful pharmacist, responsible for Goldwax; Stan Kessler, a guitarist and former Phillips producer who recently opened a $250,000 studio known as Sounds of Memphis; Lyn-Lou Recording Studio, housing the independent producing team of Dan Penn and Spooner

Oldham; and American Recording Studios, founded by Chips Moman and Don Crews in 1964.

Jerry Wexler, Atlantic Records producer who frequently travels south for recording sessions, includes two other studios in the Memphis Sound: Rick Hall's Fame Recording Studio at Muscle Shoals, Alabama, and Quin Ivy's and Marlin Greene's Quin Ivy Recording Studio at Sheffield, Alabama. Both towns are a 125-mile drive due east from Memphis on the Alabama border. In *Billboard*'s 1968 survey of the country's Hot 100 Producers, Ivy and Greene were rated number fifty-five and Rick Hall and staff, number sixteen.

Guitarist Chips Moman, a producer at Stax in its early days, has quietly established a reputation that brings artists from all over the United States to Memphis' American Recording Studios. Early in 1969 Elvis Presley flew in from Hollywood to cut seventy sides. About the same time, Dionne Warwick jetted in from New York and Moman ended as coproducer of her new LP, *Soulful*.

Buddy Killen of Nashville's Dial Records has brought Joe Tex to Moman for highly rewarding sessions. Moman has also proved himself adept at finding talent. One of his discoveries, Sandy Posey, started as a secretary and backup singer in the studio. The Box Tops, another of his finds, finished in the high twenties in *Billboard*'s 1969 survey of Top Singles Artists. Chips himself checked in at number thirty-five among the nation's Hot 100 Producers.

When Aretha Franklin first moved to Atlantic Records, Moman and his partner Tommy Cogbill cut her sessions at Muscle Shoals, with Moman playing guitar and Cogbill bass. (Cogbill, incidentally, scored at the country's number twenty-four Hot Producer.) The demand for time at American Recording Studios became so great that Moman recently opened a second studio in the eastern end of Memphis.

Discussions of the Memphis Sound inevitably involve the name of Joe Cuoghi, a much-decorated veteran of World War II, who opened a successful record shop after being mustered out of service. There are partisans who argue that the Memphis

Sound was popularized by the owner of Poplar Tunes, as he called his store at Poplar and Danny Thomas Boulevard. In 1956 he added record making to his endeavors and launched the Hi label. That same year he found Bill Black and his combo, putting Hi on R & B charts, and also on Pop, with instrumentals like "Smokey," "Don't Be Cruel," a vocal hit for Presley, and "White Silver Sands," a number-one disk. Soon a horn player named Ace Cannon was making hits for Hi, among them "Tuff." Still partial to instrumentalists, Cuoghi is currently riding with trumpeter Willie Mitchell, whose albums include *Soul Serenade* and *Solid Soul*. Some of Cuoghi's ads on Hi carry the legend, "The Label that created the Memphis Sound."

While the Memphis Sound appears to have identity in terms of the Stax family of artists mainly because one group of musicians (Booker T. and the M.G.'s) created its sonorities and texture, that identity becomes rather elusive when we seek to discover the common denominator among Bill Black, Booker T., and Willie Mitchell. Not unlike Soul, the Memphis Sound has now become a promotional handle as well as an esthetic entity. In concept if not in composition, it must undergo diffusion as more and more Memphis studios, musicians, producers, and singers seek to exploit it and the market for it widens and increases. Stax's ability to retain its identity as part of the Gulf and Western conglomerate poses questions. Unquestionably, public taste for Soul music will be the decisive factor.

C. Atlantic: The Harlem Sound

This heading is a misnomer. There is no one Atlantic or Harlem Sound, as its eight-volume *History of Rhythm and Blues* clearly reveals. Atlantic is a sound conglomerate. It has Aretha and it once had Ray Charles, also The Drifters, the Clovers, and The Coasters. It has wicked Wilson Pickett and Solomon Burke, and also jazz flutist Herbie Mann. It has Percy Sledge, Arthur Conley, and King Curtis, as well as the Rascals, Bee Gees, and Vanilla Fudge. But in *Billboard*'s year-end survey of Top R & B labels of 1968 it soared sublimely to number one both in Singles and Albums, outdistancing Motown and Stax, its nearest, hard-running competitors.

Atlantic was incorporated in October, 1947, but its first releases did not appear until the following year. They were not R & B disks. Herb Abramson and Ahmet Ertegun, the founders, had met in Washington, D.C. Ertegun, son of the Turkish ambassador to the United States, and his brother Nesuhi were jazz collectors who were able to open the doors of the embassy to frequent jam sessions. Abramson, a government employee during the war years, who was also a jazz collector, helped the brothers move the jams out of the embassy into a Washington concert hall. Thus, when Ahmet and Herb went into business they hoped to produce jazz and blues recordings.

Their first releases were, in fact, instrumental disks by jazz artists like Erroll Garner and the bands of Boyd Raeburn, Eddie Safranski, Joe Morris, and Tiny Grimes. Grimes's "Old Black Magic" and Joe Morris's "The Spider" were solid sellers, but Atlantic's first smash was an old blues known as "Drinkin' Wine Spo-dee-o-dee" by Sticks McGhee.

The label's first star was sloe-eyed Ruth Brown, daughter of a Portsmouth, Virginia, choir director, who became vocalist of the Lucky Millinder band in 1948. She was just twenty but so impressive that Cab Calloway's sister Blanche became her personal manager after hearing her once at Washington's Crystal Caverns.

Instead of bringing Ruth to the Atlantic offices for an audition, Miss Calloway arranged for her charge to be heard at her debut at the Apollo Theatre on October 29, 1948. But on that date Miss Brown lay in a hospital in Chester, Pennsylvania, recovering from two broken legs and other injuries suffered in an automobile accident. Eventually, Ruth Brown cut her first Atlantic session wearing leg braces. Out of that session—she was backed by Eddie Condon's Dixieland combo with Joe Bushkin on piano and Will Bradley on trombone—came "So Long," the record that made her an overnight star.

It is interesting that when Ahmet Ertegun met with her to discuss material, she told him she did not like blues. This is as much a comment on the times as on Miss Brown. Moreover, this was a period when black artists were not unwilling to forget their roots in order to crack the white market.

"As a result," Ertegun notes, "the blues records we made with Ruth came out like urbanized, watered-down versions of real blues. But we discovered that white kids started buying these records because the real blues were too hard for them to swallow. Distributors started telling us that they were selling these records as pop."

On the company's tenth anniversary, Ertegun observed, "What we did manage to achieve was something like the authentic blues, but cleaner, less rough, and perforce more sophisticated." Ruth Brown's diction was clean, her intonation only mildly black, and the blues coloring (occasional melisma and screechy glisses) delicate. But how she did swing. "Miss Rhythm" was a well-chosen appellation.

In 1950 Atlantic signed the first of several groups that were to become important in its history and in the development of R & B. The Clovers, who came from the Washington-Baltimore area, had a number-one hit in their first release, "Don't You Know I Love You," written by Amhet Ertegun under his pen name, Nugetre. From mid-1951 almost to the end of the decade, the Clovers produced a steady flow of best sellers, among them "One Mint Julep" and "Devil or Angel."

Listening to these disks in Atlantic's eight-volume *History of Rhythm and Blues*, one instantly hears a contrast between the Ravens and Orioles—who have a smooth pop-harmony sound like the Ink Spots and Mills Brothers—and the Clovers, whose first disk is not quite boogie, not quite bop, not quite R & B, but a rough admixture set to a propulsive riff. The tenor sax is in evidence, hardly as raucous or as exciting as it became in the hands of Sam "The Man" Taylor and King Curtis. But from the start, instead of sweet three-part Mills Brothers harmony, the Clovers worked as a typical R & B group, with a lead shouter and a rhythmic background trio. After a time, the thrust of call-and-response patterns developed into big-beat power.

The other two Atlantic groups that made history were The Drifters and The Coasters. The former came into being in what the *History of R & B* types the Golden Years, 1953 to 1955. R & B was then like an active volcano whose hot lava was beginning to run down the black mountainside into white valleys, overwhelming precursors of rock 'n' roll like Bill Haley and others.

In 1953 Atlantic signed Clyde McPhatter, who took his trenchant tenor from Billy Ward and the Dominoes to form The Drifters. Whereas the Dominoes had a gospel orientation that gave McPhatter a revival meeting leadership, The Drifters took a more secular direction that made them and him R & B giants. Scoring with "Money Honey" in late 1953, followed quickly by the calypso-gaited "Honey Love," they produced so many hits disks that almost half of Volume 4 of the *History of Rhythm and Blues* is devoted to their tracks.

Among these hits of the Big Beat years, 1958 to 1960, one finds "A Lover's Question," "There Goes My Baby," "Dance with Me," "(If You Cry) True Love, True Love," "This Magic Moment," "Save the Last Dance for Me," and "I Count My Tears." (As Nugetre's songwriting helped the Clovers account for many of their hot disks, so the team of Doc Pomus and Mort Shuman was responsible for the last four titles on The Drifters' list.)

In these records of the late fifties and early sixties, R & B had acquired a sophistication that allowed for the involvement of strings and big bands of eight reeds, five brass, and five rhythm, with tailored arrangements by Stan Applebaum, an experienced pop arranger-conductor. As McPhatter stepped out on his own with the finger-snapping "A Lover's Question," The Drifters' lead voice became Ben E. King, who soon also went single-o with the memorable "Stand By Me" and Latin-colored "Spanish Harlem."

Atlantic acquired The Coasters in 1956 through the purchase of a West Coast company, Sparks Records, whose assets also included the writing-producing team of Jerry Leiber and Mike Stoller. Originally known as the Robins and formed in 1955 by Lester Sills, now a Screen Gems-Columbia Pictures executive, The Coasters consisted of Carl Gardner, a Texan whose lead tenor is heard on "Smokey Joe's Cafe" and "Young Blood";

Billy Guy, baritone, lead on "Searchin'" and once Bip of the comic singing duo Bip and Bop; bass Bobby Nunn, who had worked with the Johnny Otis band and had a hit single, "Double Crossin' Blues," on Savoy; tenor Leon Hughes, once a member of the Four Flames; and guitarist Al Jacobs, who became permanently affiliated with the group after subbing for the regular guitarist. Two of the group, Carl Gardner and Billy Guy, were still Coasters when the group performed at Unltd!, formerly the Cafe Wha!, in New York's Greenwich Village in May of 1969.

"Smokey Joe's Cafe," cut before the Robins became The Coasters in 1956, opens Volume 3 of the *History of Rhythm and Blues*. The work of Leiber and Stoller, it is a well-made disk, with a better-integrated story-lyric than many R & B songs. The two-sided hit, "Searchin'" and "Young Blood," is likewise marked by a provocative, dramatic interplay between lead voice and group. But none of the three measure up to the two Leiber and Stoller songs and Coaster disks that appear in Volume 4.

"Yakety Yak," the Gold Record opener of the Volume, deals with the conflict between youngsters and parents who disapprove of the company their kids keep and find them lazy and neglectful of their chores. The song and the record are novel in construction. The title "Yakety Yak" appears only as a throwaway group comment at the end of each verse. Having listened to an enumeration of parental gripes and complaints, a bass voice advises, "Don't go back," and the group sneers, "Yakety yak/Yakety yak." Satirical commentary has seldom been so engagingly made.

"Charlie Brown" is another outstanding Leiber-Stoller song and Coasters record. As the group enumerates Brown's escapades (and sly attacks on authority), a deep bass voice gives expression to Charlie's not-entirely-believable innocence, "Why is everybody always pickin' on me?" The record is a hilarious three-minute dramatic comedy. Both songs suggest how far R & B had progressed from its crude postwar beginnings. Yet both records are marked by a drive, ebullience, and excitement associated with mumble-worded R & B.

Rock 'n' roll history was also made by a short-lived group called the Chords, whose seminal record release appeared on the Cat label, an Atlantic subsidiary that also disappeared after a brief existence. Insofar as I can recall—and I was personally involved in the "Sh-Boom" story—Atlantic executives did not know what to make of the record cut by the Chords. They felt that it had something. But what? And if it was a bomb, as appeared likely, why tarnish the highly respected Atlantic name with a dismal flop?

But "Sh-Boom" was not a flop. It literally made history. For one thing, it was a studio-written song, a practice adopted by many of the rock groups of today. The record label in Volume 2 of the *History of Rhythm and Blues* contains five names as the authors-composers. They are the names of the Chords.

Cut in March, 1954, "Sh-Boom" quietly sailed to the top of Los Angeles charts, outdistancing the Gaylords, Perry Como, and the Four Aces, top-selling pop artists of the day. I was then with Hill & Range Songs, a Broadway publishing firm, and accidentally learned of this development. When I heard the record itself, I must confess that I felt very much like the Atlantic executives, impressed but nonplussed. However, the fact that the disk could outsell the big name artists of the day was even more impressive.

I went to the Atlantic execs and tried to purchase the song. They would sell only 50 percent of it, and I plunked down six thousand dollars of Hill & Range's money for the slice. Within days or weeks, the same fact that had moved me motivated Mercury Records to cut the song with a new young group from Canada. They called themselves the Crewcuts, and their cover disk of "Sh-Boom" became a smash during the summer of 1954.

It antedated "Dance with Me Henry," "Tweedle Dee," and "Sincerely," all early rock 'n' roll hits, and anticipated Bill Haley's earthshaking "Rock Around the Clock" by a year. Elvis Presley did not shake up the older generation with his black, raucous voice and his suggestive hip swiveling and knee-knocking until the fall of 1955, and his first record hit, "Heartbreak Hotel," did not make number one until May, 1956. Historically, "Sh-Boom" was the first major rock 'n' roll hit.

As far as exciting solo singers are concerned, Atlantic has no shortage—from Joe Turner to Aretha Franklin. Big Joe Turner, who hailed from Kansas City, was tackling the New York scene for the second time when Atlantic signed him in 1951. A stint with Benny Goodman during the swing era was topped by an appearance at the famous Carnegie Hall Spirituals to Swing concert sponsored and produced by John Hammond. But the impact of the records he made in those years had not carried over to the years after World War II.

"Chains of Love," his first release on Atlantic, marked the beginning of a new career. A slow blues by Nugetre and Van Walls, it had a nervous, whorehouse-piano background that would have overwhelmed a less powerful vocalist than Turner.

A succession of R & B hits followed, including "Honey Hush," "Sweet Sixteen," and, in the summer of 1954, Charles Calhoun's evergreen, "Shake, Rattle and Roll." The last mentioned, audible in Volume 2 of the *History of Rhythm and Blues,* had a rolling piano background, with a burping upbeat baritone and a tubby afterbeat drum laying down the rhythm. Time has not cooled its ebullience, which moved Bill Haley and His Comets to cover Turner in 1954 and Arthur Conley to revive it in 1967. In the spring of 1956 Turner delivered a shuffle beat "Corrine, Corrina," his booming voice given a cutting edge by a girl's background group. The chick, associated originally with Cab Calloway, was still a rocking earth angel.

The career of LaVern Baker, signed by Atlantic in 1953, began before she was old enough to secure a cabaret license in Chicago, her hometown. A tour with the Todd Rhodes band and personal appearances in Europe preceded her Atlantic association. Her first big hit, the Latin-inflected "Tweedle Dee," did better for writer Winfield Scott and singer Georgia Gibbs, who covered her in the pop field, than it did for LaVern. But the excitement generated by the competition made Baker one of the highest-paid performers of the day. Atlantic's use of the male Cues behind LaVern, originally tried on Ruth Brown's hit record of "Oh, What A Dream," was then still considered a novelty. Georgia

Gibbs copied Miss Baker's record of Lincoln Chase's "Jim Dandy" two years later, but was unable to duplicate her Gold Record success with "Tweedle Dee."

In 1958 LaVern produced her first million seller, curiously not in the robust, shout type of song she had been doing, but in a 6/8 ballad, "I Cried a Tear," which was not quite a jazz waltz. The textural contrasts in her rendition are indicative of the sophistication R & B was developing at Atlantic. Her 1962 version of "See See Rider," the Ma Rainey blues, replete with a tailored score by pop arranger Ray Ellis, underscored this development.

Solomon Burke, who was signed by Atlantic in November, 1960, was celebrated in his native Philadelphia as "the Wonder Boy Preacher." At twelve he had his own church, known as Solomon's Temple, from which he broadcast his own radio show. Although his earliest recording was a spiritual, "Christmas Presents from Heaven," his first Atlantic hit, "Just Out of Reach (Of My Two Empty Arms)," gave no hint of his profound gospel orientation. In succeeding releases like "If You Need Me" and "Everybody Needs Somebody to Love," he displayed deep feeling for big ballads. But it was the sympathetic emotion of the preacher for members of his flock.

In 1964 Burke, who is an ordained minister, was crowned King of Rock 'n' Soul by Dee Jay Rockin' Robin of WEBB in Baltimore. It was a well-earned recognition of the qualities that make "Cry to Me" one of Burke's most moving records. Just as Ray Charles's "I've Got a Woman" and "What'd I Say" represent early weddings of gospel and the blues, "Cry to Me" is one of the earliest manifestations of Soul. In one segment, Burke's emotionalism climbs to such heights that the word "cry" becomes "crack" and his feelings pour forth in an uncontrolled stutter that makes him sound like a rooster cackling.

Atlantic's contribution to soul music was a mighty phase of its development, as the final section of this book will demonstrate. Three of its key figures, Ray Charles, Wilson Pickett, and Aretha Franklin, attained their majority on the label. But before it took a tough black course, in which Solomon

Burke proved the turning point, Atlantic seemed headed in a white, a soulful white, direction.

It may be coincidence that Ray Charles's departure from the label came after Atlantic's pop orientation had become clearly defined. It may also be coincidental that Atlantic's soul turn occurred after it had developed a working relationship with Stax/ Volt and the creators of the Memphis Sound. The decisive factors in the shift were nonmusical—the crisis in white-black relations that developed in the 1960s and the impact of black nationalism on Negro artists and audiences.

Volume 4 of the *History of Rhythm and Blues* covers the years 1958–60 in Atlantic's development. One is immediately struck by the marked presence of a sound not heard until then on R & B disks—violins. Not fiddles, but violins. On Drifters' records, the string choir plays sustained chords and counter-melodies, and takes an instrumental eight-bar segment ("This Magic Moment"). In "Spanish Harlem" the strings take most of a full chorus.

On Atlantic's tenth anniversary in 1958, president Ahmet Ertegun observed, "Throughout the early years we were putting out a 'popularized' R & B record that seemed to be admired. But when Clyde McPhatter returned from the army, we went much farther to the straight pop side with 'Seven Days.' This retained only vestigial touches of R & B. It was the first date on which we used arranger Ray Ellis."

Ertegun and his associates regard the use of studio musicians and written arrangements with blues singer as "one of their first and really major departures." His explanation: They had to record blues singers in New York City without the hinterland combos that rely entirely on "head arrangements." Ertegun goes on to say, "This brought about the evolution of a blues arranging style and the development of such now well-established arrangers as Jesse Stone, Howard Biggs, Budd Johnson, and later Ray Ellis. It also developed a new breed of sidemen, readers who could play real blues. A record like Ruth Brown's 'Teardrops from My Eyes,' with Budd Johnson's pop but blues-directed dance band arrangement, was quite an innovation."

Queried about the Atlantic Sound on the label's tenth anniversary, Ertegun replied, "The secret of our sound is in the arrangement itself."

Ertegun adverted to one other facet of the so-called Atlantic Sound: "One thing that has remained from the first dates we made is a prominent and clean rhythm sound, which we inherited from the jazz and country blues recordings of the past. We were, along with one or two other independent companies, the first to start cutting the drums, bass, and guitar separately. The Indian in the picture on our wall"—a reference to a well-known promotional illustration used in the Jack Kapp years at Decca—"would stand over the caption and ask, 'Where's the beat?' rather than 'Where's the melody?' " (The latter concern was Decca's.) And Atlantic's concern with the beat can hardly be considered a unique facet of an R & B label.

On Atlantic's twentieth anniversary, an entirely different type of emphasis was apparent. In June, 1968, Atlantic in association with the five hundred black members of NATRA (National Association of Television and Radio Announcers) sponsored a Madison Square Garden concert for the Martin Luther King Memorial Fund and the NATRA Summer Program for Underprivileged Children.

"Soul Together," as the show was called, featured five of Atlantic's biggest stars: Aretha Franklin, the Rascals, Sonny and Cher, Sam & Dave—Stax artists distributed by Atlantic—and Joe Tex, a Dial artist likewise distributed by Atlantic.

Not long afterward, Atlantic executive Jerry Wexler stated, "We don't do records of white kids making bad imitations of Negro singers. We give them the real thing."

Adverting to Miss Franklin's explosive emergence in 1967, he observed, "The popularity of Aretha's kind of music is connected with something else. Call it the Negro Emergence, the Black Revolution, whatever. But the fact is that Negroes are starting to make it on *their* terms. They are singing *their* songs to white audiences, so both Negroes *and* soul music are more popular."

Named Record Executive of the Year in 1968 as well as '69 in a poll of industry executives and disk jockeys, Wexler had joined Atlantic in 1953. The company was then grossing under one million a year. In 1967, its reported gross was $22.5 million, a little more than one-third of the grosses of such majors as Columbia, Capitol, and RCA. Atlantic's so-called black policy was paying off just as its popularized R & B had paid off early in its existence.

Although some of its older artists continued to deliver hits in the sixties—The Drifters had best sellers in "On Broadway" and "Up on the Roof," LaVern Baker in "See See Rider"—new artists began to build the Atlantic catalog in that decade.

In addition to Solomon Burke and Wilson Pickett, there was Barbara Lewis, who scored a number-one Smash in "Hello Stranger" (1963). Although Barbara was then still a teen-ager, her voice had a robust fullness and her delivery carried nuances characteristic of a mature singer. "Baby, I'm Yours" and "Make Me Your Baby" were succeeding chart climbers, demonstrating that Barbara was a vocalist of quality. (In the former, her voice had an oboe timbre that was both exotic and appealing.) But Miss Lewis still awaits the recognition that comes to a singer with one big smash.

With Don Covay's 1964 disk of "Mercy, Mercy," Atlantic's pipeline to the South began to gush hit platters at Memphis, Sheffield, and Muscle Shoals, shortly yielding Gold Records with Wilson Pickett, Percy Sledge, and Arthur Conley. Covay was co-writer and coproducer of the Rosemart recording of "Mercy, Mercy," whose soulful sound surfaced in a gospel service before the needle reached the terminal groove. Covay was co-writer with Steve Cropper of "Seesaw," a Stax-produced hit for him in 1965. Three years later, Aretha Franklin revived "Seesaw," having in the meantime made a million-copy seller of his song "Chain of Fools." Covay was also co-writer with Wilson Pickett of the latter's hit on Atlantic in 1964, "I'm Gonna Cry."

If there is a nonbeliever in the house who doubts the sheer force of rhythm and repetition, let him put a Wilson Pickett disk on his player and demonstrate that he can resist the suasion of Pickett's beat. His songs are as elementary as a catechism and, not infrequently, a ragbag of clichés. But he has a compelling sound, drive, and conviction. King Curtis notes

211

that he "performs in the studio just as he does on stage—jumps around, dances and the sweat pours off."

Born in Prattville, Alabama, in the same year as Otis Redding (1941), Pickett spent many years in Detroit singing spirituals.

"Since you were involved in gospel music," he was asked by *Hit Parader*, "would you consider yourself a religious person?"

His reply was, "I was at the time and I think I could be again, if I set my mind to it."

In reply to the query, "Do you think that most gospel groups are sincere about religion?" he said, "Uh! Ha! Ha! You know, I guess a human is human. Even a preacher likes that midnight dew. It's all in the line of duty, I guess."

Pickett is interesting and baffling, precisely because there's nothing hokey about him. He tells it like it is. "They're good people," he said of the Atlantic crowd. "I never worry about getting paid or getting promotion. Anywhere you go, a disk jockey can smile in your face. You know, he won't drop his head down if you walk in, because the company's taking care of business."

Because his lines are unrehearsed and unrefined, he raises some basic questions. And because his songs are the acme of simplicity and he communicates on so basic a level, he demonstrates the pure power of gospel techniques—the contagion of driving, synchronized rhythm, antiphonal voicing, hard repetition, and mounting excitement. (And let us not overlook the cotton-belt, down-home musicianship of the studio bands at Memphis and Muscle Shoals.)

On how many records does Pickett use the expression, "Git it! Git it! Git it!" snapping the words out like the flick of a whip? How often does he repeat the phrase "midnight hour," a special time for him and the title of one of his big songs and albums? And in how many songs is there lyric development beyond the title?

Listen to "I Found a Love," which comes in two parts, no less, and its very illuminating chorus, "Yeah. Yeah. Yeah. Yeah." But there's no missing the impact. Pickett is "wicked," as one of his album titles has it, and regardless of whether the song is called "Soul Dance Number Three," "Mojo Mama," or "Mustang Sally," Wilson is selling just one thing—pure, unadulterated sex. Not in word, not in concept—but the feel and sound of it.

Pickett did not give up spiritual singing until 1959, when he joined the Falcons, one of Detroit's top R & B vocal groups. During his four years as a Falcon, he not only attracted notice as a singer but proved himself a hit songwriter. Among the group's best sellers was "I Found a Love," which we wrote. By 1963 he was recording solo for Lloyd Price's Double LL label.

A song he composed and recorded led to his being signed by Atlantic. The song was "If You Need Me" and it was Solomon Burke's cover on Atlantic—it substantially outsold Pickett's Double LL disk—that stirred interest in him. "If You Need Me" was subsequently recorded by Bill Doggett, the Rolling Stones, and Tom Jones. Pickett's follow-up song, "It's Too Late," moved Atlantic to sign him.

His biggest song is "Midnight Hour," on which he collaborated with Steve Cropper during his first recording session at the Stax studio in Memphis. It was memorable session, not only because it moved Pickett from R & B into pop but because it brought out producer Jerry Wexler's hidden talents as a dancer. As Steve Cropper describes the session, "Basically, we at Stax have been one-beat accenters with an afterbeat. It was like 'boom dah' but here this was a thing that went 'um-chaw,' just the reverse as far as the accent goes. The back beat was somewhat delayed. . . . It was a good-feeling session and out of that 'Midnight Hour' date there were three other hit singles, 'Don't Fight It,' 'I'm Not Tired,' and 'It's a Man's Way.' . . . Jerry actually came out of the booth and started dancing the 'Jerk'. . . . We had the funk but he knew what the kids were doing. . . ."

By the end of 1967 Wilson Pickett was number two in a list of Top R & B Single makers. Queried about the same time concerning his hit "99½" and its possible association with civil rights, he insisted his songs did not have a message for colored people but for "all the people. I don't sing nothing about civil rights. Everybody needs rights, but they don't have to be civil. I don't march. I don't indulge in it. I contribute, though. I've given benefit shows for the Martin Luther King walk. So they can walk it out in shoes. You gotta keep contributing so they can keep walking. But Luther is a nice fellow. Now, here's fellas that are dedicated in their work. I'd go along with Martin before I'd go along with people like Malcolm X."

Put on? Sing, Wilson Pickett!

Percy Sledge, who grew up in Leighton, Alabama, became a professional singer with a group called the Esquires Combo in 1961. Working around Alabama and Mississippi, they frequently performed at fraternity parties on the campus of Ol' Miss. Early in 1966 Sledge paid a visit to Quin Ivy's Tune Town Record Shop in Sheffield, Alabama, and auditioned for the former disk jockey turned record producer. Out of the meeting came "When a Man Loves a Woman," a Quin Ivy-Marlin Greene production, that zoomed to number one, won Record of the Year awards, and launched a sensuous voice, full of gravel in the low register and steel ball bearings in the upper.

Penetrating when he takes a gospel approach, Sledge can sing with warmth and tenderness like the late Sam Cooke ("Warm and Tender Love"). In his album *The Percy Sledge Way,* he displays a wide range of styles, from Ray Charles's treatment of "Drown in My Own Tears" to Otis Redding's "I've Been Loving You Too Long (To Stop Now)" and Johnny Ace's "Pledging My Love"—all included in the LP.

The year after Sledge exploded on the music scene, Arthur Conley, an Otis Redding protégé, gave Atlantic a Gold Record in "Sweet Soul Music." Redding encountered Conley during an appearance in Baltimore when the young singer brought him a scratchy demo. He was so taken with Conley's sound that he immediately undertook his management and recorded him on his own Jotis label. Later, after two releases on Muscle Shoals' Fame label, Redding turned him over to Atlantic.

"Sweet Soul Music," written by Conley, is a triumph of the sheer excitement he can project on disk, for the song is little more than an enumeration of key soulmen, "Spotlight on Sam & Dave . . . Spotlight on Otis Redding . . . Spotlight on James Brown. . . ."

Conley is as dynamic onstage, as his tours with Stax/Volt Revues have demonstrated. Having captured the record market with "Sweet Soul Music," Conley revived the old Joe Turner hit, "Shake, Rattle and Roll," and racked up hit number two in 1967. Preferring to record at the Fame Studios in Alabama, Conley stylistically embodies a strong choke quality, an engaging feminine sound in ballads, and a soulful vitality.

Adequately to assess Atlantic's role in black music would involve us in an extended survey of the many modern jazz artists who have been and are part of the label. This material is not irrelevant but it is outside the scope of this study. Unlike Motown and Stax/Volt, Atlantic has no house or studio band. Considering the size of its roster of artists, such a setup would be impractical even if it were desired.

Among all the instrumentalists heard on a vast number of Atlantic disks, tenor saxist King Curtis is the most noteworthy. After playing the honking sideman on disks by The Coasters and Bobby Darin—not to mention innumerable artists on other labels—Curtis came up with a best-selling instrumental in 1962. "Soul Twist" was its name. It hardly suggested that his most important influence when he was growing up had been the "prez" of the cool school of jazz saxists, Lester Young.

By 1965, Curtis was a name artist on Atco, an Atlantic subsidiary, offering a soulful sax version of Ben E. King's hit, "Spanish Harlem." Since then, he has maintained a luminous position on the charts with instrumental versions of vocal R & B hits like The Drifters' "On Broadway," William Bell's "You Don't Miss Your Water," and instrumental rousers like "Memphis Soul Stew," his own composition.

That Atlantic added sophistication to R & B was hardly surprising, considering its New York locale. But Gotham was the setting of many other black independents that did not take this direction. The strong feeling of its founders for jazz undoubtedly was the reason. To call Atlantic Sound "arranged

215

R & B" or "R & B with strings" is perhaps adequate, at least as a description of its course until the early sixties. Not only scores and strings, but sophisticated lyrics that culminated in the timely satire of Leiber and Stoller, the sociological sex of Phil Spector ("Spanish Harlem"), and the refined but bald-headed blues of Nugetre. That there was an audience and a market for well-dressed R & B was apparent from the phenomenal rise of Motown. Berry Gordy began building an empire on the Atlantic formula of manicured R & B as Atlantic took a blacker course in the sixties.

If the association with the Memphis Sound was not responsible for this new course, it at least contributed mightily, as Atlantic executives were frank to acknowledge.

"Our methods here," Jerry Wexler has said, "which go back a dozen or fifteen years, served us in good stead until the Stax thing came along, and showed us that we were sort of superannuated. We had the good fortune to form a symbiotic relationship where we could feed on each other."

Out of this interplay came the new Atlantic Sound, the soul sounds of Aretha Franklin, Wilson Pickett, and Otis Redding.

The contemporary power of black sound may be partly assessed from the millions that two film companies paid for it, Paramount for the purchase of Stax/Volt and Warner Bros.-Seven Arts for Atlantic. As of this writing, and surely for as long as each record company maintains a positive balance sheet, creative direction and management remain in the hands of the founders.

13

MODERN
BLUESMEN

"Modern"—at least as far as music is concerned—is a more descriptive term than "contemporary." As a stylistic rather than a temporal concept, it poses the problem of three identities. Modern can mean Chicago bluesmen like Johnny Shines, who worked for a time as Robert Johnson's backup guitarist, and J. B. Hutto, whose idol was Elmore James, another master of the bottleneck guitar. In a sense, these are the postgraduate students of Muddy Waters, Howlin' Wolf, and the other Chicago grads of the Mississippi delta style. They bring the urbanized, electric adaptation of country blues to its peak nostalgic expression.

"Modern" can also mean bluesmen like Buddy Guy, Junior Wells, Otis Rush, James Cotton, and Albert King, who were nurtured on the sounds of the cotton-picking generation of John Lee Hooker, Lightnin' Hopkins, and Mance Lipscomb—and have since taken off from the sophisticated level to which B. B. King elevated the blues. Third generation and born to electricity like the other modernist group, they are the founders of a new school, technically more polished and harder driving than the doctorate of old.

Both of these Chicago groups have been nourished by a flourishing chain of South and West Side clubs: Theresa's, Pepper's Lounge, and Turner's Blue Lounge on the South Side,

Smoot's and Silvio's on the West Side. Successors to clubs like 708 where Buddy Guy got started in the mid-fifties, these gave Chicago of the sixties a feeling of the "live music tradition" that flourished at one time on Manhattan's Fifty-second Street, New Orleans' Bourbon Street, and Memphis' Beale Street.

Outside the Chicago orbit, there are individual and group bluesmen like Taj Mahal, Sly & the Family Stone, and the Chambers Brothers who have grown up in cosmopolitan areas and whose relationship to the blues is racial rather than environmental and who try to cope with rock-and-soul audiences.

The work of the first group is well documented in two recent collections, one produced by Pete Welding for Testament and the other by Sam B. Charters for Vanguard. *Masters of Modern Blues*, the three-record Testament compendium, presents the Johnny Shines Band in Volume 1, J. B. Hutto and the Hawks in Volume 2, and Floyd Jones/Eddie Taylor in the final set.

Born in Memphis, Tennessee, in 1915, Shines wandered with delta bluesmaster Robert Johnson from 1933 to 1935. With or without bottleneck fretting, Shines is steeped in Johnson's sound and repertoire ("Walkin' Blues," and so on).

Joseph Benjamin Hutto, born in Augusta, Georgia, in 1929, likewise exhibits a great natural kinship with Johnson, despite the fact that he was only eight when the restless, woman-crazy bluesman cut his last record session.

Eddie Taylor, born in Beneard, Mississippi, in 1923, recorded for Vee Jay under his own name from 1955 to 1957, but from 1952 into the mid-sixties appeared as a sideman on virtually every Jimmy Reed disk.

Floyd Jones, born in Arkansas in 1917, began recording in 1947 and produced a limited number of sides in a career that made him a familiar figure around the windy city's South Side bars and lounges. "On the Road," a blues he wrote and recorded in 1953, is a favorite of the Canned Heat Blues band.

Both Shines and Hutto may be heard in the Vanguard three-volume collection *Chicago/The Blues/Today*, released in 1966.

Also included are Walter Horton, rated by many as Chicago's outstanding harp player since the passing of Little Walter; Homesick James, originally of Somerville, Tennessee, and long an associate of Elmore James; and Johnny Young's South Side Blues Band. But the emphasis in this collection is on the exponents of the B. B. King tradition: Junior Wells's Chicago Blues Band kicks off Volume 1 and Jimmy Cotton and Otis Rush occupy most of Volume 2.

The overlapping of personnel among the several groups suggests the presence of a common denominator. And one does exist in the Mississippi delta roots out of which both branches of the modern blues tree have sprung. But the descendants of B. B. King display contemporary gospel-soul-jazz influences, the impact of the electric bass, and the feeling for the electric guitar as an improvisational melody instrument.

Despite his standing among bluesmen and the acceptance of his recording of "Hoodoo Man," Junior Wells was little known outside of Chicago until his Vanguard release. He actually began recording in 1953, with Muddy Waters playing guitar on sessions for State—one of many offbeat Chicago labels for which Wells recorded. Others included Chief, Profile, and Bright Star.

Born in West Memphis, Arkansas, in 1932, Wells came to Chicago in his teens. By that time, his ability as a harp man was quite apparent. Arrested for stealing a two-dollar harmonica that a pawnbroker would not sell at a discount, he so impressed a judge with his playing that the jurist paid for the instrument and dismissed the charge. Through the years, Wells has been a fixture at Theresa's, the basement bistro in Chicago's South Side ghetto. An early source of his style is to be found in "A Tribute to Sonny Boy Williamson" in the Vanguard LP. Included also is his famous "Vietcong Blues," written about his brothers in Vietnam. While social comment once was rare in the blues, contemporary life apparently makes it unavoidable for the modern bluesman.

Since 1968 Wells has recorded for the Blue Rock subsidiary of Mercury, where his debut album *You're Tuff Enough*, including the hit single "Up In Heah," suggests that soul is being added to the B. B. King synthesis of blues, gospel, and jazz.

It was at Theresa's in 1958 that Buddy Guy, born in Lettsworth, Louisiana, in 1936, met and became associated with Junior Wells. He had then been in Chicago only a short time. But he had already begun creating talk by his dazzling guitar playing at the 708 Club. Although he made recordings under his own name from 1958 on, he established his reputation as the mainstay of the Junior Wells band.

Guy had been nurtured on Texas-Louisiana blues-pickers like Mance Lipscomb and Lightnin' Hopkins. But those who heard him at Theresa's, and later at Sylvio's and the Pepper Lounge, always compared him to B. B. King. His indebtedness and his mastery are both apparent in his handling of B. B.'s own "Sweet Little Angel" in his debut album on Vanguard, *A Man and the Blues* (1968). He obviously has moved beyond his teacher. As one critic observed, "Buddy's jazz-oriented blues licks, his 'sparks,' those lightning quick 'pops' he hits you with, are his own unique property—indigenous only to the magician's hands of Mr. Guy."

For that matter, the first time Guy played on a stage with B. B., at the invitation of the King, he pursued a course like that of young Charlie Parker with Dizzy Gillespie. He demonstrated the quick ear and finger dexterity that made it possible for him to reproduce his progenitor's performance and immediately improve on it.

In the summer of 1969 Guy became the first American bluesman to tour Central and East Africa. On his return, he said, "I'm always going to do the blues because I'll make myself happy even if I make nobody else feel good." It was a reaction to his disturbing discovery that, in the urban areas of Africa, the blues failed to stir his listeners as did the more soulful and exhibitionistic performances of his brother Philip.

An African musician explains the phenomenon in this fashion: "An African can walk into town never having been to a nightclub before. Now as soon as he hears James Brown, at the very least he will be able to dance to the music."

Apparently the highly syncopated beat of 8/8 "straight time," as contemporary musicians call it, and its variant metrics, 12/8 and shuffle, "speak" to modern Congolese feet.

Peter Giraudo, who accompanied Guy on the tour, adds, "There are other reasons, too, for the overwhelming influence of Soul in urban Africa. One is the need many young Africans have to discover black people who have made it in the sense they also desire—and the richer, flashier soul performers fit this image. But just as important is . . . that traditional African people are being changed by modern Africa in the same way that black Americans from the deep South were changed by Chicago."

James Cotton is another Chicago sideman who recently stepped out on his own. It was only in 1965, after twelve and a half years with the Muddy Waters band, playing beside Otis Spann and drummer S. P. Leary, that harpist Cotton finally cut the umbilical cord. Born in Tunica, Mississippi, in 1925, he had cut sides for Sun in Memphis as early as 1954. But the single-mindedness that he had manifested in his youth kept him in the Waters fold long after he had things of his own to say. As a youth of nine, armed with thirty dollars, he had left the Mississippi cotton fields in a search for Sonny Boy Williamson (Rice Miller), whose harp playing was as magical to him as the Pied Piper's flute to the children of Hamlin. When he found Sonny Boy in Arkansas, he lied about having no family and succeeded in becoming a member of Williamson's household and mascot to the bluesman's band.

It was the Vanguard anthology *Chicago/The Blues/Today* that set the stage for Cotton's solo venture. Working with his Muddy Waters buddies as the Jimmy Cotton Blues Quartet, he recorded oldies like Williamson's "Cotton Crop Blues" and "West Helena Blues," and more recent R & B hits like Jackie Brenston's "Rocket 88." Then, in the summer of 1967, the James Cotton Blues Band made its debut on Verve/Forecast, featuring the typical blues combo of harp, guitar, piano, and drums augmented with brass and reeds. Since then the label has released two albums, *Pure Cotton* and *Cotton in Your Ears,* both superb testimonials to a gifted harpist who has made an expressive contemporary instrument of the wheezing, old country harmonica.

Referring to his own identifiable sound, Cotton has said, "I guess I get it playing from the stomach—a lot of wind. . . . Junior Wells plays more from the throat. . . ." Full, robust, and flexible, Cotton's music is a today sound that is more than a match for the amplified tonalities of electric guitar and Fender bass.

Otis Rush, whose five-piece combo also contributed to *Chicago/The Blues/Today* (Vol. 2), was born in Philadelphia, Mississippi, in 1934 and began recording in his early twenties. Nurtured on the sounds of Lightnin' Hopkins and Muddy Waters heard on his radio and later influenced by recordings of T-Bone Walker, Willie Mae Barnes, Little Walter, and B. B. King, he followed the path of an earlier generation of bluesmen and migrated to Chicago.

He was working in a packinghouse when a friend with whom he rehearsed helped him get his first club date at $2.50 a night. Through bassist-songwriter Willie Dixon, whom he met at the 708 Club, he cut his first sides for Cobra, a local record label. Dixon played the date, as he did other Cobra sessions during the next two years.

When the label folded, Rush moved to Dixon's own production base—Chess—where he made only a few sides in a two-year period. A two-year contract with Duke Records from 1962 on also yielded only two released sides. After the appearance of its anthology of blues in 1965, Vanguard took an option on Rush's services but failed to record him, ostensibly because it could not find the right material for him.

Although he can be heard in Cadet's five-volume anthology *The Blues,* the first new Otis Rush recordings appeared in the spring of 1969. A release of Cotillion Records, an Atlantic subsidiary, *Mourning in the Morning* was produced by guitarists Mike Bloomfield and Nick Gravenites. El Greco, as Gravenites is known, first heard Rush when he was a freshman at the University of Chicago and went to the 708 Club at Forty-seventh Street in the South Side ghetto. In an interview that El

Greco gave in February 1969, he confirmed that material was the major problem in recording Rush.

Nick and Mike solved it by writing eleven new blues that were eventually winnowed to the six in the album. "Blues soul-based" is their epithet for these recordings. The rest of the album consists of Chuck Willis's tender ballad "Feel So Bad," B. B. King's famous "Gambler's Blues," an instrumental version of Aretha Franklin's hit "Baby, I Love You," and remakes of two of Rush's old Cobra singles, "My Love Will Never Die" and "It Takes Time."

The album has a distinctly contemporary sound—a modern mix of Rush, Bloomfield and Gravenites's concepts, and the rhythmic push of the studio band at the Fame Studio in Muscle Shoals, Alabama. This is the studio where Aretha Franklin cut her first smash Atlantic album, where Wilson Pickett, Percy Sledge, and Clarence Carter, new Atlantic bluesman, have cut albums, and where, to El Greco's amazement, all the studio men are white southern blues musicians.

Otis Spann has been recording steadily since the early fifties when, like bassist Willie Dixon, he virtually became Chess' studio pianist. His tasteful piano is audible on disks by pioneer rhythm-and-bluesmen Howlin' Wolf, Bo Diddley, and Muddy Waters, among others. As part of Waters's band, he remained an unsung sideman for almost a decade.

In 1960 he finally stepped out on his own and recorded an album for Candid. Thereafter, he cut a Storyville LP in Copenhagen, Decca sides in London, Prestige and Vanguard disks in Chicago, and finally found a home on Bluesway in 1966. Muddy was one of three guitarists who played on his debut Bluesway LP of August 1966. His down-home pianistics are heard on both the Testament and Vanguard anthologies of modern blues, suggesting the scope of his artistry and the esteem in which he is held by two generations of bluesmen.

Born in Jackson, Mississippi, in 1931 and a half brother of Muddy Waters, Spann is a sensitive performer.

"My mother was a blues singer," he recalls, "who sang with Memphis Minnie. At the Alamo Theatre in Jackson (Mississippi), I won the twenty-five-dollar first prize. I was eight years old and sang Bessie Smith's 'Black Water Blues'. . . . I used to fight in the ring and won the Golden Gloves in the forties."

Superb as a sideman, Spann is an expressive soloist. Part of his problem is that he is a pianist, not a guitarist. The other part is a matter of personality. Just as he does not upstage soloists whom he is accompanying, so he shies, as a person, at moving into the foreground. I saw him come unannounced to the Newport Folk Festival of 1968, plead with producer George Wein for a spot in the already overcrowded program, and depart unheralded and unheard.

There has always been a less-publicized ghetto on Chicago's West Side. It took Delmark Records, which rediscovered Sleepy John Estes in the early sixties, to document its contribution to contemporary blues. Harpist Shakey Harris, once known as Cadillac Jake, produced *West Side Soul* for the Robert Koester label with Magic Sam (Maghett). Born in Grenada, Mississippi, in 1937, Maghett began making records in Chicago when he was twenty—for two years on the short-lived Cobra label, then in 1960 and 1961 on Chief.

His 1968 Delmark album incorporates blues like "All of Your Love," his first recorded song for Cobra. Meanwhile, he is noted for tunes like "Mama Mama—Talk to Your Daughter" and "I Feel So Good (I Want to Boogie)," selections that are request numbers at Sylvio's and Alex's, where Magic Sam has been a frequent resident.

According to legend, Shakey Harris was so impressed by Maghett's performance of "I Wanna Boogie" some years ago that he persuaded Muddy Waters, then at the old 708 Club, to let Magic Sam sit in with the band. Maghett became the follow-up attraction. Like Wes Montgomery, Maghett picks with his thumb. Like Buddy Guy, he rests his instrument on his hip. Like B. B. King, in whose footsteps he walks, he is powerful of voice and modern in his approach to the guitar.

Among the new generation of Chicago bluesmen, John Little-john (Funchess) has attracted notice as a slide guitarist who invests the delta bottleneck style with the sophistication of contemporary harmony. Arhoolie Records of Berkeley, California, is responsible for his debut album *John Littlejohn's Chicago Blues Stars,* released in the summer of 1969. Chris Strachwitz, the California company's dedicated bluesophile, was assisted in the production by Chicago's Willie Dixon.

Both in his vocal and string style, Littlejohn exhibits a frank adulation of the late Elmore James, represented in the album by "Catfish Blues" and the suggestive "Shake Your Money Maker." However, Littlejohn's repertoire is contemporary and catholic to the point of including Brook Benton's pop hit "Kiddio." But numbers like "What in the World You Goin' to Do" and "Slidin' Home," with the obvious play on the verb, are updated projections of the whining gliss style that the delta cotton and guitar pickers brought to Chicago in the forties.

While Chicago remains the center of contemporary blues, boasting the largest concentration of modern bluesmen, a number of contenders for the mantle of B. B. King are to be found elsewhere. Freddy King, born in Gilmer, Texas, in 1934, did cut two sides in the Windy City in 1956. But from 1960 until his recent switch to Atlantic's Cotillion label—when the spelling of his name became Freddie—he recorded for Federal, the King subsidiary in Cincinnati. Almost one hundred sides testify to the frenzy that King can muster—including a number, "Sittin' on the Boat Deck," that seems to foreshadow an Otis Redding song, "(Sitting On) The Dock of the Bay."

Since his debut Cotillion disk was produced by the tenor thunderer, saxist King Curtis, one might have anticipated an explosive platter full of lightning and decibels. But in keeping with the refinements and lettered musicianship that have become a part of modern blues, *Freddie King Is a Blues Master* is tastefully intense.

In "Hide Away" King reaches back to one of the earliest blues he recorded on Federal. An expression of indebtedness appears in "Sweet Thing" and "Blue Shadows," both audibly reminiscent of B. B. King's own versions. Contrasts of mood appear in the turn from high-flying "Funky" to the choke-guitar treatment of "Hot Tomato," a style that contrasts

225

strongly with slide guitar in that vibration of the strings is checked by the right hand, operating like a piano damper pedal. Broad-chested and bull-necked, Freddie visually communicates a sense of power that emanates from his singing and picking even when the mood is tender.

Born in West Memphis, Arkansas, in 1927, Junior Parker was one of the many poor black country boys mesmerized by the harmonica playing of Sonny Boy Williamson. The impact of Williamson was perhaps more a product of the radio than of records or personal appearances, and suggests that the role of local radio in the development of black song has not been adequately assessed. As Howlin' Wolf helped sell fertilizer as a delta disk jockey, Williamson broadcast from West Helena, Arkansas, with the King Biscuit boys, whose personnel included Elmore James and B. B. King.

Listening to his radio one day, Herman Parker learned that Williamson was to appear in the Clarksdale area where he was picking cotton. He managed to attend. Williamson, who always invited amateurs to perform, was so moved by Parker's mastery of his own style that he took him along for personal appearances in nearby towns. Legend has it that friends and audiences assumed that the two were related and began calling Herman Junior. In 1949 the ex-cotton picker also found an opportunity to play with Howlin' Wolf.

Junior cut his first sides in Memphis in 1952 for Modern Records. But the real impetus to his recording career came the following year when he cut four sides for Sam Phillips's Sun label. It was the period when Phillips was developing the stable of rockabilly singers that included Carl Perkins, Jerry Lee Lewis, Roy Orbison, Johnny Cash, and, of course, Elvis Presley. Elvis recorded Parker's "Mystery Train," which Junior had himself cut with his Blue Flames. Junior did so well with one of his other Sun sides—"Feelin' Good" hit Top Ten on R & B charts—that Don Robey brought him to Houston in 1954 for his first session on Duke, the label with which he was associated into the sixties.

The year of his first Duke releases, he went on tour with two other Robey artists—Willie Mae Thornton and the short-lived

Johnny Ace. After the latter's accidental death late that year, Parker crisscrossed the country with Bobby Bland, another Duke bluesman. Although he had substantial market items in 1957 and 1958 with "The Next Time You See Me" and "That's All Right," his biggest Duke disk came in 1962 with "Annie Get Your Yo-Yo," reminiscent of the Hank Ballard hit of the fifties. Modern bluesman though he is, Junior Parker has more of a country sound and is less polished than either harpist Junior Wells or James Cotton. He currently records for Mercury.

In the Memphis area, in the late forties and early fifties, Ike Turner was in demand as a blues pianist. When Leonard Chess first recorded Howlin' Wolf in 1948 in West Memphis, Ike Turner was at the piano, accompanying the Wolf intermittently thereafter on his RPM and Chess disks into 1952.

Turner handled the ivories on B. B. King's RPM sessions in 1950 and 1951, including the date on which King recorded his first hit, "Three O'Clock Blues." He also played Junior Parker's first date for Modern in Memphis in 1952. But this phase of Turner's work lies buried under the pile of LPs cut by Ike and Tina Turner in the sixties.

They are an attractive pair, full of deviltry and sex, and more beguiling in personal appearances than on wax. (Peaches and Herb, though sexless by comparison, remind one of them.) There has been no shortage of disks by the Turners, and on quite a number of labels, suggesting the inability of the duo to deliver with enough vocal impact to elicit long-term contracts. Since 1965 they have had albums on Warner Bros., Loma, Pompeii, A & M, Blue Thumb, and no fewer than six on Sue.

Their ability to command record producer enthusiasm, if not a continuing relationship, reached its peak with Phil Spector, flamboyant mentor of the Righteous Brothers, Crystals, and Ronettes. In 1967 Spector produced an LP with them built around his song "River Deep—Mountain High." Though Spector and other knowledgeable folk felt that the title song represented Tina's most fetching performance and had the makings of an overnight smash, it bombed in this country as a single. However, the disk made its mark on English charts, provoking the irascible Spector to take out an advertisement that read, "Benedict Arnold Was Right!" Thereupon, according to reports, he dissolved his Philles record company. Included in the album were some of the best sellers the Turners had placed on R & B charts between 1960 and 1962, their hot period, among them "It's Gonna Work Out Fine" and Ike Turner's ballad, "Fool in Love."

In their most recent album, *Outta Season*, a Blue Thumb release, they demonstrate their unabating concern with black material. The sound is contemporary, though Tina's vocals seem to lack emotional involvement, and the songs range from legendary Robert Johnson's "Dust My Broom" to Otis Redding's "I've Been Loving You Too Long."

Two groups that have been characterized as soul groups by some critics, but in my view lack the *sine qua non* of soul—audience *possession*—are the Chambers Brothers and Sly & the Family Stone. I classify them as modern bluesmen.

Considering that Sly & the Family Stone produced their first album, *A Whole New Thing,* as recently as 1967, their impact is not to be minimized. *Life,* their second album, has been characterized as "easily the most radical soul album ever issue," while *Stand!* their most recent, was typed "soul music distorted." Before he stepped out as a performer, Sly was reportedly the top-rated R & B disk jockey in the San Francisco area.

A restless and energetic young man, he worked in his spare time as a record producer for a now defunct local label. In many ways, it was his contact with the blues bands of the San Francisco Bay area that shaped his seven-piece integrated group. Employing updated "bomp-bomp" vocalizing reminiscent of early R & B, the group adds trumpet, sax, and electric piano to its musical components and produces a freewheeling mixture of rock, jazz, and blues.

With their second Epic LP, built around the hit single "Dance to the Music," Sly & the Family Stone demonstrated that *surprise* and *constant change* are their basic arranging technique. The lyrics of original songs are truncated or under-developed. A record is composed of a series of splintered sound images, involving shifting textures, fast switches from voices to instruments, and rapid changes of instrumental combinations. A flashing light show in sound is perhaps the most apt description. Only three items do not change. The tempo is fast, the dynamics are loud, and an inescapable Fender bass maintains a big electric dance beat. All else is flux—and the more unexpected the turn, the better.

Sly's most recent album represents an advance in thinking if not in technique. Featuring the hit single "Everyday People," a song of brotherhood, *Stand!* is socially oriented, dealing with problems seldom touched in the blues, problems that today require a *stand*. Its outlook is given emphasis in "Don't Call Me Nigger, Whitey," which is hardly a song, since it consists simply of the title line and its reverse, "Don't call me whitey, nigger," repeated over and over in varied speeds. Aurally the effect approximates the bouncing visual images sometimes seen on the TV screen, except that the incessant repetition is exasperating and calculatingly provocative.

Although the group's style has at times been likened to Jimi Hendrix's electrical overkill, in this album Sly seems to come closer to the freak-out technique of another socially oriented California group—Frank Zappa and the Mothers of Invention.

Unlike the Family Stone, the four Mississippi-born Chambers Brothers made their debut as a gospel group, singing spirituals in Lee County's Mt. Calvary Baptist Church. After they had all migrated to Los Angeles and were earning their livelihoods at various menial jobs, they reestablished their gospel group and began singing in different churches.

"In 1961," George E., the oldest, explains, "we all quit our jobs and went professional. We were still gospel singers and played coffeehouses and small clubs like L.A.'s Ash Grove. Then we decided to do some pop songs and blues. I turned in my gutbucket bass and got a Fender electric. We were all too busy playing different instruments to do handclaps, so we had to get a drummer."

229

In Ondine's in New York City, they found Brian Keenan, born in Manhattan and educated in London and the Bronx. And so the Chambers Brothers became an integrated group, the one white, English-looking countenance making a startling contrast sandwiched in among four black faces.

Before they came to Columbia late in 1967, they had three albums on Vault Records of Los Angeles. *Now!* and *Shout!* had neither the immediacy nor the impact that the titles suggest. But their third LP, *People Get Ready*, packed enough power to gain them entrée on a major label. *"Time Has Come,"* their first Columbia single, became a hit and yielded a Gold Record in their album of the same name.

Their second Columbia album, *A New Time—A New Day*, released late in 1968, contained the handclapping hit "I Can't Turn You Loose." Their vocal blend has gospel roots, but it is overlaid with a funky blues feeling and the energetic young drive of rock. In April 1969 they cut an album live at New York's Fillmore East. The mixture of R & B oldies, like the Fiestas' "So Fine" and Clovers' "Love, Love, Love," and pops like "Undecided" and the Joe Cuba hit "Bang Bang," emphasized the pop-rock blues direction they were taking.

The third-generation bluesman who makes the sharpest break with the migrant delta group and the succeeding post-war rhythm-and-bluesmen is the man who calls himself Taj Mahal. Speaking about his second LP on Columbia, he recently said, "It's just me playing peaceful. And lovingly."

Reviewers found precisely these qualities in *The Natch'l Blues,* as the LP is titled. "You can actually hear him smiling," one wrote.

The scope of the blues has always been as large as life. Originally a narrative outcry of poor country people against their burdens and deprivations—small and large, daily and life-long, local and racial—the blues has been marked by humor as well as sadness and pain. But qualities like peace and love? Existential the blues were. But relaxed? Not until the appearance of Taj Mahal, whose real name is Henry Sainte Claire

Fredricks-Williams, did the blues encompass the *joy* of life and not merely an acceptance of it.

Although his mother comes from South Carolina, Taj Mahal's grandfather was a conductor in the New York subways and his father "one of Brooklyn's best board-skaters." He himself was born in New York City and raised in Springfield, Massachusetts, where he eventually graduated from the University of Massachusetts with a B.A. in veterinary science. Articulate and literate, his conversation includes easy references to Eric Fromm, Aldous Huxley, and many contemporary writers.

Despite this metropolitan and cultured background, he got into the blues after first hearing some old records. He goes on to say, "It was real and it just turned me right on. My mother was into the classics and gospel music, and my father played some jazz piano and was into Basie, Ellington, and Louis Jordan. The blues just knocks me out and when it's real good it makes me vibrate. It's like a very sensuous chick and she can't even help it. It makes you realize that you're alive and there's good things in life. People should be seeing the good things because that's the only way you're going to be happy. People should be responsible and loving. If everybody's giving, then everybody is receiving."

In an article he co-authored with *Hit Parader*'s Jim Delehant, he added, "I just want to be happy. I'm not hung up with commercial success for my band. I don't care too much if I don't own things. I'd rather give something of mine to somebody who needs it."

As for the blues, he is of the opinion that they are racial rather than circumstantial or geographic in origin. "Some people think you have to be blind Lester Crawdad," he told Tom Nolan of *Rolling Stone*, "and come up from New Orleans and into Chicago to cut two sides. The Man hears it, says, 'Pretty good, give us the publishing and we'll see what we can do!' They think you have to go through that to play good blues. But you know it's not indigenous to a time or place, the music is indigenous to the *people*."

Obviously Taj Mahal did not go through the changes that

231

molded Blind Lemon, Muddy Waters, or B. B. King. His family had a two-family house in Springfield, Massachusetts. There, as in New York, he grew up in an interracial environment. His paternal grandmother and grandfather were born and raised in a Jewish neighborhood. As a boy, his father often stayed next door with Jewish neighbors.

"We were all one big family," he says, "since back before my father's time. My father spoke Yiddish, Spanish, French, Portuguese, English, just everything, and the best language he spoke was Yiddish. My mother, who came from the South, of Indian, Irish, and Negro parents, used to make gefilte fish for us. My mother's a college-educated woman working for her Ph.D. in psychology. She gave birth to six kids and has three stepchildren. My parents are happy people and they work hard. . . ."

Out of this cosmopolitan and relaxed environment has come an outlook rare among bluesmen. "Everybody is geared up to an aggressive situation," he says, "and they've got the robots to pull it off. I've managed to get out of the games that are being played. The black versus white game, the white versus black game, the black versus black game. You see, to be a black man in America, you've got to work three times as hard, keep your house three times as clean, talk fifteen times better, and then everybody may accept you. I'm getting out of that. I'd rather be myself."

He elaborates with feeling, "Compassion is a beautiful thing. It makes life much easier. In that way you can understand the weaknesses of other human beings. We're geared to love things that conform to what we understand. But that can't be because we're always meeting people who have been raised differently. Blues power is love. Through it we all know we've been down at one time or another. So we've got to get up. Like when a southern musician comes up to me and says, 'Man, you sure play beautiful.' That crosses the barrier. So it comes down to compassion through music."

The concern with compassion rather than catharsis separates Taj Mahal from today's soulmen at the same time as it places him somewhat outside the circle of old-time bluesmen. But his repertoire abounds in blues classics like Robert Johnson's "Dust My Broom," Ma Rainey's "E Z Rider" (in his spelling), and Robert Johnson's "Walkin' Blues." He makes no effort to imitate the originators, however, contending that the world that motivated them is not his.

Doing his own thing and pursuing a style that is neither sensational nor startling, Taj Mahal has managed to stir considerable attention since he cut his first two sides for Columbia in March, 1967. He was among the few contemporary bluesmen invited to the Newport Folk Festival of 1968 and was included by the Rolling Stones in their 1969 TV special.

His bizarre masquerade is, perhaps, his most striking aspect. Six feet, four inches in height, he wears a high-crowned, wide-brimmed Amish hat decorated with a linked band of pop-tops from beer cans. A knotted bandanna adorns his neck and a sheriff's badge is pinned to the left cuff of his levis. Large black shades hide his eyes and make his frequent smile two gleaming rows of white teeth. Being literate and fluent, he likes to affect the pose of an ignorant bum.

"Modern" is not a revealing epithet when applied to Jimmy Witherspoon or Arthur Prysock, both of whom are too genuinely bluesy to be described as "Oreo singers." Although the word soul appears in the titles of their recent albums, it is as inappropriate as Oreo. Both represent a type of contemporary black balladry marked by deep blues shadings. For years, each worked with a rocking blues band, Prysock with Buddy Johnson and Spoon, as he is known, with Jay McShann. The Kansas City blues-jazz style of McShann and of shouter Jimmy Rushing left indelible marks on Witherspoon. South Carolina-born Prysock, early a New Englander, is more pop than Arkansas-born Spoon, who attracted a following in the late forties with his version of a Billie Holiday perennial, " 'Tain't Nobody's Bizness If I Do." But both demonstrate the appealing, earthy qualities derived from "the most sensuous form of music we have," to use Del Shields's apt characterization of the blues.

Part III
SOUL

My Lord, He calls me,
He calls me by the thunder!
The trumpet sounds within-a my soul . . .

—TRADITIONAL SPIRITUAL

14

GOSPEL
MUSIC
AND SOUL

Twice a year, at Easter and Christmas, the Apollo Theatre turns from the profane to the sacred and schedules a run of "the Harlem Gospel Train." The stage is transformed into an old-time Baptist church, adorned with towering stained-glass windows and set with a double row of stalls. Women in shimmering white, choir robes sing to organ accompaniment as the curtains part and disclose an old black man peering anxiously toward the back of the theater.

Suddenly he extends a shaking hand and, pointing to the rear, cries out in fear, "Look over your shoulder!"

No one dares turn, for everyone knows the horror lurking in the rear. And the few intrepid souls who try to catch a glimpse never do. The Devil is too fast for them.

But the stage has been set. The voices of the choir rise as a preacher man appears to exhort them and stir the witnesses. With the sacred fire mounting, large women flip out of their seats, screaming and weaving about. A man in the second balcony, caught in the frenzy, has to be restrained by ushers from throwing himself onto the stage for Jesus. In a stage box two nurses in starched uniforms minister to those who faint or hurt themselves in falls.

"But there's no keeping hold on things now," Albert Goldman writes as a witness to the proceedings. . . . The whole theater is getting to its feet, *sixteen hundred and eighty* people are standing bolt upright, they are raising their arms straight up in the air and waving them slowly back and forth, making a multitude of crosses, making a wave offering, making a mass gesture that has the power and authority of Moses dividing the Red Sea."

Goldman concludes, "And where are you, Whitey? You're drowning at the bottom of the sea. You're sitting there so scared and so lost and so little you're going to crawl out of the Apollo Theatre like Kafka's cockroach."

Soul music had its beginnings in the dark days of the spirituals, the *sorrow songs*, as they have been called.

"In the old days," Langston Hughes explains, "the slaves had no way of protesting against their fate, without danger of being whipped or even killed, except through their songs. So into the simple lines of the spirituals, short lines repeated over and over, went all the pain and sorrow of their bondage, compressed and intensified into the very essence of sorrow itself."

But the slaves also had joyous songs, jubilant with the anticipated triumph of a Joshua who made "de walls come tumblin' down"—whence the name of the Fisk Jubilee Singers, who first made the world aware of the spirituals.

Soul music has its kinship with the blues and rhythm-and-blues. In 1928 Vocalion released a record by Georgia Tom and Tampa Red called "It's Tight Like That" whose words went:

> Now the girl I love is long and slim,
> When she gets it, it's too bad, Jim.
> It's tight like that, beedle um bum,
> It's tight like that . . .

Georgia Tom was Ma Rainey's accompanist, composer of one of her most popular songs, "Stormy Sea Blues," and a favorite of theater and tent show audiences who snapped their fingers to his ragtiming pianistics. Not long after his days with Ma Rainey, Georgia Tom was anxious to forget that he had ever written "It's Tight Like That." When the subject

238

came up, he was ready to claim, or admit, as he did on many occasions, that Tampa Red had brought the words to him and that the melody had been stolen from country blues singer Papa Charlie Jackson.

Georgia Tom, you see, was the nickname of Thomas A. Dorsey of Chicago, prominent in the early thirties in the musical life of the Pilgrim Baptist Church of Chicago and before long the distinguished composer of some of the greatest gospel songs of our time. One does not have to have religion to know such evergreen songs of faith as "Someday, Somewhere," "We Will Meet Him in the Sweet Bye and Bye," "Precious Lord," "Take My Hand," and others.

Not spirituals, not blues, not rhythm-and-blues, but gospel songs are the immediate blood relatives of Soul. In fact, blues come from another side of the family, as a Mahalia Jackson comment suggests: "Blues are the songs of despair. Gospel songs are the songs of hope. When you sing gospel, you have the feeling that there is a cure for what's wrong. . . ."

If gospel singers, in the words of the Bible, make "a joyful noise unto the Lord," soul singers make a stirring noise unto man. And the fervor of gospel becomes the frenzy of Soul.

Gospel songs are of comparatively recent origin, as the references to Thomas A. Dorsey and Mahalia Jackson would suggest. Unlike the spirituals, folk songs created by unknown groups of singers, gospel songs have come into being since the mid-twenties and are written by acknowledged lyricists and composers with strong religious feelings. Storefront churches are generally associated with gospel music. Negroes who migrated to northern cities after World War I found that they could not afford to purchase land or build churches—and so they settled for the low rentals of ghetto stores, available in profusion as the depression swept over the land.

The services conducted in these bare surroundings, especially by members of the Sanctified, Holiness, Pentecostal, and other Baptist sects, were, as Bill Johnson observed, marked by "singing and jumping as never before. The mighty rhythm rocked the churches. A deluge of new rapture completely engulfed the people and nobody knew why. The depression had sent people scurrying back to the church, and even this did not explain why they had this tremendous impulse to get out of their seats, shout, jump, and praise God in the aisles."

If I may hazard a guess, it was because going to church had to serve poor people for entertainment as well as inspiration. In the mass excitement, ecstasy, jubilation—the handclapping, the beating of a drum, the whacking of tambourines, and the voices raised in rapturous song and antiphonal shouting—the individual could lose himself in a heartwarming unity with his fellow sufferers and momentarily enjoy an escape from himself and his problems. And what about showman preachers who knew that if you made the parishioners feel happy they would give more readily?

"There is no music like that music," James Baldwin, who was himself once a Harlem storefront preacher, writes in *The Fire Next Time*, "no drama like the drama of the saints rejoicing, the sinners moaning, the tambourines racing, and all those voices coming together and crying holy unto the Lord. I have never seen anything to equal the fire and excitement that sometimes, without warning, fill a church, causing a church, as Leadbelly and others have testified, to 'rock.' Nothing that has happened to me since equals the power and the glory that I sometimes felt when. . .the church and I were one. Their pain and their joy were mine. . .and their cries of 'Amen!' and 'Hallelujah!' and 'Yes, Lord!' 'Praise His name!' 'Preach it, brother!" sustained and whipped on my solos until we became equal, wringing wet, singing and dancing, in anguish and rejoicing, at the foot of the altar.

"There was a zest and a joy and a capacity for facing and surviving disaster that are moving and very rare. Perhaps we were, all of us—pimps, whores, racketeers, church members, and children—bound together by the nature of our oppression. If so, within these limits we sometimes achieved with each other a freedom that was close to love. . . . Rage and sorrow sat in the darkness and did not stir, and we. . .forgot all about 'the man.' This is the freedom that one hears in some gospel songs."

And so a body of newly composed songs and inspirational

singers grew up during the thirties, recorded occasionally by the indie blues and jazz labels. It was not until the mid-forties that several singers, notably Sister Rosetta Tharpe and Mahalia Jackson, began to demonstrate the power of sacred song on wax. The former literally had a hit record on Decca with her own song, "Strange Things Are Happening Every Day." In the same year (1945), Mahalia Jackson recorded "Move On Up a Little Higher" for Apollo, a disk that was little known outside the ghetto market, where it became a phenomenal seller.

But even before Mahalia and Rosetta, there were the Clara Ward Singers, a high-binding, holy-rolling group that attracted national notice after an appearance at a Baptist convention in 1943. Miss Ward was then just nineteen, having been born in 1924 in Philadelphia, where she had begun singing sacred songs at five as a member of her mother's choir. Shortly before she entered high school, she was part of a trio, including mom and sis, which became a quintet on her graduation with the addition of two Baptist church friends, Marion and Henrietta Waddy.

In 1957 the Clara Ward Singers appeared at the Newport Jazz Festival and toured the country with the Big Gospel Cavalcade. The group may be heard on several record labels—Duke, Peacock, Gotham, and Savoy. (The last mentioned has the largest catalog of gospel material, not only because of what it has recorded since the late thirties but through its absorption of Gospel Record Company, a pioneer source of recorded gospel songs.)

Sister Rosetta Tharpe followed a course that paralleled Georgia Tom's career rather than Clara Ward's. Born in Cotton Plant, Arkansas, in 1921, she was at seventeen in the spotlight of Harlem's famous Cotton Club Revue, working with Cab Calloway. Into the mid-forties she continued making appearances with Calloway and Lucky Millinder's band, and as a single-o at many clubs, including Manhattan's Cafe Society.

After she began recording for Decca, her early religious training began to assert itself—as a youngster she had sung with her mother in a local church choir—and she became, in Pete Welding's view, "largely responsible for the flowering of the modern Gospel style."

Clara Ward is closer to the raucous exhibitionism of the old shouting style, while Sister Tharpe represents the movement toward the more musical expressiveness of great inner feeling, as in the Staple Singers, James Cleveland, and Mahalia Jackson. In 1949 Sister Tharpe, christened Rosetta Nubin, recorded a duet session of sacred music with her mother, Katie Bell Nubin. Many of her Decca recordings were made with Marie Knight, who is currently leading her own gospel group, records for Mercury, and has been characterized by Pete Welding as "non-pareil, outstripping any female shouter in the volcanic Gospel style."

In selecting Miss Knight's *Songs of the Gospel* for inclusion in a discography, *The Best of Blues and Roots,* Welding notes that "the runners-up include Clara Ward, with excellent LPs on a number of labels, the best being on Savoy; Marion Williams, also on Savoy; the Caravans on Gospel; the Davis Sisters, Savoy; the Gay Sisters, Savoy; the Sallie Martin Singers, Vee Jay and Song Bird; Inez Andrews and the Andrewettes, Vee Jay; and the Meditation Singers, Song Bird." Of Mahalia Jackson's Columbia album, *The World's Greatest Gospel Singer,* Welding writes, "The album title is accurate, for this set contains majestic, moving singing in the restrained Gospel style by the undisputed queen of Negro religious song."

In the New Orleans where she was born in 1911, the Queen of Gospel Singers grew up listening to the sounds of jazz and the records of Mamie Smith, Ida Cox, and Empress of the Blues Bessie Smith. But she also sang, as soon as she could carry a tune, in the choir of her father, who worked as a stevedore, an after-hours barber, and a Sunday preacher. Miss Jackson's emergence as a gospel singer came late and only after years of labor at various trades.

When she first arrived in Chicago in 1927, she worked as a hotel maid and as a date packer in a factory. Later, with the money she saved, she operated a beauty salon and a flower shop. But from her first days in the Windy City she was a regular churchgoer and choir member. Eventually her rich contralto voice made her the choir soloist and the soloist of a quintet organized by the choir director for appearances at conventions, revival meetings, and other church programs.

The fantastic acceptance of her Apollo recording of "Move On Up a Little Higher" moved her emphatically in the direction of gospel singing as a career and a calling. Switching from Apollo to Columbia Records in '54, she gained new stature and national renown when she began broadcasting her own program every Sunday evening over CBS. The suggestion that she add some nonreligious numbers or blues to her shows brought the response, "I can't let CBS dominate the Lord."

In 1957 she appeared at the Newport Jazz Festival but only at the afternoon gospel session. The following year she appeared again at Newport, performing Duke Ellington's suite *Black, Brown and Beige,* which she had recorded with the Duke. In 1959 she sang for President Eisenhower at his birthday celebration in the White House. She may be seen in the documentary film *Jazz on a Summer's Day.* Through the years, however, she has constantly refused lucrative offers for appearances in nightclubs.

"The church will be here," she has said, "when the nightclubs are gone." By the same token, she refuses to sing blues. "Anybody that sings the blues," she says, "is in a deep pit, yelling for help." Her calling, as she has said and demonstrated in years of dedicated singing, is, "in the words of David, making a joyful noise unto the Lord."

"I was Mahalia's paper boy," says James Cleveland, author of three-hundred gospel songs and, according to Herman Lubinsky of Savoy Records, the only gospel singer with an album that has sold a million copies—*In Service, Vol. 3.*

"I'd go over to her apartment on Indiana Avenue," Cleveland recalls, "and leave her paper, and then put my ear to the door to try to hear her singing. . . . I grew up in Chicago completely fascinated by Mahalia Jackson, and we get together sometimes now and laugh about how I used to follow her around."

It was another Chicagoan, Thomas A. Dorsey, who gave Cleveland his first chance to sing in public. "He was at

Pilgrim Baptist in Chicago then," the leader of the Angelic Choir recalls, "and that was my grandmother's church. I was sort of a mascot for the choir, and I'd sing louder than anybody else. Mr. Dorsey heard me and put me on a box and let me sing a song called, 'He's All I Need.'" Oh, I was about eight years old then, and had a beautiful boy soprano voice. Later on, I sang so loud and so hard I strained my voice. That's why it sounds like a foghorn now. Lots of folks call me the 'Louis Armstrong of Gospel,' you know."

New York disk jockey George Hudson, responsible for Gospel U.S.A. stage productions, has called Cleveland the King of Gospel. "Cleveland can do lots more than sing," *Ebony* magazine noted recently. "He has written dozens of gospel songs, as standard in some churches as the old great hymns. He's also a master pianist; an arranger who draws even pop and jazz artists to 'workshops' at his Los Angeles home; a choir director good enough to put together a 300-voice choir within a few days after arrival in almost any town, and a recording star with 20 or so big seller albums on the racks. A few months ago word went out that his Gospel Music Workshop of America would meet for the first time in Detroit. In came 3,000 delegates from 23 states, and all had come to learn something from 'King James.' "

King James is master of all the vocal devices of black singing—syllables stretched over many, many notes, falsetto glisses, bent notes, torn notes, excited shouts, and the changing sonorities and textures manipulated by blues and jazz singers. But he and the Angelic Choir, also the Cleveland Singers, can sing as sweetly and harmoniously as a chorus of well-tuned birds. Inescapably, there is a swinging beat, originating in his driving piano, that gets to you and makes you rock in your seat if it does not set you to finger snapping and foot tapping.

But if you doubt the immediate kinship of gospel and Soul, listen to the King and his Cleveland Singers deliver "I Don't Need Nobody Else," his updated version of "He's All I Need," the gospel song he sang as an eight-year-old boy in Georgia Tom's Chicago church.

A syncopated, up-tempo piano brings Cleveland in with

declarations of his humiliations. "I've been lied on"—*"lied on,"* the women's chorus echoes—"cheated"—*"cheated"*—"talked about"—*"talked about,"* the women respond,—"mistreated"— *"mistreated,"* the women shout. But "long as I got King Jesus," he sings, and, repeating the thought, "Just as long as I got King Jesus," his voice rises to an excited falsetto, and the women, echoing his ecstatic cry, shriek the line, *"Long, long as I got King Jesus."* And he responds, "I don't need nobody else." Soon he bears witness; he's a burden bearer, heavy-load sharer, bridge over water, doctor and a lawyer. . . and so *long, long, long, long, long, long, long*—there are seven intensifying repeats of the word—before the climactic return to "long as I got King Jesus . . ."

From Mahalia Jackson to James Cleveland to Aretha Franklin, whom King James taught gospel piano, the emotional expressiveness of gospel song has developed mainstream appeal. Once a ghetto art, it is today—as Soul—the major emotive color of the pop spectrum, as the phenomenal acceptance of "Oh, Happy Day" by the Edwin Hawkins Singers demonstrates.

Possession is the word and state that separates the black singers previously considered in this volume—except for the gospeleers—from those who follow. Possession begins with the singer. When it is potent enough, it sweeps like a tidal wave, engulfing the listener and sucking him into the emotional vortex of mass excitement and hysteria. Rooted in the blues, soul singing is in a different bag than the blues. Admittedly, they both stem from the same tradition of personal expressiveness. But the essence of the blues is a degree of *control*, reserve, detachment, and distance that make it possible for the singer to face great adversity and frustration with calm and courage. The essence of Soul is a degree of personal *involvement*, nay, extreme involvement, that emanates from the singer's feeling of rage and outrage at the adversities and frustrations of an abominable world.

One attitude and style (Blues) was natural in an era when Negroes felt that they *had* to bear whatever burdens were imposed upon them. The other (Soul) is a concomitant of a time when they are unafraid to shout out their grievances and determined to throw off unjust burdens. The middle and older generations and the Establishment have little use for Soul music. It's too loud, too raucous, too crude, too exhibitionistic, too exaggerated, and of course too emotional and lacking in restraint. The younger generation, alienated from society as are black people and resenting unjust authority, prizes the excitement, vitality, exuberance, drive, and electricity of Soul.

Nina Simone is our starter among soul singers, because her outcry against injustice is the most direct. But through her it will also become clear that soul music is not merely racial protest music. And it will become evident as we consider other soul singers that, even when the subject is love or sex, the character of soul sounds is an outgrowth of the black man's position in the contemporary scene. Like hot lava, the music wells out of a seemingly benign but really seething volcano. In short, we will discover that Soul is the projection in song of a new feeling of black dignity, self-respect, and militancy—and an unabashed search for and a return to roots.

15

NINA
SIMONE
The Rage
and Fury

Not long ago, while she was performing at the Roundtable, a swank jazz club on Manhattan's East Side, Nina Simone became so furious at the noisiness and inattention of a well-heeled audience that she stopped in the middle of a song and dashed offstage. Neither threats nor argument could persuade her to return.

An audience at Harlem's Apollo Theatre fared little better. An irritated Miss Simone interrupted her performance to lecture some unruly hecklers on the importance of good manners. Lest these incidents be construed as signs of her unconcern with audience approval, let it be noted that she wants that desperately.

However, as a critic in the *New York Post* observed, Miss Simone is "a member of a new breed of Negro entertainer—the antithesis of the posturing Uncle Tom who would do anything to win audience approval.*. . . That approval, however, must come on *her* terms and be grounded in respect for her work."

Another critic, John S. Wilson of the *New York Times*, has characterized her appearances as "essentially a battle of wills—hers against the audience."

"You're not giving one thing tonight," she chided listeners one evening at the Village Gate in New York City's Greenwich Village. "What bag are you in?"

Unconcerned? No! Demanding? Yes! The intensity of her reactions and of her performances is the result of overpowering feelings.

"Music gets me worked up," she told John Wilson. "I can't sing a song without meaning it." And the meanings of many of her songs are such that reviews of her concerts brim with words like "fury," "anger," and "rage."

"Her extraordinary faculty for communicating," Leonard Feather wrote of a UCLA concert, "is based in part on the urgent topicality of her songs, and in equal measure on the power, sometimes tantamount to fury, with which she drives home her point. . . . Though anger is by no means her only emotion, a great proportion of the material she uses . . . carries an urgent social message. . . . 'Four Women,' as always, was the most compelling story, told with a rage that had her listeners, black and white, cheering. . . ."

Released in 1966 in her album *Wild Is the Wind,* "Four Women" is a mordant satire on skin color and the effect of gradations of white and black on the attitudes and situations of four women. Radio stations in New York and Philadelphia manifested a strange paternalism and banned Nina's disk on the ground that it might offend black listeners! (The same reason was given years ago when stations banned a disk by Oscar Brown called "Black Boy" with a lyric by the Pulitzer Prize-winning Negress Gwendolyn Brooks.)

"Mississippi Goddam!" another of Nina's controversial songs never enjoyed the sound of any radio exposure. Its blasphemous title gave the stations an easy out. But Nina Simone was so upset that she would not make any concessions. The writing of the song was motivated by the Sunday school bombing in Birmingham, Alabama, in which four little girls lost their lives. As Nina was working on a commemorative song in her "tree home"—as she calls the isolation chamber over the garage at her Mt. Vernon, New York, house—James Meredith was shot in Mississippi:

> Alabama's got me upset [she wrote]
> Tennessee made me lose my rest
> And everybody knows about Mississippi—Goddam!

"All my life," she told John Wilson, "I've wanted to shout out my feeling of being imprisoned. I've known about the silence that makes that prison, as any Negro does."

Well, Miss Simone has begun "shouting out" as a songwriter only recently, although she discovered as far back as 1959 that she could write. Nineteen fifty-nine was the year in which Miss Simone came to public notice through a Bethlehem recording of "I Love You, Porgy" from the George Gershwin opera *Porgy and Bess*. During the recording session, two songs were scrapped by Bethlehem executives. To meet the emergency and fill the available recording time—union rates were the same for three hours and a maximum of four songs—Nina, who had not tried her hand at composing, improvised or composed two new songs.

The realization that she could sing came at an even more critical moment. During the summer of 1954, she decided to get a job in a nightclub. The Philadelphia music studio at which she worked as accompanist for vocal students was closed for the summer and her private piano students were also taking a recess. After a brief search, she found a spot in an Atlantic City bar that paid the handsome sum of ninety dollars a week. On her first night, she was approached by the owner, who wanted to know why she was not singing. Without realizing it, she had been hired as a singing pianist. During her second set that night, she sang—and has been singing ever since.

It was while she was working at this bar that Eunice Kathleen Waymon, as she had been christened in Tryon, North Carolina, in February, 1935, became Nina Simone. She had a double motive. She was planning to return to the Philadelphia music studio at summer's end, and she thought it would be better if the parents of her students did not know that she had entertained in a bar. And then there was the possible displeasure of her father, who was a handyman by day and an ordained minister at night and on Sundays. Accordingly, she chose Nina (*girl* in Spanish), a nickname by which she had been known as a child, and Simone because it seemed to go well with Nina.

The route to the vocal studio in Philadelphia had been comparatively direct, considering that Nina was the sixth of eight children and grew up in conditions of poverty that compelled her mother to work as a daytime housekeeper.

"When I was a child," Miss Simone has said, "nobody was ever proud of me, and my people were never proud of themselves or of anything they'd ever done." That they should have been, and might have been, was complicated by one fact: in the town of Tryon, Nina was, in her own words, "the most outstandingly talented little girl—and I was colored."

Nina manifested unusual musical talent so early in life that a white woman for whom her mother did housework arranged for her to receive piano lessons. Her teacher continued instructing her free of charge when her benefactor stopped paying for the lessons. It was as exciting for a little girl to receive such recognition as her first recital proved a cruel experience. Nina can never forget that recital. It was in the "white library."

"There was a big hassle," she recalls, not without a stab of pain, "about where my mother and father sat. That hurt me. Mis' Mazzie"—her teacher's name was Mrs. Lawrence Mazzanovich—"never knew how tense and scared those white people made me. I was split in half. I loved Bach. But the music was no joy, no pleasure."

Regardless of her inner ambivalence and tensions, Eunice Kathleen Waymon played so well that Mrs. Mazzanovich established a fund to guarantee her studies. As a result of contributions by white and black audiences at church and school recitals, she was able to attend the Allen High School for Girls in Asheville, North Carolina, where she distinguished herself academically and in extracurricular activities, and was valedictorian of her graduating class in 1950.

The fund established by Mis' Mazzie also enabled her to attend the Juilliard School of Music in New York City. Here she studied piano and theory with Carl Friedberg, a noted keyboard pedagogue, and seemed headed for a classical concert career. After she began working at Arlene Smith's Studio in Philadelphia (where her family had moved), she studied at the Curtis Institute, receiving instruction from the celebrated music educator Vladimir Sokoloff.

A major turning point in her career came when she decided to forget about becoming a concert pianist. "That's a very high goal to have," she has said. "Study eight hours a day. I didn't even think about it. I just got into it. I was very young. As I got older, though, I wanted a life of my own. Classical training was very demanding and thorough. It was a very sheltered existence. Even though I heard blues and gospel on the radio sometimes, it was always back to the piano and study and give recitals."

Miss Simone does not mention the additional demands made on a Negro seeking a concert career. But she gave up the idea during her working days in Philadelphia.

The second turning point of her career came in 1966 after the death of the four little girls in the Birmingham Sunday school bombing. Before then, she had recorded albums that allowed her to display her artistry as a pianist and her unique singing style. *In Concert* exemplifies one facet and *I Put A Spell on You* the other. Critics like Leonard Feather did not consider her a jazz pianist, although she improvised with extraordinary facility and taste. Her keyboard influences, by the way, are Oscar Peterson, Art Tatum, and Horace Silver, while her musical influences—after Bach—are John Coltrane, Dizzy Gillespie, and Miles Davis.

As a singer, she early manifested a kind of absorption in her material that transformed everything she touched with hugely personal emotions. In a song like "I Put a Spell on You," her voice takes on a searing tenor sax quality that cuts like a whiplash. She scats like a witch with an oboe and stutters like a disbelieving preacher. And in "Ne Me Quitte Pas"— Jacques Brel's intense songs excite her—her anguished pleading is overwhelming in its tenderness.

Since 1966 the very titles of her albums indicate a new emphasis in her expressive outlook and style: *High Priestess of Soul, Sings the Blues!* and *Silk and Soul*. Her own compositions during this period include a setting of Langston Hughes's troubling poem "Backlash Blues." "Turning Point" in *Silk and Soul* deals with a little girl made conscious of race for the first time: "Can't she come over and play with me, ma? What?

251

Oh . . ." Quite recently, she wrote the moving song, "I Wish I Knew How It Would Feel to Be Free."

"Go Limp" is a narrative ballad on which she collaborated with Alex Comfort, whose lyric tells of a girl on a freedom march:

> With a brick in my handbag
> And a smile on my face
> And barbed wire in my underwear
> To shut out disgrace.

Miss Simone has an acid sense of humor, even though her face is not made for smiling or easy laughter.

The anger and fury now apparent in her work are really not new. Long before 1966, Miss Simone frequently performed "Strange Fruit," originally recorded by one of her idols, Billie Holiday. (She treasures a short note she received from Billie about her debut recording of *Porgy and Bess*.) And Nina did the antilynching classic with a suppressed sense of indignation that reached its peak in a display of rage seldom heard in a nightclub. But even when she was performing tender ballads like "Little Girl Blue," she delivered them with a mesmerizing intensity that held audiences spellbound. Miss Simone has always been inside her songs and has generally been able to penetrate the inner recesses of her listeners. This is subtle possession and as potent as the psychedelic variety of James Brown and Aretha Franklin.

Reviewing a joyous two days of jazz at Berkeley in May 1969, a *New York Times* observer reported, "Nina Simone's set was, perhaps, the emotional high point of the festival. Without compromise, but also with humor, she sang songs to black beauty and was so convincing in her person that the whole audience, white and black, responded thunderously."

16

JAMES BROWN
The Frenzy
and the Sex

He calls himself "America's No. 1 Soul Brother." But he has also been typed as "the last great figure in the history of Negro dance" (*Newsweek*), "the greatest demagogue in the history of Negro entertainment" (the *New York Times*), "a great stage lover" (ditto), "the most exciting performer on records and on stage today" (*Music Business*), "a ranking black capitalist" (*Look*), and "the first black man in the 30-year history of *Cash Box* magazine to be cited as Best Male Vocalist on Single Pop Records."

The man who is all these things was born poor-black in the red clay hills of the Georgia-Carolina border sometime between 1930 and 1934. An only child, he knew little about his father or mother. He left school in the seventh grade. By that time he had picked cotton, washed cars, danced for coins from soldiers at Fort Gordon (near Augusta), and shined shoes outside a Macon radio station he now owns.

Only five of America's 528 R & B stations are owned by black men. Brown owns two and is considering the purchase of four more. He also owns a record production company, considerable real estate, a music publishing company, and sundry personal effects (five hundred suits, three hundred pairs of shoes, six cars, a twin-engine Lear jet, and a castle cum drawbridge-and-moat in St. Albans, New York). With a staff of eighty-five people, his payroll is reported at $1.1 million.

In 1968 his gross from one-nighters was calculated at $2.5 million, of which 10 percent reportedly went to black charities and ghetto youth groups. Said to be worth more than $3 million, he is in the process of developing a chain of black-managed restaurants to be known as Gold Platters, Inc.

Since 1964 he has been singing a song from the musical *Pickwick* titled "If I Ruled the World." He has sung it so frequently—he uses the words "If I had the world"—that it is almost his theme song. And well it might be, considering how much of the world he has been able to possess. But has he?

In April, 1969, after an informal visit with Macon's Mayor Ronnie Thompson, a onetime gospel singer, he announced that he was moving from New York, where he was "just another of the big numbers," to Macon, where he was "treated as a man."

And when he returned from Vietnam in June, 1968, the first major performer of his race to have visited the fighting front, he told reporters, "We had to fight to do this show, period! . . . I could only take eight of my band, but I saw plenty of empty seats on the plane in economy class—well, they said transportation was hard to come by—I won't argue the point. But, gentlemen, I'll tell you the whole thing in a nutshell. To me, America is still the greatest country in the world—but we don't have to fight with each other. Otherwise, we'll blow it."

And he continued, "I drew more people than Bob Hope at one place—thirty-eight thousand soldiers, but Hope got six months' preparation and I get a day and a half—and I've been trying to get over there for a year now. . . . Go back? Sure! But first class! I went economy. Why? I don't know. . . . The USO does. . . . I spent thirty-five hundred dollars of my own money. . . ."

Gold Platters—the real thing, not plates of food—accounted for the fantastic change in Brown's status and outlook, a change, he constantly tells his black audiences, that is possible for any man in the ghetto. It took less than twenty years if you figure from the time he left a Toccoa, Georgia, church where he sang spirituals. (He was then on parole from a three-year reform school sentence for car theft and breaking and entering.) It took less than ten years if you reckon from his first big hit record, "Please, Please, Please," released by King of Cincinnati in 1956.

Since then, largely unknown in the white world, he has been one of the most consistent sellers of records in music business. The Top Ten of R & B charts include "Think," "Baby You're Right," "Bewildered!" "I Don't Mind," "Lost Someone," "Prisoner of Love," a revival, and "Ain't That a Groove." In the same period, Brown had number ones in "Try Me" (1958), "I Got You" (1965), "Papa's Got a Brand New Bag" (1965), and "It's a Man's Man's World" (1966). Even "Don't Be A Drop Out," a song he wrote to promote high school attendance after touring the San Francisco ghetto, invaded the Top Ten.

As for albums, there was such a demand for Brown LPs that King rushed out more than fifteen. All became best sellers. Included were *Pure Dynamite, Cold Sweat,* and *Raw Soul,* their very titles indicative of the Brown bag of explosives.

But the record market is only one facet of a career that has encompassed the most grueling schedule of personal appearances ever attempted by a performer. Not a few artists, white as well as black, have given up income and renown rather than submit to the destructive demands of life on the road.

But Brown, who was once a prizefighter under the tutelage of ex-champ Beau Jack, has a stamina and ambition that boosted his road gross from half a million in 1963 to two and a half million dollars in 1968. It is said that he travels 335 days a year. Music biz pros will tell you that there is no substitute for "meeting the people," a type of promotion that works even with books, as the author of *Valley of the Dolls* has demonstrated.

The almost magical power Brown wields over black audiences and record buyers was well illustrated in the days following the assassination of Martin Luther King, Jr. He was scheduled to play the Boston Garden when news of King's murder was flashed to the world. He immediately canceled his show and was planning to return to New York when a call came from the mayor of Boston. Worried that the murder of the black leader would set off riots, the mayor asked for Brown's help in calming his people.

All through the day, announcements were made at regular intervals in Boston that Soul Brother No. 1 would appear on TV. And that night Brown was visible on the television tube for six consecutive hours, a period when blacks were little interested in going out on the streets of Boston.

The following day, the mayor of Washington, D.C., was on the phone asking for Brown's help in cooling the Negroes of the nation's capital. Brown flew down and went out on the streets to talk to gangs of looters. That night he appeared on Washington TV.

"This is the greatest country in the world," he told his viewers. "If we destroy it, we're out of our heads. We've come too far to throw it away. You gotta fight with dignity."

The potency of his charisma in preventing riots on a smaller scale was demonstrated at Yankee Stadium, where he appeared after his return from Vietnam. At one point, kids began rushing the stage, anxious merely to touch Soul Brother No. 1. In an effort to protect him, guards and police raced to surround him. The situation was rapidly deteriorating into a riotous clamor when Brown managed to get to a mike. First he ordered all guards and police off the stage. Then slowly and patiently he talked the excited crowd back into their seats.

His remarkable ability to sway his soul brothers was given quiet recognition when he took his chair at a White House dinner to which he had been invited by the President of the United States. His place card bore the personal message, "Thanks much for what you are doing for your country." It was handwritten and signed "Lyndon B. Johnson."

Yet when he returned from Vietnam in June, 1968, and a crowd of blacks waited with placards at Kennedy Airport to greet him, a *Village Voice* reporter encountered two white nuns who said, "Oh, we all thought that Mr. Brown was a fighter—with a nickname like Mr. Dynamite."

The *Village Voice* man approached two second-generation Italians from Wilkes-Barre, Pennsylvania, who were seeing their uncle off to Rome. They laughed and confessed, "We thought it was Rap Brown. We were looking for his sneakers."

Despite the millions of records he has sold and the thousands of appearances he has made all over the United States, Brown is not very well known among whites. Astounding as this may at first appear, it is not too surprising considering his limited exposure on TV and in white clubs. Until recently, this limitation was the consequence of Brown's style. Unlike Ray Charles, Diana Ross, and other black singing stars, Brown has not gone commercial. As an artist and a pro, he is capable of adapting if he wishes.

Listen to his singing of "Mona Lisa" in his *Cold Sweat* album, and it is clear that he can handle a ballad tenderly and sweetly. His only departure from a comparatively straight reading is in the intensity produced by the shrill timbre of his voice and his personalized spacing of the lyric.

Contrast "Mona Lisa" with "Come Rain or Come Shine" in the same album, where he lets himself go, and the shrillness of his voice peaks in shrieks and screams, words disappear in banshee wails and the stuttered repetition of syllables, and the final word becomes one long, extended, snake-hissed "shi-i-i-i-i-ne." As a matter of curiosity, listen also to his rendition of "I Love You, Porgy," where he is so overcome by emotion that he confuses Porgy with Bess—literally has Porgy singing to himself—and manages surprisingly to find a happy ending for the tragic pair.

In short, Mr. Dynamite does not have to whine and screech like a jungle cat, he does not have to grunt, howl, or use tense falsetto, he does not have to stutter like a stammerer in spasm. But this is Soul and this is James Brown. And when he does appear, as he has begun to, in New York's Copa or L.A.'s Cocoanut Grove, he does not make concessions to his white listeners but compels them to accept him on his own terms. He is closer in this respect to Aretha Franklin than to Nina Simone, whose classical keyboard training gives her a ready point of contact.

Even when he handles white material, his version is so black it sounds like another song. Take as an instance "Prisoner of Love," the song co-authored, introduced by, and associated with Russ Columbo—and a hit for Perry Como in 1946. At no time does Brown use the entire title phrase. Instead, he repeats over and over, "I'm just a prisoner . . . don't let me be a prisoner." He phrases and manipulates the melody so freely that only the chord sequence keeps us aware of the song's original form.

The record ends on a series of feline wails, as a vocal group develops a rhythmic ostinato against which Brown hurls free phrases, some so soft they are inaudible gasps, while others rise into uncontrolled shrieks. The insistent omission of the terminal word of the title, "Prisoner of Love," gives the song unexpected social overtones, and the elongated ending succeeds in communicating the prisoner's search for an escape route that does not exist.

Commenting on Brown's in-person impact, Albert Goldman has said in the *New York Times,* "Mr. Dynamite is a great stage lover, a man who can take on thousands of women at a time and reduce them to screaming jelly. In fact, he goes after the women in the audience a lot more directly than do most entertainers. When he does one of his slow drags, like 'It's a Man's World,' the rapport between him and the girls reaches scandalous proportions. He shouts with killing sincerity, 'Just be there when I get the notion!' and the screams come back from the house like an enormous trumpet section screeching in on cue. . . ."

Mass erotic frenzy reaches such heights of soulful interplay that, in the view of rock critic Richard Goldstein, Brown's stage presentations and his record style are "really constructed around the attainment of orgasm." At times, the female response has the ecstatic spillover of an attained peak, as it did with Sinatra in the mid-forties.

But there is another factor that enters into Brown's in-person appearances, a quasi-religious quality. At the end of a show, he rushes back onstage, his face drenched with the sweat of exhaustion, and collapses. His attendants throw a bespangled robe over him. In a matter of seconds, the robe rises and Brown flies forth like a phoenix emerging from a fiery pyre. He races offstage and again returns to collapse, to be covered with another bespangled robe, and to rise. The convulsive ritual has been compared by some reviewers to an enactment of the Crucifixion. The analogy is sound. But I take the ritual, Brown's falls and risings, to represent Jesus at the stations of the cross.

Whether one regards his style as orgiastic religion or sanctified sex, it is compounded of extremes of emotion, excitement, and expression that are characteristic of gospel meets. It is the blackest black. And that's the way Soul Brother No. 1 wants it to remain. In his spoken words as well as his songs, he makes an emphatic identification with his soul brothers.

"Without you there wouldn't be a James Brown," he told his Yankee Stadium audience. "This evening's event should serve as a reminder of what black people can do if they get together. . . . You know, that marquee tonight says James Brown—now, that's not a baseball team or a football team, but a soul brother! And I thank *you*!"

At another moment in the show, after he had talked the boisterous crowd into settling down, he said, "I can't see you not enjoyin' it—a man gets where I am—look, I am you. I never want to be nothing but you, a soul brother, and that's what I identify with. . . . Two-thirds of tonight's money will go to the ghettos . . . and we're doing it ourselves. . . ."

In 1968 Brown made his position emphatic in a song he wrote and recorded, "Say It Loud—I'm Black and I'm Proud."

But there are soul brothers with whom Brown does not identify—the militants. "I'm a racist," he has said, "when it comes to freedom. I can't rest until the black man in America is let out of jail, until his dollar's as good as the next man's." He has no illusion that the prison doors will swing open easily, and he warns, "This country's gonna blow in two years unless the white man wakes up. The black man's got to be set free. He's got to be treated as a man. I don't say hire a cat 'cause he's black. Just hire him if he's right. This country is like a crap game. I'll lose my money to any man long as the game is fair. But if I find the dice are crooked, I'll turn over the table. What we need are programs that are so out of sight they'll leave the militants with their mouths open. A

259

militant is just a cat that's never been allowed to be a man."

H. Rap Brown, one of the militants, inevitably found reason to question some of Brown's activities, and dismissed him in none-too-complimentary fashion as the "Roy Wilkins of the music world." Rap Brown did not approve of James Brown's role in helping the Establishment cool the April, 1968, riots in Boston and Washington. He was suspicious of Soul Brother No. 1's acceptance of an invitation to the White House. And he was so critical of a new James Brown recording, "America Is My Home," that Mr. Dynamite felt called upon to reply:

"I was talkin' about the land, the country, not the government. There's no country can beat us if we get the race problem fixed. This is *home*. We can't leave. Never found another nation yet that could make hard ice cream or decent soul food."

But another militant, playwright-author LeRoi Jones, speaking at a Black Power conference in the fall of 1968, named James Brown "our number-one black poet." There was an intimation that he perhaps needed guidance in areas outside the esthetic.

As for his esthetic accomplishment, James Brown long ago earned the right to call himself Soul Brother No. 1. Our criterion for admitting artists to the select circle of the soul stirrers is audience reaction. It is not enough for the performer to resort to extreme forms of expression, since these can be fabricated. What counts is the response of the listener. Does the expressiveness provoke strong vocal and physical reactions? In a word, does the possessed achieve possession? James Brown does—and how!

17

JIMI HENDRIX
Reactive Noise and the Big Nasty

Jimi Hendrix was named Artist of the Year for 1968 by two publications as far apart as the moon and Mars. But the grounds for their choice were strikingly similar.

Billboard wrote: "His second U.S. tour showed he was second to none in appeal and excitement. . . . His impact extends far beyond his songwriting. His fusing of the highly-amplified music of today with the purer sound of the blues places him at the forefront of today's major pop music trend."

That underground arbiter of the pure in rock—*Rolling Stones*—chose him for "creativity, electricity and calls above and beyond the call of duty. . . . Blues players, jazz players, rock players—all were agreed that Hendrix' improvisations transcended category and constituted music as imaginative and alive as rock and roll has known. Jimi, more than any other player, has extended the voice of amplified guitar to an incredible range of new emotive sounds."

Hendrix has had other titles bestowed upon him. He has been described as "the Black Elvis," "the Wilt Chamberlain of electric guitar players," "a genuine nightmare," "brash buccaneer with a wa-wa," "the most spectacular electric guitarist in the world," and the "Wild Man of Pop." He has himself characterized his music as "ugly," while others call it "violent."

At the Monterey Pop Festival in 1967 he went The Who

one better. Instead of breaking his guitar to pieces, he doused his instrument with lighter fluid and set it on fire. But word had already preceded his arrival here—after tours in England and France—that he picked his guitar with his teeth as if he were eating the strings and played it with his tongue. That he sometimes threw himself supine and, holding the instrument on his belly like an upright phallus, pumped it as he lay on his back. And that, as a clincher, he played the instrument behind his back, shoved it forward between his legs, strummed on it violently, and then propelled it from his groin as if it were coming climactically out of his fly.

His trademark has been described by Michael Lydon as "careless, slovenly, and blatantly erotic arrogance," but Tom Phillips, in a review of his first album, *Are You Experienced,* was sharper in suggesting that Hendrix carried eroticism to the point of degeneracy. There's a hint of it in the face, even if he "cries easy," as he told an interviewer, and others have found him "a shy and introverted man away from the stage." It's suggested by the big, bushy mane of uncombed hair. And perhaps it's audible in the thundering volume at which his group plays—"top volume," as Lydon described it, "the bass and drums building a wall of black noise heard as much by pressure on the eyeballs as with the ears."

I am including the Jimi Hendrix Experience in the soul category because he represents a type of visual and audible extremism implicit in Soul. But he is also so much a product and instance of gimmickry that he warns us of the thin line dividing authenticity from fabrication. Where does true emotion begin and the put-on, through mastery of all the audible and visual embodiments, end?

A man's scars and the dues he has paid cannot be disregarded. Born James Marshall Hendrix in the black ghetto of Seattle, Washington, in 1946, he was kicked out of Garfield High School, as he tells it, for holding hands in art class with a white girl. (Elsewhere he has said that he quit high school at sixteen to join the paratroopers, and "man, was I bored!")

Having learned guitar through listening to records of Muddy Waters, Elmore James, B. B. King, and Chuck Berry, he became an itinerant bluesman, "sleepin' outside between them tall tenements [with] rats runnin' all across your chest and cockroaches stealin' your last candy bar from your pockets."

A gig in the backup band of the Isley Brothers eventually brought him to Nashville where, after playing the small black clubs, he joined a package show starring B. B. King, Sam Cooke, Solomon Burke, and Chuck Jackson. Missing the show bus one day, he found himself stranded in Kansas City, Missouri.

Apologetically, he observes, "When you're running around starving on the road, you'll play almost anything. I was more or less forced into like a Top 40 bag."

Drifting to Atlanta, Georgia, he joined a Little Richard tour. One of his vivid, if unpleasant, memories involves an altercation over some fancy shirts that he and another guy donned " 'cause we were tired of wearing the uniform." As he tells it, "Little Richard called a meeting. 'I am Little Richard, I am Little Richard,' he said, 'the king, the King of Rock and Rhythm. I am the only one allowed to be pretty. Take off those shirts.' Man, it was like that. Bad pay, lousy living, and getting burned."

The tour with Little Richard took him out to the coast, where he played the Fillmore in the backup band of Ike and Tina Turner. After a time, he drifted back to New York and lost himself in the R & B gigs of King Curtis and the twist music of Joey Dee and the Starlighters. Curtis has said that he was "tough to work with, very moody." But Jimi also begged his way onto Harlem bandstands, where he got burned, apparently because of his wild hairdo.

"I couldn't stand it there," he later said, "because they talk about you worse than anyplace else!" And so, strangely, he became a refugee from Harlem, drifting downtown to the Village, where no one at the Cafe Wha! bothered about his unconventional hairdo or music. No one, that is, until Charles Bryant Chandler, ex-member of the British Animals, and Mike Jeffrey, the group's manager, came in one night and began urging him to come to England.

"I said I might as well go," he later told Valerie Wilmer

in a London interview, "because nothing much was happening. We were making something near three dollars a night and you *know* we were starving! I only hope that the guys I left behind are doing all right. The way I left was kinda wrong—they all thought they were going, but this way it was much easier for me to go alone. I feel kinda rotten about leaving just like that because we weren't living much, you dig?"

Jimmy James, as he then called himself, left his Blue Flame combo in August, 1966. By October 12, the Jimi Hendrix Experience had been formed in London, with Noel Redding, a guitarist who switched to bass, and Mitch Mitchell, a drummer devotee of explosive Elvin Jones, completing the trio. "Hey Joe," the group's first disk, made number four on British charts, and their second and third platters, "Purple Haze" and "Wind Cries Mary," likewise were fast and big chart climbers. Perhaps these disks and the group's overly loud, electrified, loose-jointed, every-man-for-himself style of playing might have made them the overnight sensation they became. But showmanship and weird stage antics played their roles in transforming an unknown of '66 into '68's artist of the year. There was also some astute promotion, as Charles Chandler admitted.

From the first photograph session after the group was formed, only the "more gruesome shots which made him look like a big nasty" were chosen for circulation. Chandler early set about promoting Hendrix as the big bogeyman of all time.

"It was in Munich in their first experimental appearances," Chandler told Keith Altham in a *Hit Parader* interview, "that I realized his enormous visual attraction, and there that the 'smashing routine' really began by accident. Jimi was pulled offstage by a few overenthusiastic fans. As he jumped back onstage, he threw his guitar before him. When he picked it up, he saw that it had cracked and several of the strings were broken. He just went balmy and smashed everything in sight. The German audience loved it and we decided to keep it in as part of the act when there was a good press about or the occasion demanded it."

In this period, Chandler also encouraged Hendrix to be outspoken in press interviews, not to be concerned about unconventional things he might say or frank revelations he might make. Hendrix thereupon went about saying that he was the world's worst singer and that he hoped to be appreciated only for his guitar playing, assertions that greatly impressed sentimental press people and netted him large coverage.

Following the conquest of England and the Continent, stage three in the campaign to put Hendrix across as a topflight star was the American album market. Against the advice of sage show biz promoters, Hendrix was made part of a tour of the Monkees, a group whose following (built via their TV show) reportedly consisted largely of subteen boppers. Conceding that the incongruous booking was like putting Count Dracula on with Snow White, Chandler explains that they hoped for a big publicity break. Partly because the Jimi Hendrix Experience received no advance billing and partly because the Monkees were the star attraction, the publicity did not come until it had been decided that the tour was a mistake and Hendrix should leave it.

"We concocted the story," Chandler admits, "about the Daughters of the American Revolution objecting to Jimi's act and saying it was obscene. That did the trick—and we hit every newspaper in the country, with Jimi coming up with little gems about how he had been replaced by Mickey Mouse." The underground American press immediately jumped to the defense of "someone who had affronted the dignity of the Establishment," and the Experience had it made with the hippies and west coasters.

But the initial impact on American audiences, Chandler contends, was made at Monterey. And Keith Altham adds, "I can vouch for that myself, as I was there when Hendrix brought a ten thousand capacity crowd to its feet with his guitar antics and incredible improvisation."

Charisma and visual antics have a carry-over impact on records played at home. But there must be something in the grooves to command the audience that Hendrix has been able to reach. By August, 1968, his acceptance was apparent in two albums, both selling in such quantities that they were in the Top Twenty: *Are You Experienced* at number 10 and

Axis: Bold As Love at number sixteen. The third album, a double LP titled *Electric Ladyland,* became the first to reach number one—and that was achieved in a record-breaking interval of five weeks. Having previously demonstrated his craft as a songwriter, Hendrix here proved his point as a record producer.

Rock producer Tom Wilson said, "He combines the phantasmagoric splendor of a Hieronymus Bosch painting with the funky essence of rhythm and blues. The cat is out of sight."

By virtue of his possessive power over listeners, Hendrix warrants a soul tag. But in a large sense he is in another bag.

Eric Barrett, who handles his sound equipment, recently said, "Jimi is the master of feedback. He plays both amplifiers full up at volume ten. . . . He destroys at least two speakers whenever he plays. . . . Then there's the wah-wah pedal. Most people just touch it with their foot. Jimi jumps on it with his full weight so I carry about three extra wah-wah pedals and ten extra fuzz boxes. . . . He ruins a lot of tremolo bars, too. He bends the strings with the bar, and they get bent way past the distortion level. That starts the feedback. . . . The pickups in the guitar amplify all the strings bending. That's how he gets that terrifying roar. . . . Jimi also burns up a lot of tubes because of the great volume. . . . One night he burned out four amplifiers. You see, his amplifiers are turned full up and pushing what they're supposed to, but then all the speakers are pushing plus the fuzz and the wah-wah, so there's often more power than the amplifiers can take. . . ."

And there's more volume than even an experienced sound man can take. "I think I've gone deaf," Eric Barrett told *Hit Parader's* Jim Delehant, "from standing near the cabinets. I'm going home to Scotland for two weeks to see if my hearing comes back to normal."

What Jimi Hendrix has done is to take the "wall of sound" concept developed in the early sixties by Righteous Brothers producer Phil Spector and others, and transform it into what is now known as "reactive music." Behind the ear-shattering volume is a feeling and a philosophy as well as the search for aural excitement. Jimi and his cohorts are trying to shut out a stinking world by enveloping themselves and the audience in their own impenetrable sound.

"Man, the world's a bring-down," Jimi is saying. "If we play loud enough, maybe we can drown it out."

There's sex in *Electric Ladyland*. In "Crosstown Traffic," Jimi tells his girl, "Ninety miles an hour is the speed I drive," but "it's so hard to get through you." There's also the escapism of "1983: A Merman I Should Be," where, as the universe is about to be destroyed by war, he and his lady kiss it off by flight into the science fiction or fantasy world of life in the sea. Throughout, there's constant use of manipulated electronic sound, phasing, tape loop, feedback, fuzz, and high-amp volume.

Not too long ago, Hendrix told an interviewer, "Once in a while I like to listen to that soul stuff, but I don't like to play it too much anymore. Soul isn't adventurous enough. It's just the one same thing." He added, "What I hate is society trying to put everything and everybody into little tight cellophane compartments. . . . They don't get me in any cellophane cage. Nobody cages me."

18

OTIS REDDING
Tough and
Soulfully Tender

In the summer of 1967, Otis Redding told an interviewer that he wanted "to fill the silent void caused by Sam Cooke's death." He was just twenty-six years old then and on the verge of rising out of black ghetto music skies into the milky way of pop superstardom. On what turned out to be his last session—he was dead in a plane crash less than six months after the interview—Otis recorded "Shake," a song written by Cooke and recorded by him at what accidentally became *his* last session. (Curiously, just three years separated the two tragedies. Cooke was shot on December 11, 1964, and Otis was at the bottom of Wisconsin's Lake Monona on December 10, 1967.)

Sam Cooke was one of two major influences on Redding's vocal style. Cooke gave Otis a feeling for soul in its tenderer, quieter, and more introspective moments. But Cooke had swagger and ego that linked him with the other major Redding influence. Little Richard, the first of the orgiastic rhythm-and-bluesmen, was a Macon resident whose frenzies bombarded the ears of young Otis as he was growing up in the Georgia town.

One gave depth to Redding's emotional expressiveness, the other excitement. The two influences combined to make him a commanding figure on stage. Rock critic Jon Landau once saw Redding perform at a revue in Boston.

"The audience," he later wrote, "was overwhelmingly black and sat through two and a half hours of soul music before Redding made his appearance. The crowd was growing restive and had heard many singers say, 'Let me see you clap your hands,' and all that. Then Redding came on. The first thing he did was say, 'Let me see you clap your hands.' You immediately forgot the preceding two and a half hours and clapped your hands. . . . Then he said, 'Shake,' and kept on repeating it until everybody said it."

Those who attended the Monterey Pop Festival in the summer of 1967 witnessed a similar spectacle. Redding once again did not come on stage until quite late, nearly 1 A.M. By then the audience had heard and seen enough to make it tired and tough. But Redding dashed onstage with that half grin and big, self-amused mouthful of teeth, kicked the band off with four solid beats, and had the crowd screaming within seconds.

Jazz critic Ralph J. Gleason, who heard Redding in a San Francisco club, wrote, "In person, everything Redding does is an all-out powerhouse, total emotional explosion. He may start singing 'Try a Little Tenderness' with tenderness, but it always ends up 'Sock it to me, baby'. . . . He can work listeners into a frenzy more quickly than any night club performer of his time."

Born in Dawson, Georgia, the son of a Baptist minister, Redding imbibed gospel influences in his earliest years and, being a child of the 1940s, grew up with the sound of rock 'n' roll and R & B in his ears. As a high school student in Macon, he was so impressed by the adulation showered on Little Richard, a local luminary, that he determined to become a performer. By then Redding, who was a natural musician, could play as many as five instruments, and was singing as well as playing gigs around town.

Phil Walden, who today heads one of the largest R & B management businesses in the world and shortly was to become his manager, first met Redding when he booked a band for a rush party at Mercer University in Macon. Otis was the band vocalist. Through Walden, Redding became acquainted with another local band, Johnny Jenkins and the Pinetoppers. It was a fortunate association, for Jenkins was an Atlantic artist through whom Redding accidentally made his first recording. Jenkins cut his sides at the Stax/Volt Studio in Memphis, where Redding drove him in 1962.

In a tribute Stax/Volt producer-guitarist Steve Cropper wrote after Redding's death, he recalled his first contact with Otis: "At the time [in 1962] Otis was sort of a road manager, singer, driver for Johnny Jenkins. One day they came to the studio to cut a bunch of sides. Otis was just sitting over in the corner all day long and every once in a while he'd say, 'Man, I sure would like to cut a song.' After we finished Jenkins, we said, 'OK, let's see what this guy's got. He's been sitting here all day and he seems real interested.' "

The song Redding cut that fateful day was "These Arms of Mine." It became his first release and was only moderately successful. More significantly, it led to an association with the Memphis Sound and with Cropper, who collaborated with him on his first Stax/Volt release and other songs, including the posthumous award winner "(Sitting on) The Dock of the Bay."

While Redding contributed much to the Memphis Sound, the Stax/Volt influence was critical in his career. Motown and the Detroit Sound represented a major market breakthrough of black artists and recording power, but largely on white terms. Coming at a later stage in the black invasion of pop, the Memphis Sound represented the mopping up phase of the operation. It was possible for the M.G.'s of Booker T. to be half white and half black because all were blues oriented and their common orientation was black, not white.

Redding's earliest recordings reveal an interest in sentimental ballads. It earned him the sobriquet of "Mr. Pitiful," after a song he wrote with Steve Cropper and his first best seller on Stax. The instrumental background of the record is sock black, but Redding, except for the intense, supplicating quality of his voice, is not blues oriented. While *Pain in My Heart*, his first album (1963), showed the influence of Little Richard's shout style, it pointed in a direction that could have led to Brook Benton rather than Ray Charles.

The Stax/Volt influence was astringent. You hear a different singer in "I've Been Loving You Too Long," a slow-drag ballad he wrote with Jerry Butler. Still the suppliant lover, he now delivers with a violent intensity that compels him to worry syllables beyond endurance and to end the disk on an unending stream of endearments. In "Respect," his hit of that year (1965) and later Aretha Franklin's, he writes with an earthy ferocity that yields one of the classic ballads of our time:

> I'm out to give you all of my money
> And all I'm askin' in return, Honey,
> Is to give me my propers when I get home . . .

And what's that? Sweet words? A kiss? No, baby:

> Whip it/ whip it/ whip it to me when I get home . . .

Never was the concept of "respect" given a more honest and more realistic domestic definition. To the man of the house, respect is warm, willing, freely given, exciting sex.

The Sam Cooke-ballad influence and charisma remained, stirring Otis to record "Try a Little Tenderness" when he heard his idol's version in the album *Sam Cooke at the Copa.* However, there's nothing sentimental about Otis's treatment. The record builds to the white-heat intensity of his up-tempo stomp pieces.

The year 1966 also found him cutting and making a best seller of the Rolling Stones' "Satisfaction," hardly a song of mawkish emotion and, in Redding's reading, caked with Memphis mud.

Redding had been making records for less than five years when a new airplane he bought took his life, and also the lives of four of the Bar-Kays, his backup band, Yet in that brief period his impact was so great that, two months before his death, an English trade paper, *Melody Maker,* named him the World's No. 1 Male Vocalist, a title that had been monopolized during the preceding ten years by Elvis Presley. The British broadcasting industry reacted quickly, as did the national radio network of France. The BBC flew a crew to Redding's Georgia ranch—a three-hundred-acre farm he bought with music money near Macon—and filmed a TV documentary. It provoked Ralph J. Gleason to ask in the *San Francisco Chronicle* why Redding had not received similar recognition in his own country and to suggest that there was still a color lag in the United States.

That Aretha Franklin could make a number-one pop hit of Otis's song "Respect" and he could make only a Top Ten R & B best seller of it is less a reflection on Redding than on the development of the market. It is a manifestation of the difference in black temper and white taste between 1965 and 1968. The promise of wider acceptance, anticipated by those who heard Redding at Monterey, was perhaps realized sooner than anyone expected, but not soon enough for Otis to be a witness.

In a year-end survey that appeared in December, 1968, he was among the Top Five Singles Artists, just behind Aretha, Gary Puckett, the Beatles, and James Brown. "(Sitting on) The Dock of the Bay" had already gone to number one on R & B charts. Posthumously, it captured a Grammy as the Best R & B Song of the year, won another Grammy for him personally for Best R & B Performance, and gave him the only Gold Record of his abbreviated life.

There are some, like Robert Shelton of the *New York Times*, who feel that Redding's "true magic came alive on stage where a torrent of motion, gesture and total involvement would be unleashed." Regardless, the most ironic aspect of his regrettably early death is that, among soul singers, he most communicated an infectious *joie de vivre*—the joy and excitement of living. He was a tough singer who could be soulfully tender.

Since Redding's death, four posthumous albums have been released. All are outstanding sellers and the demand for his disks displays no diminution. In fact, so large a cult has grown up around him that a writer in *Rolling Stone* urged young record buyers not to forget the live soul singers, who could use the enthusiasm they were showering on "the Kennedy of rock, the mythic hero cut down in the prime of life. . . ."

19

ARETHA
FRANKLIN
Lady Soul

In *Aretha Arrives,* her second Atlantic album, Miss Franklin sings a swinger written by her sister Carolyn, "Ain't Nobody (Gonna Turn Me Around)." Nobody can say that Columbia Records did not try. From 1961, for five years after John Hammond had signed her, she recorded jazz tunes, pretty standards, and torch ballads, the white equivalent of heartbreak blues—nine albums of them. A few sold, but everybody, including Aretha, knew that something was missing. At the same time, Miss Franklin made the rounds of the nightclub circuit—not the big plush white spots but the small jazz clubs and rhythm-and-blues bars.

"I sang a lot to the floor," she has said. "I was afraid."

What did she fear? The failure properly to assess this admission has led some critics into egregious errors of interpretation. For example, Albert Goldman wrote in the *New York Times,* "More than any other singer in the soul bag, she makes salvation seem erotic and the erotic seem like our salvation." How far Mr. Goldman is off the mark may be judged from a succeeding statement in which, evaluating her album *Lady Soul,* he observes, "Regrettably [*sic*] . . . the most noticeable tendency is a regression towards traditional gospel style."

On the basis of his emphasis, the *Times* captioned a five-column photograph of Aretha "Queen of Soul has the gift of a 'natural woman.'" And this is the rub. Miss Franklin does not look like a natural woman in that picture, or in most photos of her that have appeared. She looks like what she is and what accounted for her fears when she sang in nightclubs. Aretha looks like a comparatively young girl. I was about to say young, immature girl. But I am not trying to judge, only to describe her, and to fathom an enigma that has not yet been critically solved. Aretha was afraid because the role of a nightclub "chantoosie," torch singer, femme fatale—call it what you will—was entirely foreign to her and her background.

Things were moving too fast for Aretha, as they have been for much of her life. And she just has not been able to catch up. (I was about to say "until recently" when word came of her fiasco engagement at Caesar's Palace in Las Vegas where, after three days, management and Aretha agreed to terminate her appearances. She could not go on the first night. She went on the second night, but her performance was apparently unsatisfactory. Amid rumblings of contributory domestic difficulties—her husband is her manager—Sinatra was hastily called in to fill out the unexpired portion of her engagement.)

It comes as a surprise to learn that Aretha is the mother of three children—aged six, nine, and ten—all of them born before she was out of her teens. It does not come as a surprise that Aretha is shy, withdrawn, and prone to live in a shell.

"She sleeps until afternoon," according to friends, "then mopes in front of the television set, chain-smoking and snacking compulsively. . . . Most of her socializing is confined to the small circle of girlhood friends with whom, until a couple of years ago, she spent Wednesday nights skating at the Arcadia Roller Rink (in Detroit)."

Friends do not add, though they well might, that she was not the most popular of girls and hardly the type the boys buzzed about. Aretha was a nice girl, but also a troubled girl. Growing up in a middle-class ghetto just outside the poor black neighborhood that nourished Diana Ross, Smokey Robinson, and other Motown artists, she missed both maternal and paternal love.

Mama ran out on the family when Aretha was six and died

when she was ten—two shocks that left ineradicable scars. Papa is the high-binding and high-living Reverend C. L. Franklin, pastor of Detroit's flourishing New Bethel Baptist Church. A fiery gospel preacher who has recorded fifty-two volumes of his sermons for Chess Records, he is a charmer whose sacred calling somehow has not interfered with other, more mundane interests. In 1967 he paid a twenty-five-thousand-dollar fine for failing to file federal tax returns that would have shown an income of more than seventy-six thousand dollars between 1959 and 1962. Mahalia Jackson, who knows the family well, has said, "After Aretha's mama died, the whole family wanted for love."

Nor does it come as a shock when Aretha tells a *Time* reporter, "I might be just 26, but I'm an old woman in disguise—26 goin' on 65. Trying to grow up is hurting, you know. You make mistakes. You try to learn from them, and when you don't, it hurts even more. And I've been hurt—hurt bad."

Among the things that hurt was a circumstance that hurts all people of her color, just being black. By the time she was a ripe fourteen, Aretha was a featured performer with her father's gospel caravan, traveling across country by car for whistle-stop appearances.

An older brother, Cecil, now assistant pastor of the New Bethel Baptist Church, explains, "Driving eight or ten hours trying to make a gig, and being hungry and passing restaurants along the road, and having to go off the highway into some little city to find a place to eat because you're black—that had its effect."

Time adds an understandable postscript: "And the post-performance parties among older troupers in hotel rooms where the liquor and the sex were plentiful—they had their effect, too."

All these torturous experiences would seem to be emotional grist for a great blues singer, another heart-torn Billie Holiday. They could have been and might have been, save for one thing: Aretha was the sensitive, immature daughter of a preacher. Gospel ideas as well as gospel music were her heritage. It was not only what she had learned in church from the time she could raise her voice. The great religious singers of her race—Mahalia Jackson, Clara Ward, Sam Cooke (during his gospel-singing days)—were all guests in her father's house.

Commenting on James Cleveland, a longtime dedicated gospel shouter who stayed with the Franklins for a time, she has said, "He showed me some real nice chords, and I liked his deep, deep sound. There's a whole lot of earthiness in the way he sings, and what he was feelin' I was feelin', but I didn't know how to put it across. The more I watched him, the more I got out of it."

When Aretha, inspired by the example of Sam Cooke, decided at eighteen to venture into the pop field, she was an introverted, deeply inhibited girl. Although she had made some religious tracks for the Checker label, a Chess subsidiary, she was encouraged by Teddy Wilson's bassist, Major "Mule" Holly, to audition for Columbia. Her first releases after she was signed were R & B. As time went on the company's choice of material called upon her ample vocal artistry but slighted her emotional and experiential resources. This is a mistake with any singer, but particularly a young singer.

As Aretha puts it, "If a song's about something I've experienced or that could've happened to me, it's good. But if it's alien to me, I couldn't lend anything to it. Because that's what soul is about—just living and having to get along." The ballads, jazz tunes, and standards she cut for Columbia were obviously "alien" to her, later causing her to say, "It wasn't really me."

Toward the end of her five-year contract, Columbia made an effort to correct its mistakes by hiring a new black producer for her. Cognizant of her great talent, the company offered her a new contract despite the limited sales of her disks. Fortunately for Aretha, she and Ted White, her manager-husband, decided to leave the label and, after some discussions, to move to Atlantic. Signed in November, 1966, she was flown to the Fame Studios at Muscle Shoals, Alabama, for her first Atlantic session.

Her producer at the new label, Jerry Wexler, recently explained the reason for not recording her in New York: "Everybody who knows the South, the real South, knows that, despite the Klan and the lynchings and the brutality, the liberated southern white is a hell of a lot closer to the Negro soul than the northern white liberal. . . . And besides, this is the Memphis Sound. To think that only Negroes were brought up in this musical tradition would be a form of Crow Jim."

Backed by one of the best rhythm sections in the business, a group that combined gospel-and-blues roots with sterling innate musicianship, Aretha cut—literally delivered herself of—one of the most perfect soul disks ever made. "I Never Loved a Man the Way I Love You" became a runaway hit, easily aggregating the totals that made it a Gold Record. The important consideration here was that the musical background, the production guidance, and the studio environment (Aretha was born in Memphis and moved north to Buffalo and Detroit when she was two) all combined to tap the gospel vein that was her natural expressive style.

From the opening gospel piano chords, played by Aretha herself, to the closing, repetitive cries of "Lord, Lord, I ain't never, ain't never, I ain't never loved a man . . ." we are at a church service that builds in intensity. The organ that enters after a time is a church organ, and the horns, making sharp, antiphonal responses like a compulsive choir, raise the emotional heat until Aretha explodes in the breathless—a cappella —self-harmonized words—"loved a man the way I love you." The record has the rare quality of leaving you before you are ready to leave it.

The gospel frame is Aretha's, but the record also has the supreme authority of autobiography:

> I don't know why I let you do these things to me . . .
> The way you treat me is a shame . . .
> My friends keep telling me that you ain't no good . . .

Not long after she made this recording, her husband "roughed her up in public" at Atlanta's Regency Hyatt House Hotel. "It was not the first such incident," *Time* noted.

And Mahalia Jackson says diplomatically, "I don't think she's happy. Somebody else is making her sing the blues."

That is what observers at the abortive Caesar's Palace engagement in June, 1969, were also saying. Aretha refuses to share her problems with the public or with friends, though she did tell Mahalia at one point, "I'm gonna make a gospel record and tell Jesus I cannot bear these burdens alone."

In her first year with Atlantic Aretha had so many chart records that she finished 1967 as the number-one R & B Artist, ahead of James Brown, The Supremes, the Temptations, Wilson Pickett, and Stevie Wonder. Among the disks that contributed to this achievement were Otis Redding's "Respect," "Baby, I Love You," and Don Covay's "Chain of Fools," all of which were certified Gold Records. By the end of 1968 she had moved, after other million-copy records like "Since You've Been Gone," to the pinnacle of number-one Pop Singles Artist.

Like much of contemporary pop and Rock, Soul songs are plain-talking songs:

> Don't send me no doctor fillin' me up with all of those pills;
> Got me a man named Dr. Feelgood and, oh yeah,
> That man takes cares of all my pains and my ills.

For poor men and women whose lives are an around-the-week routine of exhausting labor, there are few pleasures, and sex is generally more absorbing than TV or alcohol. It is a point of reference on many of Aretha's disks. But the strange thing is that Aretha is not a sexy, sensual, or erotic singer. When she sings a line like "Whip it to me when you get home," or, as she prefers, "Sock it to me," she burdens the simple aches of the flesh with more complex feelings and yearnings.

Listen to the opening of "You Are My Sunshine," where she performs a freestyle rabbinical chant against the doom-like reverberating bass notes of the piano and the antiphonal cries of a female trio that sounds like the Furies.

"They tell me that into each life some rain must fall," she chants, and adds, almost as a painful afterthought, "And I've had enough rain in my life . . . but now I've got a little love around me to keep the rain off . . ."

If one part of Aretha is the powerful-voiced gospel shouter, wailing of Jesus and jubilation, the other is the little girl hungering for love and crying out in anguish for the man who will say, "Never let me go."

Having found ways of adapting gospel-styled frenzy to profane expressiveness, she has now become one of the great blues-ballad singers of our day. Aretha is not Erotic Soul but, as one of her Gold albums calls her, *Lady Soul*. She communicates the yearning of young people for warmth, for tenderness, for making it together emotionally as well as sexually —and the hurt of not making it.

This burden of her singing virtuosity does not prevent her from turning Madison Square Garden, as Robert Shelton of the *New York Times* put it, into a "Soularium filled with the heat and light of free expression." Or, as John Wilson noted concerning her appearance at sedate Lincoln Center: "By the time that Aretha got to her last number, she had most of the people who filled Philharmonic Hall on their feet, clapping and cheering as she sang."

20

RAY CHARLES
Soul Supreme

Not only Aretha but an entire generation of gospel-shouting, blues-singing black artists walk in the capacious footsteps of Ray Charles, whose career encompasses all the major developments in black music of the past two decades, and who pioneered the rise of Soul.

Beginning with a Nat "King" Cole type of trio, he went on to form a band that honked out R & B disks, beat out rock 'n' roll platters, and improvised jazz records. Having achieved a fusion of sex and salvation, the sacred and the secular, the jubilation of gospel and the earthiness of the blues, he boldly invaded the hills of Tennessee and carved out a niche in country-and-western music.

Today, he seems to be concerned with the so-called good music of the twenties and thirties, the hit show tunes like Rodgers and Hart's "I Didn't Know What Time It Was," the Gershwins' "Love Is Here to Stay," and, incredible though it may appear, Rudolf Friml's "Indian Love Call"—but also Andy Razaf and Eubie Blake's hit from *Blackbirds of 1930*, "Memories of You."

Despite this mixing of genres, materials, and styles, Ray Charles has managed to remain soulful Ray Charles, a monolith of a man and musician about whom even the demanding jazz critic, Whitney Balliett of *The New Yorker*, recently wrote, "He has done what no other jazz performer has done—remained incorruptible while becoming nationally revered." And Balliett amplifies, "He is a ballad singer who, like Billie Holiday, usually turns dross to gold. He is also a nonpareil down-home blues singer and gospel singer, the father of all rock singers, the only country-and-western singer to sublimate his materials, and a funny novelty singer. But no matter where he turns, he is a jazz singer."

In Balliett's eyes, the highest accolade: Jazz Singer. In our view, Ray Charles is Soul Singer pioneer and supreme.

Regardless of the quality or character of the material, once it has moved through the coils of the Ray Charles music distillery it comes out with the unmistakable aura, bouquet, and taste of the Genius, as he has been called with little exaggeration. The ability to overwhelm pop music history and make it part of one's biography, and to make one's black biography part of history—this is the mark of the soul singer.

In 1966, when the music world was celebrating his twentieth year in show business, a special resolution honoring Charles was introduced on the floor of the U. S. House of Representatives. It was one of the few times a black singer had been so honored. Unlike many such commendatory gestures, the tribute contained words of truth: "The pain of his early life," the resolution read in part, "and the hardships he has overcome are part of the Ray Charles sound."

If Aretha Franklin's outcry is for love denied, Ray's anguish is partly that of the blind man—and black—the blind man inescapably and permanently dependent on others in a mean world of hustlers. And Charles has had to contend with his "friends" as well as exploiters.

"Sure, he's got a wife and three kids," a former sideman told Nat Hentoff. "But how often does he see them? On the road the man hasn't a soul to lean on. It's no wonder he's restless, suspicious, often irritable, and so desperately committed to his music. Oh, he likes to laugh and get his kicks. But the music is the only way he gets full release."

Blind from the age of six, fatherless at fifteen and alone at seventeen when his mother died, Charles studied music at a school for the blind in St. Augustine, Florida. Though blessed with perfect pitch, he had to learn music notation through Braille, an enervatingly slow process requiring an extraordinary exercise of memory. Undaunted, he mastered piano, sax, and trumpet as well as the demanding craft of arranging. With the death of his mother in 1947, he faced the same chilling alternative as all blind blacks since the Civil War: whether to beg for a living or sing-and-play. So he followed the course of the Blind Lemon Jeffersons and Blind Blakes, except that he became a traveling musician. Through Florida, Tennessee, and the southern states, he worked (and starved) with hillbilly and R & B bands.

"I've known the worst kind of despair," he has said, recalling some of the experiences of those years, "I remember being paid once with a tin of jam. When I tried to open it in my hotel room, I was so tormented by hunger that I jabbed the can opener into the top too quickly, and everything inside fell on the floor."

The music brought rewards, and it also brought associations that made a drug addict of Charles before he was out of his teens. (Thinking for a moment of those moralists who like to associate narcotics with music and musicians, how does a blind man get drugs and use the paraphernalia of addiction if they fiteers?) The drug habit was to plague Charles until 1965, when are not supplied by pushers who get them from criminal pro- he voluntarily entered a California clinic.

The West Coast proved rewarding at an even earlier date. It was in Seattle, Washington, that Charles was able to gain the acceptance that made his King Cole-type trio the first black jazz group to appear on a sponsored TV show in the Northwest. In 1951–52 Charles also made his first recordings, cutting not jazz but R & B for Swing Time, a California label that also found Oklahoma bluesman Lowell Fulson.

Charles's recordings quickly bounded onto R & B charts: "Kiss Me Baby" in 1952 and (shades of the Beatles' first American smash) a song called "Baby, Let Me Hold Your Hand," which went to number one in '51. It was from Swing

Time that Atlantic purchased Ray's contract for two thousand dollars.

"Recording Ray Charles," Atlantic producer Jerry Wexler has said, "is like putting a meter on fresh air—ain't nothin' to it—just open up the pots." By the time Charles's first album appeared in 1956—now known as *Hallelujah! I Love Her So* but originally bearing only Ray's name and the subtitle *Rock and Roll*—he had had so many disk clicks that the LP was truly a collection of hits. Incidentally, it was not the typical "best" album of one or two sellers and a series of nondescript tracks to pad out the required number. Among these early Charles gems were "Don't You Know" ('54); "Greenbacks," the humorous but brutally frank exposé of love for pay; "I Got a Woman" and "This Little Girl of Mine" ('55); and "Drown in My Own Tears" and "Hallelujah! I Love, Her So" ('56).

Special interest attaches to two of the 1955 songs. "I Got a Woman" and "This Little Girl of Mine" mark a turning point in Charles's work and in the development of R & B. As Ahmet Ertegun, president of Atlantic, recalls the sequence of events, a phone call came in one day from Charles, who was then playing with his band at the Royal Peacock Club in Atlanta. He sounded so excited and was so anxious to have them hear some new songs that Ertegun and Wexler flew down to the Georgia capital the following day. Since there were no recording studios in Atlanta then, they went to a local radio station to make the records.

"We had to stop every half hour or so," Wexler recalls, "while the station gave the news, because the control room was where they were broadcasting the news! I'll never forget. It was three hours before we could even get a balance. We didn't record a single note. But before the session was over, we had 'I Got a Woman,' 'Come Back Baby,' and 'Greenbacks.' And before we left Atlanta, we also had 'This Little Girl of Mine.' "

"What makes these sessions historically important is that this was the first time," Ertegun explains, "that someone had

283

the audacity to mix sacred and secular black music. Ray had taken the gospel hymn 'My Jesus Is All the World to Me' and rewritten it as 'I Got A Woman.' He had taken another gospel song made famous by Clara Ward, 'This Little Light of Mine,' and converted it into 'This Little Girl of Mine.' "

Now, at the present enlightened moment in the history of the black cultural revolution, this act of apostasy may not appear as impressive as it did in 1955. To evaluate the boldness of Charles's move, consider the comment of Big Bill Broonzy, hardly a pillar of Establishment or middle-class values.

"Ray Charles is mixin' the blues with spirituals," Big Bill said. "That's wrong. . . . He's got a good voice but it's a church voice. He should be singin' in church."

For whites to realize the potency of the separation between gospel and blues requires a major act of identification. One sang gospel to celebrate the spiritual joys of the afterlife. Blues was a medium to confront and conquer the torments of this life. Gospel songs were chanted in the sacred environs of a church. Blues, sometimes known as "devil songs," were sung in honky-tonks, juke joints, bars, and you-name-it. The two types were as far apart as heaven and hell. And they differed even in form; the blues were a set chord sequence of twelve bars, while gospel patterns followed a large variety of chord changes in eight- and sixteen-bar patterns.

Disregarding the traditional separation, Charles had boldly crossed the bridge and, kneeling at the feet of "baby" instead of the altar of Jesus, had crossed from spiritual into sensual ecstasy. His conversion occurred at just about the time that white southerners like Elvis Presley, Buddy Holly, and Jerry Lee Lewis began to cross from hillbilly into the blues. Young white record listeners were as receptive to Ray Charles as young black buyers were to Elvis Presley. This was a moment when pop music was integrated at the performing and listening levels.

Having established a foothold in the pop field, Charles seemed to veer away from it during 1957 and '58 as he produced instrumental jazz albums that made him a central figure at the Newport Jazz Festival of 1958. These LPs also won him the *Down Beat* International Critics Award as a new star in jazz, as well as the Grand Prix du Disque of the French Academy.

In 1959, however, Charles came back stronger than sin with "What'd I Say," a disk that went to the top as if heaven and hell were turned upside down. Ahmet Ertegun regards this record as the most important of Charles's career, not because it was the biggest and fastest seller he had had up to then but because of its subject matter and approach.

Ray's earlier fusion of gospel and blues, of jubilation and ecstasy, here reaches a climax in the frank exaltation of the flesh. Possessed of a rather sly sense of humor, Ray points up the sexual connotations of his lyric by pretending to be unaware of what he has said: "What'd I say?" But the simulated revival meeting on wax, with the antiphonal responses of the congregation to preacher Charles, leaves no doubt that everything became all right once the gal learned how to put out right and without reserve.

Having left Atlantic for an ABC record deal that initially gave him a higher royalty rate, and the publishing rights to all his original songs (later his own Tangerine Records would acquire his masters and lease distribution rights to ABC), Charles made another sharp turn in his accelerating record career.

One day he phoned Sid Feller, his A & R producer in New York, and requested that recordings of all the great country-and-western songs be put on a tape for him. Through repeated plays of taped songs, Charles generally chooses his material for recording, learns songs, and works out his arrangements. Sensing what Charles was contemplating, Feller went to the president of ABC Records, who got on the long-distance phone to L. A. and pleaded with Charles not to do it.

"All these stories you hear about Ray being led around by the nose because he's blind," the ABC president later said, "they're just not true. When he wanted to do his first country-and-western album, we said to him, 'Don't do it.' When the distributors got his recording of 'I Can't Stop Loving You,' they called up asking, 'What is this? A joke?'"

The so-called joke sold more than two million records, yielded two albums of country-and-western songs, each of which sold a million, and led to Charles's becoming the first Negro to be named among the Top Ten performers by the C & W Music Association of Nashville. With white southern youngsters doing blues-styled recordings of country songs, it was no more than natural for a southern black man to bring his brand of soul to play on C & W material.

But "I Can't Stop Loving You" and other country songs of heartbreak recorded by Charles had a significance above and beyond their market impact. Perhaps they appealed so strongly because they flowed from a deep recess of Ray Charles's being. When he was arrested in 1961 for possession of narcotics, a police reporter for the *Indianapolis Times* came to see him.

"He appeared very disturbed and lonely," Rick Johnson recalls. "He sat down on the bench in city jail and began to cry softly and then lost all control of himself. I asked him how he got started on narcotics. 'I started using stuff when I was sixteen and first started in show business,' he told me. Then Ray broke off and began to cry again. 'I don't know what to do about my wife and kids. I've got a month's work to do, and I have to do it. I really need help. I'd like to go to Lexington [the federal narcotics hospital]. I guess I've always wanted to go, but it was easier the other way. A guy like me has to have something to keep going.' "

If any word can be summoned to describe Charles's emotional state, anguish surely is it. You can see it in the handsome, crop-haired, eye-shaded face of the man whose white clenched teeth frequently suggest the joyous shouter but at other times communicate an inescapable feeling of inner torment. This is the Soul of Ray Charles, sandy-voiced celebrant of the pleasures of the flesh and the agonizing frustrations and loneliness of the sightless.

"To me Ray Charles is a soulful musician," pianist Ramsey Lewis has said. "Not the piano playing so much, but his singing. He makes me feel the story he's telling. And he does it in a simple form . . . all the time. Now, that's real soul."

And James Baldwin has said, "Ray Charles, who is a great

tragic artist, makes of a genuinely religious confession something triumphant and liberating. He tells us that he cried so
loud he gave the blues to his neighbor next door. . . ."

Ray Charles was the pioneer. Soul was his bag because
that was the way an inspired, musically talented, black, blind
man had to go.

21

OF CHITLINS,
BLUE-EYED SOUL,
AND BLACK
CAPITALISTS

Pop music today is like a satellite drawn by the huge gravitational pull of black sound. Black artists like brash Jimi Hendrix, troubled Aretha Franklin, explosive James Brown, and young Stevie Wonder vault to the top of best-seller lists. In the country's plush clubs, hotel rooms, and college concert halls, there is a growing demand for the Little Richards, Fats Dominos, Chuck Berrys, and all the black stars of the R & B era. And the number of white cats imitating spades continues to multiply both here and abroad.

Blue-eyed Soul, as the latter phenomenon has come to be known, is a sociopsychological as well as a musical development. Alienated from their own sound culture, young white performers seek to master the style of an alien culture. They find excitement, electricity, and exhilaration in today's soulmen and the rhythm-and-bluesmen of the early fifties. In turn, young audiences respond to the drive of imitation black and indigenous black music. What stirs listeners, perhaps, is the sheer *sensuality* of black song.

"To be sensual," James Baldwin has said in *The Fire Next Time*, "is to respect and rejoice in the force of life, or life itself, and to be *present* in all that one does, from the effort of living to the breaking of bread."

And Taj Mahal has aptly said, "Blues happens to be a very

sensual, down-into-the-body music, and that's why it's catching on. People want real things."

But young listeners also take black to their bosoms out of sympathy for the underdog and outcast (like themselves?) and as a gesture of defiance to the older generation.

The pioneer R & B creators, today enjoying a long overdue acceptance in their own land, credit the British for their new mass popularity. And well they should, since the English rock groups recorded their hits, adapted their styles, and built live audiences for them. But even if the fire of acceptance was ignited by the British, the kindling was done over a period of years by young, white Americans.

What was rock 'n' roll in its initial stage if not a form of blue-eyed soul? To be sure, there is a difference. The rock-billy crowd—Elvis Presley, Jerry Lee Lewis, Buddy Holly, to name a few—*fused* rhythm-and-blues with hillbilly. They did not try to sound black but worked at *adapting* black.

The Righteous Brothers were cats of another color. Until a Negro group identified them as "our blue-eyed soul brothers," incidentally giving rise to the descriptive phrase, so many black jockeys had played their records that they easily made black charts. (In 1965 "Unchained Melody" and "You've Got That Loving Feeling" both made Top Ten among R & B singles.)

"You should have seen his face drop," the general manager of station WWRL in New York said of Rocky G., a leading R & B disk jockey, "when he found out that the Brothers were not really Negroes."

Soon quite a number of individual singers and groups sounded black though they were white. Among these one finds Mitch Ryder and the Detroit Wheels, Wayne Cochran, Vanilla Fudge, Soul Survivors, Magnificent Men, Box Tops, Tim Hardin, the Young Rascals (now the Rascals), Janis Joplin, and Tom Jones.

On the instrumental level, there was a proliferation of white blues bands. In England there was John Mayall's Blues-breakers, Fleetwood Mac, Ten Years After, and Savoy Brown. Here in the United States we had Paul Butterfield Blues

Band, the Electric Flag: An American Music Band, Steve Miller Blues Band, Charles D. Musselwhite Blues Band, Candymen, Canned Heat, Dirty Blues Band, Blues Project, Blood, Sweat and Tears (who recently had a hit single in "Spinning Wheel"), and many others.

Like the white men who donned blackface and imitated Negro song and dance in the era of the minstrel shows, all these singers and instrumentalists find an irresistible vitality in black music that turns them into carbon copies. The minstrel show embodied a not inconsequential degree of burlesque, mockery, and put-down. But the white imitators of today are motivated by admiration, empathy, and possibly a sense of guilt.

"Preposterous!" was the cry of many a black reader when *Newsweek* advanced the guilt theory in a cover story on "The Rebirth of the Blues."

"White big business," one reader wrote, "has managed to exploit blacks for more than 300 years, and certainly it views the blues as one more salable commodity."

Blue-eyed soulmen, however, face problems other than a questioning of their motives.

Reverse race prejudice, Crow Jim instead of Jim Crow, is one. A member of the Dirty Blues Band explains, "In some instances we can relate more to a white audience than to a colored because . . . some colored audiences resented the fact that we played their music."

The Righteous Brothers had earlier encountered similar situations. "A lot of rhythm-and-blues stations," one of the Brothers admitted, "won't play Righteous Brothers records. They used to. But the records got yanked. 'Little Latin Lupe Lu' was getting a lot of air time—but once we went around to visit the stations and they found we were white . . . that was it, man, that was it."

Esthetic and psychological considerations, as well as economic, are involved. A style, a sound, a sonority, a mode of expression and locutions can all be persuasively imitated. But there are severe limits. Nina Simone suggests one.

"My people," she has said, "have very subtle slang, inflections, and ways of saying things that have little to do with words. If you're from the same place, you'll feel the jargon and know exactly what's happening. Same with any neighborhood cat. What he sees and hears and feels and lives make him what he is. That's what blues is."

Initially, the black creators could not reach white listeners precisely because of these idiomatic subtleties. By the same token, white imitators could and did because they were either unaware of or eliminated the noncommunicative elements.

Pete Welding raises another issue with respect to the exponents of what he calls the "mock-tough school of blue vocalizing." Describing the technique as one of swallowing syllables, mispronouncing words, and distorting sounds, all in an attempt to approximate "what the vocalist assumes are the speech patterns and inflections of uneducated field hands," Welding concludes that this is "taking pleasure from another's misfortune."

Obviously we are involved here with questions of identity, personal experience, and genuine feeling. All the imitators are aware of the gap between their lives and the black experience.

The lead singer of the Hollywood-based Dirty Blues Band asserts, "I've had a lot of hard luck. I'm singing from what I feel myself."

The British Fleetwood Mac try to toughen themselves by confining their gigs to small, shabby clubs in London's East End and North England tenderloins. This is "method" playing with a vengeance. Thus we have the ersatz spectacle of singers and musicians who are literally turning the creative process upside down. Instead of playing the kind of music they live, they are trying to live the kind of music they play.

Empathy is a powerful force. But since style comes from genuine feeling and genuine feeling comes from life lived, not shared vicariously, blue-eyed soul is esthetically in a box canyon. The more slavish the imitation, the more devitalized the music.

"Now, I could play a tune," Taj Mahal has said, "just exactly like Robert Johnson. But what would be the point of that? This is 1969, not 1926."

Black sound is the product of centuries of enslavement, segregation, cultural submergence, rootlessness, and lack of pride and identity. The act of seeking a sense of the black experience by eating chitlins and so-called soul food is ludicrous.

"These white kids who play the blues," Taj Mahal has said, "they don't understand but they are doing the same thing as their fathers did . . . but on a different level. They're taking somebody else's thing, their music, and using it. Now, I'm not against someone who plays and plays and plays until he finally gets down to where the real him gets in touch with it and he can play what's *inside* of him finally. . . ."

To use the black experience for understanding and illumination . . . to probe black sound for expressive elements . . . to seek the feel of *Blues* and Soul—these are unobjectionable, but only as means to an end. As ends, those procedures become evasion and escapism for blue-eyed soulmen. The great music of the black people has come out of their insides, and this will be the source of whatever greatness there is in the new generations of white artists. Study the black experience. But play the white one. Eventually people and music will be color-blind. But until then, the keynotes, musically and economically, are respect and equality.

Three recent developments pose problems and/or hold promises for the future of Soul.

1. Paralleling the white man's effort to capitalize on black sound is the black man's bead on the white market. The Staple Singers "refine" their gospel style to reach a bigger audience. The Supremes and other Motown artists record show tunes to gain entry into the white nightclub circuit. From a psychological as well as an economic point of view, the motivation is understandable. But in the process of gaining an audience, are these singers losing their Souls? The pun is intended. Or, having reached a new audience, will they lead it to an appreciation of their own musical culture? And what about the audience whose shared experience nurtured their art?

2. Jazz critic Leonard Feather recently confronted Ray

Charles with the words of a recording executive who had said, "If any artist can't sell one hundred thousand records, we are not interested." Charles's comment was, "I don't find that so callous. It's the way things have to be. With the production costs as they are nowadays, most artists can't break even unless they sell fifty to a hundred thousand. Even back in the 1950s, Atlantic didn't hire me to experiment with. They hired me to make money and they had a good idea of what my potential was."

Observing that Charles was as far from Uncle Tommery as from militancy and spoke in the "temperate terms of a middle-class moderate," Feather concluded that Charles's views were "those of a black capitalist and realist, a ghetto graduate who may actually believe in the American dream."

Whether they believe in the American dream or not, it has come true for James Brown, Aretha Franklin, and Jimi Hendrix. The talents of these artists have produced revenues that have completely removed them from the nagging economics tearing at the mass of their brethren, white as well as black. They have become black capitalists—a desirable condition in a society where black ownership in radio and recording does not exceed one-tenth of one percent.

James Brown has made an overt effort to use his wealth not only to buy radio stations, but to provide necessities for needy blacks and to stimulate black ownership of small business (the latter, incidentally, a project to which his namesake in films is also dedicating himself).

But if we believe that great singing is the product of deep, genuine feeling, what will happen to the expressive art of these black capitalists? Wealth does not eliminate emotional problems, as we have seen in the recent travail of Aretha Franklin. It may reduce but it does not eliminate the solitude of Ray Charles's blindness, nor his irritating (to him) dependence on others.

However, there are inherent dangers that luxurious living, obsequiousness of associates, and a feeling of power, which frequently attend the acquisition of great wealth, may destroy the common touch. There is the further danger that Soul may be reduced from an overpowering emotional force to a mere musical quantity or style. In his latter days, Hemingway was castigated for doing an imitation of Hemingway. And not long ago Ray Charles was criticized for mimicking himself rather than singing out of an intensely felt need.

For Charles as for the other black artists who have come into the big money, it is a situation fraught with challenge. The future of Soul is at stake.

3. *Mourning in the Morning*, Otis Rush's 1969 release on Atlantic, was cut, like Aretha Franklin's first smash Atlantic LP and disks of Wilson Pickett and Percy Sledge, at the Fame Studios in Muscle Shoals, Alabama. Nick Gravenites, who coproduced the Otis Rush album, returned to New York with an unquenchable flow of excited epithets for the musicianship of the studio band. What amazed him most was, in his words, that "the basic rhythm section down there at Muscle Shoals is an all-white cracker band!"

Is this a form of blue-eyed Soul? Unquestionably, it is. The world of the Memphis white musician is not the world of the Memphis black musician. But the musical tradition, like the sound of the spoken word, is the same. And not only for the present generation of white Memphis cats but for an earlier group: Presley and the rockabilly songsters of the fifties. As Aretha Franklin's producer and other New York producers who have worked in Nashville, Memphis, and Muscle Shoals have pointed out, the liberated white southerner has a natural feeling for black Soul. It is an outgrowth of a shared environment and shared experience, even if the parties started out by being at opposite sides of the bandstand.

An Otis Rush record session at Muscle Shoals is a mix, as American pop music has often been a mix of black originators and white polishers, black style and white experience. Expressive song of the future depends on the richness of that mixture —and the more integrated our society, economically as well as musically, the richer the mixture.

Discography

Only albums are cited, and these are listed for each chapter in alphabetical order under artist names. Titles of albums appear in italics. When an artist's name appears in italics, it means that the album carries no other title. Regrettably, there are artists and groups that have not survived the R & B era of single releases.

1. **Soul Is . . .**
   James Brown. *Say It Loud, I'm Black and I'm Proud.* King 5-1047.
   José Feliciano. *Souled.* RCA Victor LSP 4045.
   Otis Redding. *Dictionary of Soul.* Atco S 33-287.

2. **Country Blues and Bottleneck Bluesmen**
   The Bill Broonzy Story. Verve MG-V 3000-5.
   Sleepy John Estes, 1929–40. RBF RF 8.
   John Lee Hooker. *The Blues.* Crown CLP 5157.
   Lightnin' Hopkins. *Early Recordings.* Arhoolie R 2007.
   Son House, with J. D. Short. *Delta Blues.* Folkways 31028.
   Mississippi John Hurt. *Folk Songs and Blues.* Piedmont PLP 13157.
   Skip James. *Greatest of the Delta Blues Singers.* Melodeon MLP 7321.
   Blind Lemon Jefferson, 1926–9. Biograph 12000.
   Robert Johnson. *Delta Blues.* Columbia CL 1654.
   Huddie "Leadbelly" Ledbetter. *Memorial.* Stinson 17/19/48/51.
   Mance Lipscomb. *Texas Sharecropper & Songster.* Arhoolie 1001.
   Brownie McGhee & Sonny Terry. Fantasy 3254.
   Charlie Patton & the Country Blue. Origin Jazz Library 1/7
   Speckled Red. *Dirty Dozens.* Delmark 601.
   Bukka White. Arhoolie 1019/20.
   Josh White. *Sings the Blues.* Stinson SLP 14/15.
   Sonny Boy Williamson. *The "Original."* Blues Classics BC 9.

3. **Classic Blues**
   The Great Blues Singers. Riverside RLP 1032.
   The Immortal Ma Rainey. Milestone MLP 201.
   The Bessie Smith Story. 4 Columbia CL 855/8.
   Victoria Spivey. *Recorded Legacy of the Blues.* Spivey 2001.
   Women of the Blues. RCA Victor LPV 534.

4. **The Blues Is . . .**
   The Blues. 5 Cadet 4026/27/4034/4042/4051.
   Blues Roots/Chicago, 1930s. RBF 16.
   Blues Roots/Mississippi. RBF 14.

5. **The Jazz Singers**
   Louis Armstrong. *Autobiography.* 4 Decca DX 155.
   Louis Armstrong Story. 4 Columbia CL 851/4.
   Cab Calloway. *Blues.* Vocalion 73820.
   Best of Ella Fitzgerald. 2 Decca DXS 7156.
   Billie Holiday. *Golden Years.* 3 Columbia C 3L 21.
   Billie Holiday. *Golden Years, Vol. 2.* 3 Columbia C 3L 40.
   Essential Billie Holiday. Verve 68410.
   Billie Holiday Story. 2 Decca DXS 7161.
   Carmen McRae. Vocalion 3697.
   Sarah Vaughan. *All Time Favorites.* Mercury 16123.
   Fats Waller. *Ain't Misbehavin'.* RCA Victor LPM 1246.
   Best of Nancy Wilson. Capitol SKAO 2947.

6. **Black Pop and the Oreo Singers**
   Harry Belafonte. *Calypso.* RCA Victor LSP 1248.
   Brook Benton. *Golden Hits.* Mercury 60607.
   Leroy Carr. *Blues Before Sunrise.* Columbia CL 1799.
   Chubby Checker. *Twist.* Cameo P 7001.
   Nat "King" Cole Story. 3 Capitol SWCL 1613.
   Sam Cooke. *Best, Vol. 2.* RCA Victor LSP 3373.
   Sammy Davis, Jr. *Treasury of Hits.* Reprise 96096.
   Fats Domino. *Sings Million Record Hits.* Imperial 12103.
   Billy Eckstine. *Golden Hits.* Mercury 60796.
   Fifth Dimension. Soul City 92000.
   Roy Hamilton. Epic BN 26009.
   Al Hibbler. *Greatest Hits.* Decca 75068.
   Lena Horne. *Lovely & Alive.* RCA Victor LSP 2587.
   The Impressions. *Best.* ABC S 654.
   The Ink Spots. *Best.* 2 Decca DXS 7182.
   Damita Jo. *If You Go Away.* Epic BN 26244.
   Johnny Mathis. *More Greatest Hits.* Columbia CS 8150.
   Mills Brothers. *Best.* 2 Decca DXS 7193.
   The Platters. *Encore of Golden Hits.* Mercury 60243.
   Lloyd Price. *Mr. Personality.* ABC S 297.
   Lou Rawls. *Best.* Capitol SKAO 2948.
   Della Reese. *Classic Della.* RCA Victor LSP 2419.

O. C. Smith. *Hickory Holler Revisited.* Columbia CS 9680.
Dionne Warwick. *Golden Hits, Vol. 1.* Scepter S 565.
Dinah Washington. *What a Diff'rence.* Mercury 60158.
Ethel Waters. *On Stage & Screen.* Columbia CL 2792.
Joe Williams. *Everyday I Have The Blues.* Roulette R 52033.
Jackie Wilson. *Greatest Hits.* Brunswick 754140.

7. **Rhythm-and-Blues Is . . .**
Anthology of Rhythm and Blues, Vol. 1. Columbia CS 9802.
Eighteen King Size Rhythm & Blues Hits. Columbia CS 9467.
History of Rhythm & Blues, 1947-60. 4 Atlantic S 8161/4.
History of Rhythm & Blues. 1961-67. 4 Atlantic S 8193/4, S 8208/9.
This Is How It All Began: The Specialty Story, Vol. 1. Specialty
SPS 2117.

8. **West Coast R & B Record Companies**
Johnny Ace. *Memorial Album.* Duke DLP 71.
Bobby Bland. *Call On Me.* Duke 77.
Lowell Fulson. Arhoolie 2003.
Percy Mayfield. Tangerine S 1505.
Willie Mae Thornton. *Big Mama Thornton.* Arhoolie 1028.
Aaron T-Bone Walker. *T-Bone Blues.* Atlantic 8020.
Larry Williams. *Original Golden Blue Greats.* Liberty 7572.

9. **Midwest R & B Record Giants**
Hank Ballard. *Greatest Jukebox Hits.* King 541.
Earl Bostic. *Best.* King 500.
Jerry Butler. *Golden Hits Live.* Mercury 61151.
Bo Diddley. *16 All Time Greatest Hits.* Checker 2989.
Dominoes ⎤
Bill Doggett ⎟ *18 King Size Rhythm & Blues Hits.* Columbia
Wynonie Harris ⎬ CS 9467.
Ivory Joe Hunter ⎟ *Anthology of Rhythm and Blues, Vol. 1.*
Bullmoose Jackson ⎦ Columbia CS 9802.
Etta James. Cadet S 4013.
Gladys Knight & the Pips. Soul S 706.
Little Milton. *"'Grits Ain't Groceries."* Checker LPS 3011.
Jimmy Reed. *New Jimmy Reed Album.* Bluesway S 6004.
Memphis Slim. *Chicago Boogie Woogie, Vol. 3.* Folkways 3536.
'Howlin' Wolf. *Moanin' in the Moonlight.* Chess 1434.

10. **East Coast R & B Record Scene**
Faye Adams. *Original Golden Greats, Vol. 5.* Liberty 7525.
Nappy Brown. Savoy 14002.
The Crows. *Oldies But Goodies, Vol. 2.* OSR 8852.
The Dovells. *You Can't Sit Down.* Cameo P 7025.
Little Esther. *Esther Phillips.* Atlantic S 8102.
Isley Brothers. *It's Our Thing.* T Neck TNS 3001.
Isley Brothers. *Twist and Shout.* Wand 653.

Chuck Jackson. *Encore*. Wand 665.
The Larks. *Super Oldies*. Capitol T 2562.
The Orioles. *History of Rhythm & Blues, Vol. 1*. Atco S 8161.
The Orlons. *Biggest Hits*. Cameo 1061.
Johnny Otis. *Cold Shot*. Kent 534.
The Penguins. *Decades of Golden Groups*. Mercury S 2-602.
The Ravens. *Write Me a Letter*. Regent 6062.
The Ronettes. Phillies S 4006.
Five Royales. *18 King Size Rhythm & Blues Hits*. Columbia CS 9467.
Dee Dee Sharp. *Biggest Hits*. Cameo 1062.
The Shirelles. *Greatest Hits*. Scepter S 507.
The Tymes. *So Much In Love*. Cameo P 7032.

11. **The Foremost Rhythm-and-Bluesmen**
    Chuck Berry. *Concerto in B. Goode*. Mercury SR 61223.
    Chuck Berry. *Golden Decade*. 2 Chess LPS 1514D.
    Heavy Heads. Various Artists. Chess LPS 1522.
    B. B. King. *Blues in My Heart*. Crown 5309.
    B. B. King. *Live at the Regal*. ABC S 509.
    Little Richard. *Here's Little Richard*. Specialty 2100.
    Little Richard. *Greatest Hits*. Okeh 14121.
    Muddy Waters. *Down on Stovall's Plantation*. Testament 2210.
    Muddy Waters. *Electric Mud*. Cadet CS 314.

12. **The Big Three of R & B**
    A. Motown: The Detroit Sound
       The Four Tops. *Greatest Hits*. Motown S 662.
       Marvin Gaye. *Greatest Hits*. 2 Tamla S 252/278.
       Martha and the Vandellas. *Greatest Hits*. Gordy SLP 917.
       The Marvelettes. *Greatest Hits*. Tamla S 253.
       The Motown Sound. Various Artists. Motown 651/661/666.
       Smokey Robinson and The Miracles. *Greatest Hits*. 2 Tamla S 254.
       Diana Ross and The Supremes. *Greatest Hits*. Motown SLP 2-663.
       The Temptations. *Greatest Hits*. Motown S 919.
       Junior Walker & All Stars. Soul S 710.
       Mary Wells. *Greatest Hits*. Motown SLP 616.
       Stevie Wonder. *Greatest Hits*. Tamla SLP 282.

    B. Stax: The Memphis Sound
       Booker T. and the MG's. *Best* Atlantic S 8202.
       Eddie Floyd. *Knock on Wood*. Atlantic 7714.
       Albert King. *Blues*. Atlantic S 8213.
       Albert King. *Years Gone By*. Stax STS 2010.
       Sam & Dave. *Best*. Atlantic S 8218.
       Carla Thomas. *Gee Whiz*. Atlantic S 8057.
       Rufus Thomas. Atlantic S 7704.

    C. Atlantic: The Harlem Sound
       LaVern Baker. *Blues Ballads*. Atlantic 8030.

298

Ruth Brown. Atlantic 8004.
Solomon Burke. *The Best of Solomon Burke.* Atlantic SD 8109.
The Chords. *History of Rhythm & Blues, Vol. 2.* Atlantic SD 8162.
The Clovers. Atlantic 8009/1248.
The Coasters. *Greatest Hits.* Atco 33-111.
Arthur Conley. *Shake, Rattle & Roll.* Atco S 33-320.
Don Covay. *Mercy!* Atlantic S 8104.
The Drifters. *Golden Hits.* Atlantic SD 8153.
Barbara Lewis. *Workin'.* Atlantic S 8173.
Wilson Pickett. *The Best of Wilson Pickett.* Atlatnic SD 8151.
Percy Sledge. *Best.* Atlantic S 8210.
Joe Tex. *Best* Atlantic SD 8144.
Big Joe Turner. *The Best of Joe Tex.* Atlantic SD 8144.

13. **Modern Bluesmen**
Chambers Brothers. Columbia CS 9522.
Chicago/The Blues!/Today! 3 Vanguard VSO 79216/17/18.
James Cotton. *Pure Cotton.* Verve Forecast FTS 3038.
Buddy Guy. *A Man and the Blues.* Vanguard VSD 79272.
J. B. Hutto. *Masters of Modern Blues, Vol. 2.* Testament T 2213.
Floyd Jones. *Masters of Modern Blues, Vol. 3.* Testament T 2214.
Freddy King. *Is a Blues Master.* Cotillion 9004.
John Littlejohn. *Chicago Blues Stars.* Arhoolie 1043.
Magic Sam. *West Side Soul.* Delmark DS 615.
Taj Mahal. *Natch'l Blues.* Columbia CS 9698.
Junior Parker. *Baby Please.* Mercury 16401.
Arthur Prysock. *Art & Soul.* Verve V6-5009.
Otis Rush. *Mourning in the Morning.* Cotillion 9006.
Johnny Shines. *Masters of Modern Blues, Vol. 1.* Testament T 2212.
Sly and the Family Stone. *Stand!* Epic BN 26456.
Otis Spann. Archive of Folk & Jazz Music 216.
Eddie Taylor. *Masters of Modern Blues, Vol. 3.* Testament T 2214.
Ike and Tina Turner. *Greatest Hits.* Warner Bros. S 1810.
Junior Wells. *You're Tuff Enough.* Blue Rock SRB 64002.

14. **Gospel Music**
James Cleveland. *With Angelic Choir, Vol. 3.* Savoy 14076.
Mahalia Jackson. *The World's Greatest Gospel Singer.* Columbia
    CL 644.
Marie Knight. *Songs of the Gospel.* Mercury MG 20196.
Negro Religious Songs & Services. Library of Congress AAFS 1 10.
Staple Singers. *Uncloudy Day.* Vee Jay LP 5000.
Sister Rosetta Tharpe. *Gospel Train.* Decca DL 8782.
Clara Ward Singers. *Lord Touch Me.* Savoy 14006.
Jimmy Witherspoon. *A Spoonful of Soul.* Verve V6-5050.

15. **Nina Simone: The Rage and Fury**
Nina Simone. *Best of.* Philips PHS 600-298.

Nina Simone. *Best.* Bethlehem 6028.
Nina Simone. *To Love Somebody.* RCA Victor LSP 4152.

16. **James Brown: The Frenzy and the Sex**
James Brown. *Cold Sweat.* King 1020.
James Brown. *Gettin' Down to It.* King 5-1051.
James Brown. *Please, Please, Please.* King 909.
James Brown. *The Unbeatable 16 Hits.* King 919.

17. **Jimi Hendrix: Reactive Noise and the Big Nasty**
Jimi Hendrix Experience. Reprise S 6261 S
Jimi Hendrix Experience. *Axis.* Reprise 6281.
Jimi Hendrix Experience. *Electric Ladyland.* 2 Reprise S 6307.

18. **Otis Redding: Tough and Soulfully Tender**
Otis Redding. Atco 33-161.
Otis Redding. *History.* Atco S 33-290.
Otis Redding. *Sings Soul.* Atco S 33-284.

19. **Aretha Franklin: Lady Soul**
Aretha Franklin. *Arrives.* Atlantic S 8150.
Aretha Franklin. *I Never Loved a Man.* Atlantic S 8139.
Aretha Franklin. *Soul '69.* Atlantic S 8212.

20. **Ray Charles: Soul Supreme**
Ray Charles. *Doing His Thing.* Tangerine/ABC Records ABC S 695.
Ray Charles. *Great Hits.* Atlantic 7101.
Ray Charles. *Hallelujah I Love Her So!* Atlantic 8006
Ray Charles. *Modern Sounds in Country & Western Music, Vol. 1.*
    ABC Records ABCS 435.
Ray Charles. *What'd I Say.* Atlantic 8029.